Simone Weil

D0769091

Simone Weil

~Interpretations of a Life

EDITED BY GEORGE ABBOTT WHITE

The University of Massachusetts Press

Amherst, 1981

COLLEGE OF THE SEQUOIAS
LIBRARY

Copyright © 1981 by George Abbott White
All rights reserved
Printed in the United States of America
LC 81-7460   ISBN 0-87023-343-2   344-0 pbk
Library of Congress Cataloging in Publication Data
appear on the last page of this book.
Earlier versions of the essays by Staughton Lynd,
Michael K. Ferber, Conor Cruise O'Brien, and
Joseph H. Summers appeared in a limited edition
entitled *Simone Weil: Live Like Her?*, edited by
George Abbott White, copyright © 1976 by the
Technology and Culture Seminar, Massachusetts
Institute of Technology, Cambridge, Mass.
J. M. Cameron's essay originally appeared in an
earlier version in the *New York Review of Books*.
Reprinted by permission from the *New York Review
of Books*. Copyright © 1977 Nyrev, Inc.

DOROTHY DAY
1897–1980

Contents

Acknowledgments   ix

Introduction   GEORGE ABBOTT WHITE   1

The Jagged Edge: A Biographical Essay on Simone Weil
MICHELE MURRAY   13

Simone Weil's Mind   ROBERT COLES   29

The Life and Death of Simone Weil   J. M. CAMERON   35

Simone Weil: Last Things   MICHELE MURRAY   47

Simone Weil's *Iliad*   MICHAEL K. FERBER   63

Notes on Simone Weil's *Iliad*   JOSEPH H. SUMMERS   87

Patriotism and *The Need for Roots:* The Antipolitics of
Simone Weil   CONOR CRUISE O'BRIEN   95

Marxism-Leninism and the Language of *Politics* Magazine:
The First New Left . . . and the Third   STAUGHTON LYND   111

Simone Weil's Work Experiences: From Wigan Pier to
Chrystie Street   GEORGE ABBOTT WHITE   137

Simone Weil's Bibliography: Some Reflections on
Publishing and Criticism   GEORGE ABBOTT WHITE   181

Notes on Contributors   195

Index   199

Acknowledgments

The more one tries to know Simone Weil and the ideas and issues she engaged, the clearer it becomes that *one* can not do it; it can only be done collectively. Since standard scholarly protocol requires either a rugged individualism or nearly anonymous identification in these matters, the attempt in this acknowledgment will be to give this larger community the recognition it deserves.

My own interest in Simone Weil began, as did so many interests, in conversation with Tony Stoneburner, now of the English Department at Denison University. Almost twenty years ago at the University of Michigan, Professor Stoneburner introduced me to Weil's essay on *The Iliad* and since then, he has encouraged my reading of her work with the intent of making certain "personalist" connections between her life and work and my life and work. As a result, Simone Weil has become one of my guides when thinking about issues of war and peace, factory work and union organizing, the function of monastic communities and the nature of the ancient world. I suspect that I have inherited her bias against the Roman Empire (though I continue to be fascinated by the history of Roman Britain), and in a similar vein and over the arguments of my wife and several of our friends, I have few positive feelings for the potential of the State, in any of its forms. Simone Weil's skepticism has made me examine my own teaching again and again, and I have come away grateful for having had teachers, like Tony Stoneburner, who have "lived like her" in their determination to raise difficult questions and to offer, as necessary, the partial and personal solutions of their own lives, without embarrassment or apology.

This collection of essays then, grew from those early conversations, my own work and Civil Rights experiences, and from two symposia on Simone Weil, one at the Massachusetts Institute of Technology during the academic year 1975–76, and one at Princeton University, in the spring of 1978. I made several visits to England and Europe related to Simone Weil; most particularly those made during the summers of 1975 and 1980 were essential, not only from the point of information gathered, but in terms of gaining perspectives, in the actual physical context of where she lived and worked.

In England, August 1975, I was hosted by several Simone Weil enthusiasts including David and Marion Raper of Bishop's Stortford, Patricia Little of Southampton (now of Dublin), and Vernon Sproxton of London. Professor Raper wrote a lucid dissertation on Simone Weil's view of the Old Testament, edited a very useful collection of her religious writings, *Gateway to God* (London: Fontana Books, 1974), and he provided me with an understanding of the circumstances surrounding the publication of Simone Weil's writings. Professor Little compiled—and continues to compile—the essential bibliography, *Simone Weil: A Bibliography* (London: Grant & Cutler, 1973; Supplement, 1980). Mr. Sproxton is the producer of religious programming at the BBC, and, in addition to a number of full-length programs on figures such as Luther and Gandhi, has made the evocative documentary "Simone Weil: Pilgrim of the Absolute."

Anthony Sheil of Anthony Sheil Associates, Ltd., kindly provided me with office space in London in 1975, and Ralph and Marion Miliband in 1980 generously provided me with a base from which to explore places in London and Kent familiar to Simone Weil. The engraver and letterer Edgar Holloway made his workshop available to me at the Guild Workshops, Ditchling Common, Sussex, on both visits, and his conversations and those of his wife, the late Monica Holloway, on Eric Gill's first intentional community have helped me to develop an understanding of the relationship between Simone Weil and that writer and worker in wood and stone. Professor Richard Ellmann was my host both summers at New College, and my only regret is that I could not persuade his wife, Mary, to complete the essay on Simone Weil she and I once sketched out.

While in England I also received most helpful correspondence from the Rev. David Anderson, who had written the concise biography, *Simone Weil* (London: SCM Press, Ltd., 1971), and from Sir Isaiah Berlin and Professor George Steiner. Mrs. J. Percival, Archivist, thoughtfully made me aware of the extent of Sir Richard Rees's papers at the Library, University College, London, and it was Ms. G. M. Furlong who was my guide through them in the Manuscripts and Rare Books Room, D.M.S. Watson Library, where those relating to Simone Weil are actually housed.

The Department of Humanities, Massachusetts Institute of Technology, invited me as a Visiting Lecturer in 1975–76 for the purpose of conducting a seminar on Simone Weil in the fall of 1975, and organizing a public lecture series on Simone Weil throughout that academic year. The Rev. John Crocker, Jr., then the Episcopal chaplain at MIT, and now of Trinity Church, Princeton, encouraged this project from initial discussions with professors Henry Hanham and Bruce Mazlish through to the daily administrative tasks of running the seminar and locating the lecturers, often on the same day. To his support were added the skills of members of his staff, particularly Ms. Jane Sauer and Ms. Suzanne Strutt. Without their continual assistance the seminar and lecture series might well have taken place, but precisely *where* would have been less certain.

The MIT seminar on Simone Weil enrolled students from Harvard-Radcliffe, the Harvard Divinity School, the Episcopal Divinity School, as well as from Wellesley College. Here, Professor Alan Heimert of Harvard University was invaluable in his support. Understanding that those who make forays into teaching and scholarship require rooms of their own, Professor Heimert, as Master of Eliot House, Harvard College, has provided me with one since 1973, offered me the resources of a fine library nearby, and has even gone to the extraordinary length of allowing me periodically to assemble audiences of undergraduates for such courses as I might attempt in my own and their education. For this course, he and his administrative associate, Ms. Edie Holway, did yeoman service, and, as always, I had the thoughtfulness of Dr. Laura Gordon Fisher, Senior Tutor of Eliot House.

In the spring of 1978, Professor Mark Blasius, of the Politics Department of Princeton University, organized with great effort a twő-day symposium on Simone Weil that brought me to Stevenson College, along with Professor Andre Weil, Susan Sontag, and Professor Sheldon S. Wolin. The lectures, discussions, and informal conversations that followed still remain vivid to me.

Invitations for the MIT lecture series and for this collection of critical essays generated a large correspondence, mostly sympathetic, but in any event one that made me aware of the sense of responsibility an invitation to speak or write about Simone Weil created. I therefore wish to thank: Henry David Aiken, Fran Ansley, Hannah Arendt, Harvey Cox, Dorothy Day, Barbara Deming, M. I. Finley, the Rev. Harvey H. Guthrie, Jr., Elizabeth Hardwick, Michael Harrington, George Kateb, Alfred Kazin, Merloyd Lawrence, Denise Levertov, Dwight Macdonald, Alasdaire MacIntyre, Mary McCarthy, Alice Mayhew, Philip Morrison, James H. Murray, Walker Percy, Adrienne Rich, Philip Rieff, Arthur Rosenthal, John Schaar, Theodore Solotaroff, Susan Sontag, Peter Steinfels, William Stringfellow, U. T. Summers, Mark Taylor, Helen Vendler, M. T. Wilcox, Gary Wills, and Howard Zinn. In a more specialized but no less personal way I have had essential photographic assistance as well as critical insight from Christopher Seiberling.

As Simone Weil's brother helped Sir Richard Rees through his translating of her writings relating to science and mathematics, so my brother, Dr. Marvin Hart White—formerly Senior Engineer at the Westinghouse Research Laboratories, Baltimore, and now Fairchild Professor of Electrical Engineering, Le High University—helped me through the teaching of these writings in the MIT seminar by carefully annotating the collection known as *On Science, Necessity and the Love of God*. His diagrams helped to clarify the relationship between certain of her ethical concerns and specific scientific principles. And with respect to mathematics and science, he also explained with great patience what I should have remembered from my own undergraduate studies.

Particular thanks are due to Professor J. Allen Smith of the Rutgers University Law School who, in August 1980, took time from his own vacation to conduct my wife and me on tour in France, with attention to those places where Simone Weil lived or worked. His wise counsel, along with that of friends and colleagues John D. Stoeckle, M.D., Professor Austin Warren, and Chester A. Pearlman, Jr., M.D. was invaluable.

Friends and colleagues in the Newton Public Schools and at Cambridge-Somerville Catholic Charities were invaluable—especially superintendent Aaron Fink, Lillian Radlo, Dr. Thomas P. O'conor, Robert V. Frost, Dr. Paul Welch, Douglas Worth, and Woody Crowther. Harold W. Walsh deserves special mention.

The publication of this collection of essays would not have been possible without the diligence of my agent, Julian Bach, or without the foresight and faithfulness of Leone Stein, Director of the University of Massachusetts Press. Nor would it have been as "coherent"—Sir Richard's word—without the determination of Professor Robert Tucker, an editor of the *Massachusetts Review*. He, with his cheerfulness and skill, has made what was a working relationship into a friendship, and I thank Simone Weil for that too. Ms. Pam Campbell copyedited the manuscript for the Press with rare attention to detail. Ms. Mary Mendell translated conversation into splendid typography, and Frank Morrissey was the watchful proofreader.

My wife, Professor Ann Withorn, has been almost wholly without enthusiasm for Simone Weil since I announced this project to her. And yet she has listened carefully to most of what is in this book, and in many others relating to Simone Weil. I would like to believe that her stern skepticism has prevented me from making Simone Weil into something she is not.

Beth Kleiner, Zoe Quan, Harte Weiner, Marion Redonnet, Peter Harbeck, John Dorfman, Joe Crocker, Helenmarie Zachritz, Tom Harbinek, Nick Herman, Penny Greer, Maureen Kemeza, and Dan Jiggits were students in F21.935 at MIT. I can only hope I learned a measure of what they had to teach.

G. A. W.
Eliot House, Harvard University
Easter 1981

Introduction

Simone Weil was born in Paris in 1909 and died in Grosvenor Sanatorium just across the English Channel—Ashford, Kent—in 1943. We have always been clear about those dates, and reasonably clear about many others in her brief, searching, painful life. With her it is not so much the life as what it meant that has been so very unclear; unclear and troubling enough to have provoked over the forty years after her death a discussion characterized by extraordinary claims and extraordinary denials, by inaccuracy, hagiography, violence, inappropriateness, and outright nonsense. And the bulk of it, when spoken aloud or actually written, has come from those whom Simone Weil respected least and mistrusted most, those she endlessly confronted and made uncomfortable: middle-class academics and intellectuals, especially those seeking power or justifying the power they had already gained.

If in France today there are those who regard Simone Weil as "Sainte Simone," it is worth recalling that de Gaulle while in London with the Free French during World War II pronounced her as "mad" and likely never read the manuscript of her prophetic *Need for Roots.* Reprinting her penetrating essay "Factory Work" in *Politics* magazine immediately after that war, Dwight Macdonald also felt it necessary to editorialize in a postscript that "the remedies suggested appear as superficial as the evils previously analyzed are profound." The *Times Literary Supplement* has given each of her posthumous English-language collections of essays, journals, and letters respectful attention, yet Oxford University's Sir Isaiah Berlin will not write about her and Cambridge University's George Steiner regards Simone Weil as "culty" and "perverse." One feminist journal, *Soundings,* is sensitive to her pivotal essay, "The *Iliad,* or, The Poem of Force," while *Ms.* magazine headlines her as THE RED VIRGIN. No left journal in America has featured her extensive writings on the trade union situation while scarcely an issue of *The Catholic Worker* is without a quotation from or a reference to that work. Even the jacket of Simone Petrement's comprehensive biography, *Simone Weil: A Life* (New York: Pantheon, 1976), must make us aware that "she was as illuminating in her thought and in her quest for spiritual purity as she was unrelenting in her need for martyrdom."

Contradictory views—though of course all are correct. Hers *was* a body at home with ascetic detachment and discipline as well as with assembly-line engagement with chaos. Hers *was* a mind at home with Greek philosophy and mathematics as well as with the intricacies of Communist Party reversals and Hitler's *realpolitik.* Hers *was* a spirit at home with Benedictine plainsong as well as with Baptist spirituals. Simone Weil was also demanding, ridiculous, stubborn, abrasive, extreme.

Of course, with such sharp divisions and such striking polarities, how could any assessment of her life be otherwise? Avoiding the divisions would be dishonest, understating the polarities would be misleading. Moreover, as Elizabeth Hardwick suggested from the front page of the *New York Times Book Review* in 1976, the narrative of a personality in such contradiction ("breaking intensity") can only result in a certain soft confusion about the subject; regrettably, the necessary balancing of biography must "obscure" and "blur" the exemplary (but hopelessly complicated and essentially inaccessible) life. Of course.

Fortunately for Simone Weil and for those who wish to learn a measure of what she struggled so long and so hard to learn, her second major biographer refused to accept this all too contemporarily American, academically intellectual, tough-minded liberal, pseudo-psychoanalytic, coolly objective notion of biography-as-balanced-contradictions. Friends and foes may persist in this kind of spectacle; Simone Petrement, however, had the good sense and the skill to present contradictions dialectically.

For any reader of that essential survey of Simone Weil, the results become fourfold.

First, in spite of a silent abridgment of slightly less than half of the two volumes originally published in France in 1973, Simone Weil's early, original, remarkably penetrating insights into each of our oppressive twentieth century *isms*—colonialism, imperialism, state socialism, totalitarianism, nationalism, racism, sexism, scientism, secularism—emerge in all their intended provocativeness.

Second, given a clean translation into English, it is clear for those who wish to see that the meaning of Simone Weil's life is neither blurred nor obscured by the particulars of that life which, in true Platonic fashion, she herself regarded as intimations and finite, though quite real all the same. The meaning of her life is simply unbearable to accept, because accepting those insights and accepting that exemplary life would require nothing less than our radically changing our own.

Third, one thinks of George Orwell and T. E. Lawrence in England, F. O. Matthiessen and Dorothy Day in America, Ignazio Silone in Italy, but almost alone among the intellectuals of her time (and our own, sad to say), Simone Weil went beyond brilliant but cerebral insights into oppression, by choosing to engage the more fundamental question of injustice itself. And like them, in Camus's phrase, she "paid up personally."

Finally, when she wrote to a former lycée student in 1934: "Culture is a privilege that . . . gives power to the class that possesses it . . . let us try to undermine this privilege by relating complicated knowledge to the commonest knowledge," she was carrying the engagement a step further. She and those of similar privilege were not mere spectators in the vast industry of injustice. If their privilege was a self-deprivation, it was also, she now understood, part of the problem. It was this understanding of privilege and its relation to oppression and injustice that she would deepen and refine, insisting upon its centrality until the end of her life.

Herein lies the great value of insisting that a life must be viewed in its totality before judgments can be made. Formerly, Simone Weil's life was paraded as a series of extraordinary conversion experiences: initially, we were shown youthful involvement in studies, then Marxism-Leninism, trade unionism, pacifism, the Spanish Civil War, then exile to America, entering the ranks of the Free French in London and, at the end, an intense involvement with religion some have characterized as mystical. Now, the experiences are not denied; though presented dialectically, they appear less gaudy conversions, more impressive transmutations, less wild oscillations, something more like a steady progression.

To ask Toward what end? only highlights what a truly comprehensive view entails. That is, seeing the full sweep of her engagements—mental and physical—allows the linking of Simone Weil's extensive work experiences in factory and field to her thoughtful encounters with the Catholic Church. Without such linking, the earlier tendency was to minimize or patronizingly misunderstand the work experiences in their importance and to castigate or mystify into religiosity the experiences with Catholicism.

On her deathbed Simone Weil would remain uncertain as to why people oppressed one another, but when she stood at her shearing machine in a Paris factory in December 1934 it was not "experience" alone she needed; it was, a comprehensive view of her life might argue, that she had reached a theoretical impasse as to how the machine becomes a part of this world's terrible oppression. Nine months and three factories later, having experienced burns, filth, cuts, infections, fatigue (but not fear), Simone Weil had come to the understanding that there was a direct line of "reasoning" from our modern division and extreme specialization of labor (Taylorism) to the original separation of intellectual from manual labor that Karl Marx inveighed against when he saw it had developed two thousand years earlier in her beloved classical Greece.

"The capital fact is not the suffering," she wrote, "but the humiliation." She went on to agree with Marx that "the liberation of the workers must be accomplished in the work itself, and that the work, in order to become that of a free man, must be pervaded by thought, invention, and judgment." Yet Simone Weil learned enough in her time spent with the machines to disagree with Marx's belief in "the liberating powers of the revolution." And she disagreed even more with his theory of "the infinite development of the productive forces after the revolution." Neither, she had learned by her own excruciating experiences, would up-root injustice and both, in fact, would only prolong it, because they reinforced a fundamental illusion about the nature of injustice.

Her own manual labor righted an experiential balance in her life, to be certain, opening Simone Weil to the absolute correct-ness of particular aspects of Marx. But she could not agree with him—nor could additional manual labor in vineyard after vine-yard convince her—that injustice was exterior to man, rooted in the material environment alone. It was the Church, on three memorable occasions (at the Blessing of the Fleet in a poor vil-lage in Portugal, while kneeling in Saint Francis's little chapel at Assisi, and while attending services from Palm Sunday to Easter Tuesday at Solesmes), that righted a balance on another plane, a plane that transcended the material environment while allow-ing her to see the essential connection between the two realms.

"A laborer," she then wrote, "burns up his own flesh and trans-forms it into energy like a machine burning coal. He transforms his own flesh and blood into the fruits of his labor, food and wine. . . . Manual labor," she concluded, "is either a degrading servitude or a sacrifice."

Learning what this "sacrifice" meant was the most difficult les-son of all the lessons Simone Weil had to learn. Learning this, she knew at last what working people have always known—in-cluding the ultimate residence of injustice—and accepted through faith. Perhaps trivial to some but precious and redeeming to us, this lesson. After all, as a farm woman said, "All the intellectuals we knew put barriers between themselves and the peasants. Si-mone Weil threw down these barriers and put herself on our level."

The essays that follow were assembled in order to engage Simone Weil from a very wide perspective, from particular and divergent personal, religious, political, and social orientations. They were written by "intellectuals," that is, by people who regard ideas in certain ways and who have attempted to use them in certain ways. In October 1975, Dr. Robert Coles gave the first lecture in an

MIT series on Simone Weil, and her brother, Andre, the distinguished mathematician at the Institute for Advanced Study, Princeton, was invited as the respondent. Although Professor Weil disclaimed "being an authority on Simone Weil or her writing," his own perspective remains an important, even though a neglected one, and it serves as a valuable commentary on these essays.

"Dr. Coles referred to Simone Weil's 'contempt' for intellectuals [in his lecture]," Professor Weil noted. "Well, I don't think Dr. Coles meant it in quite that simplistic a way." Professor Weil continued,

In the first place, Simone Weil knew very well that she was one—an intellectual—and couldn't help it, because she had that particular training to a very high degree. She had a professional philosophical training which was always quite beyond me, because my mind is one of the most *un*philosophical in existence.

She had that training, and it was immediately clear to anyone who discussed any topic with her, because with that training she could out-talk anyone who tried to discuss any of her views.

Many people had this painful experience. For example, she had a discussion with a priest of which this priest, as I discovered only later, had a somewhat painful recollection. And at the time my sister told me that quite probably she was sent by God to earth in order to make some Catholics, and particularly Catholic priests, do their purgatory while on earth!

This is to demonstrate that her philosophic training showed in her dialectical powers in any kind of philosophic discussion. And there is no doubt that in many ways she transcended this philosophic training. She never uses technical philosophic language, for example, and she wrote in a very simple and beautiful French. Some have said they find her hard reading, however, since her *thought* is sometimes difficult. . . .

Dr. Coles's essay on Simone Weil's mind in this collection accepts her brother's position as a given, but develops the distinction between that mind and other minds of her time, namely, that as an intellectual she was not only critical, but *self*-critical. In turning her considerable powers upon such abstractions as the State or such concrete ills as the racist attitude of France toward her colonies, Simone Weil joined the very small group of intellectuals—whom Coles discusses as well—who also submitted their own intellects to self-criticism.

Several essays in this collection consider Simone Weil's attempt to understand the workings of certain *systems,* whether ancient or modern. Professor Cameron questions Simone Weil's understanding of Gnosticism, Michele Murray questions Simone Weil's understanding of Catholicism, Staughton Lynd questions Simone Weil's understanding of Marxism and of Marxism-Leninism. As to her own system, Andre Weil had remarked:

I think that [Coles] rightly said that in Simone Weil's writings one should not seek a system. One can say a little more about that observation: In an unpublished essay she has expressed herself on philosophical systems. As I remember it now . . . she wrote in that essay that since the purpose of philosophy was to react to the contradictions which are just there, any attempt to build up a philosophical system is false and un-philosophical, *a priori.* The purpose of philosophy, as she conceived it, was not to resolve contradictions in the foolish manner in which some people say, Yes, there is a Thesis, and here is an Antithesis, and then on top of them is a Synthesis. . . . No, she did not believe in synthesis; she did not have the belief that if she lived long enough she would some day discover some wonderful synthesis.

For all her intellectual resources, Simone Weil could be perfectly human in her tendency to use her intellectual resources to run past or to run over contradictions, and she was as capable as any of pushing thought, pure thought, beyond supporting data in her attempt to make what she took to be important "connections." In the area of science and mathematics, Professor Weil commented, "She did not know much mathematics, naturally," he added, "because she had no special talent for mathematics." Further,

She was convinced (as many philosophers are) that the existence of mathematics is of supreme philosophical importance. This attitude goes back quite definitely to Plato, perhaps further . . . and she decided that instead of making a useless effort to get the gist of contemporary mathematics (not the New Math, for heaven's sake!), instead of getting into this spirit through studying textbooks which give you bad mathematics, what a philosopher must do is to get into the spirit of live mathematics which can be followed without too much trouble, by beginning elsewhere. Therefore, she solved the problem quite reasonably by reading some of Archimedes's easier writings, by reading Viète—the classical French algebraist of the 16th century—and she tried to read some later writers.

But she tried not to go beyond what she could actually follow in the way of live mathematics. She had no intention of getting any deep insight into mathematics as such. Her interest was in trying to discover from her point of view a satisfactory answer to the question, What is mathematics? To some extent I think she answered that question.

But in her attempt to extrapolate from what she had learned, she could make serious errors. "I may mention one very specific point [by way of example]," said Professor Weil, "where she got the idea that contemporary physicists had been entirely on the wrong road, which is a technical point concerning quantum mechanics."

There was some correspondence between us on that. She came to this understanding while she was in Marseilles and I was in America with the Quakers at Haverford College. She wrote to me about difficulties and objections, and I tried to help her, but her views were entirely mistaken [on this technical point].

It is the question of whether discontinuity in quantum theory arises from the fact that probability theory started from discontinuous probabilities. And she asked whether a theory of continuous probabilities might solve this problem? And of course physicists are perfectly well aware of this theory, and this is perfectly trivial from their point of view, and her idea on this specific point was totally mistaken and not worth discussing.

Even Simone Weil's errors, however, could provide illumination in other areas, or encourage a larger truth, as several essays demonstrate. Professor Ferber in his analysis of her essay "The Iliad, or The Poem of Force," for example, makes some telling points not only on her handling of the Greek text, but on her understanding of basic elements of Greek culture and the implications her understanding had for what she went on to say about power. On the other hand, both Professors Ferber and Summers agree that what arises from Simone Weil's argument about Homer's poem had enormous value for her own time and for the future, as a commentary on power and violence and the nature of war. And in spite of the caustic skepticism of Simone Weil's views concerning politics and politicians, Conor Cruise O'Brien must admit the ways in which such skepticism has great positive value in the conduct of "practical" political affairs, given the current dangers inherent in various nationalisms and uncritical notions of patriotism and the glories of the State.

Michele Murray subjects Simone Weil's personal motivations to harsh scrutiny, and both Professor Cameron and Dr. Coles raise grave doubts about the meaning of Simone Weil's last days. All, however, might have nodded in agreement with Professor Weil when he said, "[As far as finally making a system] she probably didn't mean to live long enough. I remember her saying in a letter to me—I don't remember what I had written to her to provoke the response—she wrote, 'the future has no more need for me than I have for it.'" He continued,

The second part of this statement, that was her own outlook. About the first part of this statement, she may not have realized herself when she was writing, how much she had to say. At other times, she seems to have realized it. In another letter, to Father Perrin, I believe, she says something like this: that a certain number of essential truths seem to have descended upon her and she does not know how they came to do that, but since the truths have descended upon *her,* she feels it her duty, her mission, to pass them on to the outside world and to future generations, for what they may be worth. But obviously she felt they were worth something.

Each of the writers in this collection has made an effort at identifying precisely what those truths were. While Conor Cruise O'Brien may find certain of her ethical positions remarkable, Staughton Lynd locates her value, to some extent, in her work with trade unionists in the 1930s, and the editor of this collection, in her work experiences in factory and field. What may be the unifying element in each of these seemingly divergent responses to her life and her writings is that none of the writers believes that one of these truths *necessarily* has excluded the others, and that however Simone Weil went about discovering or embodying these truths, the sense of her willing herself to this activity was absent. Simone Weil was, in short, *called*.

The notion of vocation appears to have evaporated from our culture; moderns no longer feel themselves bound by such archaic and self-limiting beliefs. Simone Weil would have found *that* belief absurd, though her brother concluded his remarks, responding to the statement that perhaps his sister's vocation was that of a saint, by engaging such a possibility, saying

I must clarify this statement even further as, taken out of context, it may be misleading.

In ordinary language, it is true the word "saint" is normally taken as a laudatory word—what a fine person he is, she is. They are saints. One may also, in an entirely different context, use the word "saint" not as laudatory or as pejorative, but simply as a statement of fact, of a certain person's inclinations toward this or that type of activity.

I happen to be a mathematician. From a very early age I didn't have to ask whether I was a mathematician, because I was one. Gauguin was a painter, and eventually discovered that he had to sacrifice, to give up, a number of very important human values to this "business" of his which was to be a painter. My sister was convinced that some people are born to be a carpenter or a mechanic, and that these vocations were equal to more intellectual or high-sounding vocations, that these men performed tasks with as much intrinsic value as those born to be poets or philosophers. In that very specific sense, I think it is reasonable to use the word "saint" as describing a certain kind of inclination toward types of activities—be they physical, mental, social or whatever.

This can be typified by a number of well-known examples. Because the examples will normally be taken from the "better" specimens, the more famous ones, however, the word is associated with lauditative ideas. Well, there is no doubt that Saint Francis or Saint Theresa can be named. He was a great man, and she was a great woman. But many of us have in our acquaintance people who have this kind of urge, and at a very low and poor level, just as there are bad painters whose vocation is indisputable. There are people who have the clear vocation to be composers, and have this urge so strongly they cannot do anything else . . . and they have never written a bar of good music. This can very well happen. It has nothing to do with using the word "saint" as a judgment of quality.

A religious man would have said God put her into the world for that purpose. That again is quite meaningless, but her vocation or role or business in life from a very early age was to be a saint, and from an early age she trained herself quite consciously for that purpose. It is another thing, a matter of personal views or feelings, to decide whether beyond this, she was a good saint, a mediocre saint, a first-class saint, or a third-class saint!

What possible use then, can be made of Simone Weil's life? Some readers will be loath to "use" her. For them, she must remain one of those all-too rare intellects, austere, subtle, powerful, and splendid in its isolation. Others will either reject her example (as historian, political theorist, literary critic, social activist, pedagogue, religious seeker) or shy away, as suggested earlier, from its radical implications for the course of their lives.

Anyone who reads Simone Weil carefully, however, will not be able to avoid the sense that, despite a mind capable of the highest abstractions and a spirit capable of the farthest reaches of consciousness, this woman also had a concrete sense of the mundane here-and-now, and a complex but immediate sense of utility. She *meant* her writings and her life to be taken seriously and she meant them to be taken literally and transformed—like the flesh and blood that she saw become productive labor—into something useful, in this world, on this earth.

But what use has a political analyst outside a party, or a bureaucracy, or a government? What use has a religious seeker outside a denomination, or the Church? What use has an intellectual bearing the stigmata of industrial and agricultural labor, and the high visibility of one who has constantly criticized intellectuals and even the intellect itself? What use has a classicist who abhors Rome, someone French who admires poetry by George Herbert, a clumsy woman in a male-dominated mechanized and technologically defined world?

Perhaps awareness on the part of readers that a world (or a society) that does *not* value the usefulness of such an individual, that goes so far as to define him/her as "outside," may very well be a world most needful of such an individual if only to provide another perspective, an alternative vision of what might be possible.

Like that other eternal question raiser, Hannah Arendt, Simone Weil was also concerned with power and more than merely puzzled as to why groups found it necessary to make people as characterless and submissive as possible, and why some people found it necessary to identify with such power while others resisted or disobeyed. Simone Weil's examination of *The Iliad* is her most dramatic examination of this process of domination. In respectful but piteous detail she demonstrates how supposedly intelligent men so willfully blind themselves, why it is they become so utterly un-self-conscious as to submit to domination while they place the lives of their loved ones at such enormous risk.

Simone Weil was aware that she was outside. Is it not just possible that a primary use of her would be to discover why she was outside? And not by focusing on her as the problem, but by seeing her disciplined, courageous withdrawal from so many seductive centers of power as part of the solution?

This collection, it is hoped, will advance such a use.

The Jagged Edge: A Biographical Essay on Simone Weil

~

MICHELE MURRAY

We have to learn that personal suffering is a more effective key, a more rewarding principle for exploring the world in thought and action, than personal good fortune.—Dietrich Bonhoeffer

The trajectories of Simone Weil's life—from agnosticism to faith, from middle-class comfort to identification with the poor, from intellectual accomplishment to radical distrust of the dominant intellect—are not singular. Other men and women have found circumstance and conviction moving them on one or the other of these paths. Weil's uniqueness is found in her having traveled on all three simultaneously, moved by a psychological need to unify her life absolutely, to test her ideas with her body, and to think nothing but what was rooted in her experience. That she failed and left behind a record of a truncated life and a collection of fragmentary writings is not surprising; from Nietzsche through Wittgenstein and Bonhoeffer, ours has been a century of the fragmentary and the suggestive, the graveyard of philosophical systems. Her failure indicates, perhaps, the limits of her pure and powerful enterprise.

It is this power and single-minded attention to living out the consequences of her beliefs that lifts her from the realm of merely representative figures and compels our special attention.

Simone Weil was born in Paris in 1909; her father was a doctor and her family was solidly middle class. To give weight to the acts of the adult woman, it is important to remember what the Paris of her childhood was like, in those years before World

War I cut across and effectively ended a particular way of life. In 1909, for example, Paris was the home of Picasso and Apollinaire, Gertrude Stein was living in her atelier, 27 rue Fleurus, Rilke had served as Rodin's secretary only a few years before and was working on his *Notebooks of Malte Laurids Brigge* with its vision of Paris as the city of death, and the Ballets Russe paid its first visit to western Europe during that summer. Paris was also a city of luxury and of good bourgeois comfort that seemed as if it would last forever. Simone Weil did not leave behind any autobiographical notes, but her near-contemporaries, Jean-Paul Sartre, Simone de Beauvoir, and Clara Malraux, have all written of the muffled order of bourgeois life, of the restrictions and rigidities which surrounded this comfort, and of the price it exacted from rebellious youth by that final authority, the family.

The Weil family was not so rigid. Both parents were interested in intellectual matters, and Simone's older brother, Andre, the only other child, was a mathematical prodigy. Simone herself, although manifesting a brilliant intelligence at an early age, never lost her sense that her own powers were inferior compared to her brother's genius. The Weils, however, were close, and Simone had the extraordinary good fortune of having the emotional support of her parents throughout her life.

Paris in 1909 was still under the shadow of the Dreyfus Case. Although the Weils were nominally Jewish, they were well assimilated and did not offer their children any religious upbringing. We do not know how the Dreyfus Case affected them. Simone did not think of herself as Jewish, and although she has been written of as a Jew who wrote harshly about Israel, she can be considered Jewish only in the most general racial terms or in Sartre's formulation that a Jew is one who is seen as a Jew by others. The family was patriotically French and committed to the secular state of the Third Republic.

More significant, in the light of Simone Weil's life, was the division of Paris into Black and Red, Right and Left, rich and poor. Beneath the calmness of the grands boulevards, there was a city of bitter workers who were unable to forget the bloody repression that followed the Commune in 1870-71, a proletariat cut off from any share in middle-class prosperity, and an underworld of anarchist assassinations, illiteracy, and crime. The two Frances that had existed since the French Revolution were further apart than ever in 1909, and on either side of the split, class passions were strong. Not many crossed the barrier. Simone Weil was one who did.

She claimed to have become aware of God and of Jesus Christ in her childhood, despite her agnostic upbringing, and she did reveal a precocious streak of asceticism, as well as keen powers of observation, when she refused to wear socks because poor children did not have them or to eat sugar during World War I when the soldiers at the front did not have it. From where did her particular moral conscience come?

Perhaps it came from childlike feelings of exclusion and a childlike awareness of all that she possessed; perhaps from a sense that who she was had nothing to do with individual talent, that she was literally the *product* of a rich cultural life which nourished a certain class of people throughout Europe, which opened doors, which gave, with an infant's food, a tangled mix of customs and ideas that depended upon money, certainly, but also on family continuity and stability, on a conjunction of circumstances that America has not experienced, except possibly in some patrician New England families. A sense that it was, somehow, all more than one deserved—the ease that comes from knowing who you are, the security and certainty that springs from a solid family life, the comfort that comes with servants and the ability to travel, see, and experience. Parents exist as models of achievement, there is access to music, to nature during long summer holidays, to the finest schooling and books, to a wide range of successful and intelligent adults, and to friendship with other gifted children. High standards are set and upheld, and the means for achieving them are present. And yet the direction, somehow, seems wrong.

Neither such feelings nor awareness, poor health nor a belief in her own intellectual inferiority kept Simone Weil from compiling a splendid record at school and claiming first place in the nationwide examinations for the Ecole Normale Superieure, which had only recently been opened to women. Simone de Beauvoir gained second place in the same examination, with thirty men following both women on the list. Once there, Weil did brilliantly at the Ecole Normale, which is considered to be the crown of the French educational system. Its method of instruction, with strict emphasis upon logic and philosophy, suited her temperament, which was given to speculation and abstract reasoning, and she continued to study with Alain, who had been her teacher at the Lycée Henri IV and whose ideas continued to influence her to the end of her life.

What is most interesting about Simone Weil at nineteen, however, is not her scholastic achievement; she was not the only gifted student at the Ecole Normale, nor were her accomplishments highly regarded by all her instructors, some of whom categorized her as eccentric and excessively individualistic. What *is* striking is her concern with political and social problems and her belief that in order to understand them, she had to go beyond an intellectual grasp and, regardless of the consequences to her career, join her life with that of the workers. This she attempted to do.

That is not an ordinary decision even today [1973], when professors and students openly engage in political action, but in 1928 or 1929, and in a France far more rigidly stratified by class than the United States ever was, such direct action—including action in the streets—was neither customary nor understood. In her memoirs, Simone de Beauvoir writes that, for her and Sartre, politics was far away in those years, they felt that they lived a charmed life, and they gave no thought to the difficulties of the working class.

Such distance was not possible for Simone Weil. While still at the Ecole Normale, she was known as the "Red Virgin"—for her outspoken support of left wing and pacifist movements—and as "the Categorical Imperative in skirts"—for her humorless, irritating philosophical argumentation. It was at this time that she had her first prolonged stint of physical labor when she assisted in a harvest during her summer holidays, displaying the same wish for the hardest work and the fewest comforts that she was to show throughout her life.

Graduating from the Ecole Normale in 1931 with the highest

rank, that of agregée, she was entitled to a post as a teacher in a lycée, and received an appointment to the small industrial town of Le Puy from a Minister of Education who wanted her as far from Paris as possible. From then until 1934 she taught at a number of lycées in provincial towns and engaged in political activity on behalf of the unemployed and striking workers at a time when France was going through a period of great political agitation. Her presence at the head of workers' delegations was invariably criticized by right-thinking citizens who believed implicitly that teachers were members of the middle class and had no business associating with workers. The citizens were especially critical of Mlle. Weil whose low monotonous voice, carelessness about dress, incessant smoking, awkward gait, and imposing intellectual presence made her an easy target.

Indeed, reading the class notes that her pupils took, it is difficult to see how any of these ordinary young women ever understood her lectures in philosophy, mathematics, and the history of science. She was remote, not at all warm, preoccupied with her thoughts and political activities. Nevertheless, her students were attracted to her, sensing the force of her personality and also, perhaps, finding in her rebellious figure a focus for their own opposition to the parental order.

Since Simone had understood from the beginning that she would incur the disapproval of the authorities, her superiors in school and at the Ministry of Education, as well as the local establishment, she was not deterred by their opposition from following a course she perceived as correct. Although at this time she indicated no interest in religion, she lived with utmost austerity. In each town she would choose a small room in an unassuming neighborhood, move in with her papers, books, and cigarettes, refuse heat or other extras, eat as little as possible, and contribute the larger share of her pay to workers' causes.

In addition to her teaching and political activity, she was busy writing articles, which were striking in their prescient analysis of totalitarian regimes, the nature of the coming war, and the underlying structures of the democratic and capitalist societies of the West. She had been a Marxist, but soon found doctrinaire Marxian formulations inadequate to explain what she had seen and understood of the conditions around her, and she boldly advanced her own analyses based on an examination of the language used by governments to conceal the social reality from the people, buttressing her position with classical Greek thought.

It was her personal style of political involvement that was (rightly) perceived as threatening by supporters of the existing social order, for the example of Simone's utter commitment could have proven contagious to the young people she taught. That they were not infected, despite their admiration, was to a large degree the result of Simone's eccentricities, which isolated her to such a degree from the experiences and emotions of ordinary people that no prolonged emotional exchange was possible. Even the workers she helped found her pride and exigency both irritating and amusing, and they could never take her as seriously as she took herself. And no more than the bourgeoisie, did they believe in her attempts to identify with the working class and the poor.

The gap between the way Simone regarded her work and the way that others looked at her was an increasing problem all her life. Of course, this is a difficulty that everyone faces but it was acute in Simone's case because she set herself such impossibly high standards, she was so manifestly full of both good will and outstanding intelligence, she was so audacious in her desires—and yet, she was so clumsy, so frail, so isolated in her gifts, as well as in her pride.

When she determined to erase the class barriers between her and the workers by abandoning, at least temporarily, a teaching career and doing factory work, she crossed from a marginal knowledge of the sufferings of the poor to another world that marked her forever, as she later stated, with "the brand of a slave" never to be effaced from her soul. This extraordinary act, which was the linchpin of her life, made a return to her former mode of living impossible. She began in December 1934, working with heavy machinery at a Paris factory, and remained in that job for four months despite her immediate recognition that she lacked the physical strength for such a job. She could not keep up with her companions, the noise gave her headaches, she was continually fatigued.

At the end of the work day, she could not think or write in her journal; only on Saturday afternoons and Sundays could she recover some measure of intellectual power. In March she was laid off and did not find another job until April—this time as a packer in a particularly filthy and depressing small shop, from which she was dismissed after a month because she was unable to keep up with the minimum piecework demand. Before she found her third job, at the Renault works, again after a month of unemployment, she applied for a teaching job to begin the following year, perhaps acknowledging that her experiment could be no more than that; she was incapable of continuing this brutal labor without utterly destroying herself.

In any case she had learned what she needed to know. For the rest of her life her writings were marked by this knowledge earned by the flesh. It was the background against which all of her later ideas were developed. Although she had not yet been touched by religious imperatives, she was prepared to receive Christianity by her feeling that she had become a slave, for she later wrote that she recognized in Christianity the religion of slaves and she knew it as the religion for her.

She returned to teaching in Bourges in 1935–36, but it was not the same; she was relatively indifferent to her pupils, her irritating mannerisms increased, and she lived even more frugally. She put more of her passion into reading her beloved Greek authors, and she alienated many with her relentless curiosity, which seemed almost inhuman in its intensity and disregard for the personal. She was never conscious of her insensitivity, however, and seemed unaware that she amused others by her single-minded concerns. In her life, both at this time and later, were raised the eternal questions of the relationship between prophets and their society.

Of course ordinary people are usually condemned for refusing to heed the words of the prophets in their midst, whether Jeremiah, John the Baptist, or Simone Weil, but just how can an ordinary person relate to someone like Simone, someone who had entirely sublimated her emotional and sexual development, and whose intelligence enabled her to grasp ideas far beyond the understanding of those about her? Add to this her clumsiness, her untidiness, her ugliness—for by now the beautiful child had become an ugly woman who dressed in ill-fitting clothes and spoke strangely, peering at the world from behind thick glasses, constantly smoking, her fingers stained with nicotine, her rasping cough a regular accompaniment to her monologues—and she was unlikely to appeal to anyone lacking her gifts and her obsessions.

With the outbreak of the Spanish Civil War in July 1936, Simone felt that here was another experience she had to share, and she contrived to get to Spain, not to fight—for at this time she still retained the pacifism she later abandoned as artificial—but to share the dangers of her working-class comrades. It says much for her intensity that she managed to get sent to the front by men who had—and rightly so—no confidence in her ability to do anything practical in a war. The doubts of her friends were justified when, assigned to cook for a battalion at the front lines, this undomestic woman upset a pot of boiling oil over her leg and had to be taken to a hospital at Sitges, where she learned a good deal about the actual conduct of the war, as distinct from the official version of events, from wounded men brought in for treatment and surgery. Having lost her confidence in the rightness of the Loyalist cause after hearing that the atrocities they practiced were no different in kind from those of Franco's troops, she returned to Paris at the end of September with her leg still unhealed, more isolated than ever from accepted leftist opinion.

Her experiences in Spain, on top of those in the factories, destroyed her already poor health; she never again held a regular teaching post, although she continued writing widely on political and social subjects, and warned repeatedly of the coming war and of the dangers of *any* totalitarian regime. But from 1937 on, she moves into another sphere, the religious one, without abandoning her earlier preoccupation with the social, yet moving it into the background as she emphasized the need to live in conformity with the will of God. Discovering this will became her chief work.

Here, a visit to Italy in 1937 was decisive—she had always been attracted by the figure of St. Francis, and in Assisi was forced to her knees, as she later wrote, although she was not yet sure to whom she was praying. Afraid, in her scrupulosity, that if she read the New Testament she would unconsciously be influenced by it, she had refrained from reading the Gospels. Her second and crucial experience occurred in Easter Week at Solesmes Monastery, famous for the purity of the Gregorian chant of its Benedictine monks. Driven almost to insanity by one of the headaches that plagued her, she found herself carried out past pain while listening to the chant, writing that Christ entered her soul "once and for all" at this time. An Englishman also at Solesmes introduced her to the English metaphysical poets, and it was while she was reciting George Herbert's poem, "Love bade me welcome while my Soule drew back," that, in her words, "Christ Himself came down and He took me."

Such a mystical experience has different consequences for different people. For Simone, it meant an attempt that lasted until her death in 1943 to express perfectly what she took to be God's will and to understand intellectually what this meant. This is the Simone Weil who has received the most attention, and it is this Simone who has proved most attractive to those who are without conventional religious belief yet feel attracted to spiritual matters. She has been pictured as a "secular saint," a forerunner of a new type of religion which would be in the world rather than in the churches, and as a prophet, along with Dietrich Bonhoeffer, of a new religionless Christianity. A reading of her writings during these last five years is immensely problematical, but this cannot be separated from the atmosphere in which they were first received.

The first book of Simone Weil published in English—*Waiting for God*—appeared in America during one of our periodic "religious revivals." The year was 1951 and ecstatic reviews and enthusiasm about sainthood were propelling college students and intellectuals to buy the essays. No more can 1951 be brought back than 1937, and the catchwords of the Silent Generation and McCarthyism risk the danger of taking the political element of life, which is a small part for most, as a metaphor for all of life—a mistake Simone Weil never made.

For those who cared about art and literature, the religious

revival of the 1950s was a time of extraordinary, almost embarrassing zeal. The influence of T. S. Eliot was at its apogee in the universities; the poet Allen Tate had become a Catholic (as had Robert Lowell earlier); Jacques Maritain's *Creative Intuition in Art and Poetry* would attempt to yoke together scholastic philosophy and modern art; and Thomas Merton's *The Seven Story Mountain* laid out, in overwrought language, the course of a brilliant young man's abandonment of secularism and positivism in favor of Catholicism and the silence of Trappist austerity. His example filled the spare monasteries of contemplative orders with young people eager to dedicate their lives to something more than getting and spending. Then, as in the early 1970s, mysticism was the operative word, but it was mysticism of a different kind that drew ardent young souls (and I use those three words deliberately, for that was the diction of those days) toward God.

How else could one explain the popularity of Julian of Norwich, an English mystic of the fourteenth century, whose mention in Eliot's *Four Quartets* had sent enthusiasts to other Eliot poems, or of other English mystical works, *The Cloud of Unknowing* and the writings of Richard Rolle chief among them (this latter reissued by the Newman Press in charming little books covered in cornflower blue). A new bookshop, graced with tasteful art and liturgical objects to complement the books, opened on Third Avenue in New York City in the shadow of the yet-to-be-pulled-down elevated, and there one found the writings of St. John of the Cross in three thick volumes with dusty rose jackets and dauntingly small type. On Sunday evenings at St. Thomas More Church on New York's East Side, the increasingly larger number of liturgists gathered to chant Compline—in Latin, of course—in the Gregorian mode. But the chief religious influence came, in those days immediately after the emotional excitement and the exhaustion of World War II, from the French.

Maritain, of course, was the conduit for a good deal of this, the French writer having been in residence at Princeton University during the war and thereafter. But the enthusiasm so many felt for Claudel, Peguy, Mauriac, Marcel, and Bernanos did not depend upon the influence of one person, or even of several. It was a reaction to the inward turning that marked postwar America, and it signaled a renewed appreciation of la belle France free again. Among people of certain temperaments, it was a reaction against that *other* intellectual movement that had blown to America on the westerlies once the French were free—existentialism—which seemed to offer no firm basis for values and to have no room for metaphysical or religious experiences. To some, it appeared hopelessly barren and utterly joyless in its insistence on man to the exclusion of any possibility of God. (Kierkegaard's influence would come, but later, and the religious existentialism of Marcel and Buber was still in the shadows of Sartre.) We might gauge the distance or the temper, by noting that today's Conor Cruise O'Brien—politician, diplomat, and passionate opponent of colonialism, racism, and terrorism—was the author, as Donat O'Donnell, of the superb book, *Maria Cross,* a study of Catholic novelists, which took its name from the temptress of Mauriac's *Desert of Love.*

To some degree, this religious revival was a conservative one, looking for a return to a stable social order based on rural life and harmony with nature. Such had never existed, but a shadow order had, which was built on the labor of the rural poor and sustained because of the depressions that followed upon World War I in Europe and America; but the upheavals of World War II had destroyed forever the possibility of any reconstruction of that social order. Simone Weil had addressed herself to just this painful situation in the book she wrote at the behest of her superiors among the Free French while in London, *The Need for Roots.* It was no longer a question of words or ideas, however. And as the impossibility of returning to the land became ever clearer, so did the need grow more pressing. The ring may sound familiar to those in the mid-seventies who remembered a back-to-the-land movement, not among hippies, but among midwestern Catholics even earlier, in the late 1930s and early 1940s, fostered by St. John's Abbey, the great Benedictine foundation in Minnesota. Abigail McCarthy's *Private Faces, Public Places,* has pages devoted to recollections of this desire for a wholeness that was to be exemplified by combining farming with intellectual work in the rural surroundings that were thought to be more spiritual than the noisy, secular, industrial life of the cities.

Technology and a clever American instrumentalism veiled as "pragmatism" in the workplace and "realism" in domestic and foreign policy, were readying for the onslaught against the old religious order, which was determined to hold its own, with its weapons of prayer and literature. One piece of that, one weapon, was Simone Weil.

Simone Weil was born—for Americans—in this atmosphere, and she was used—by Americans—in a number of ways, not all of them intended or conscious. Very quickly then, the force of her personality touched life after life. Leslie Fiedler recorded his admiration for this woman, and Catholics rushed to claim for one of their own this woman whose refusal of baptism was seen as only a "minor blot" on an "essentially" Catholic spiritual nature. After *Waiting for God,* there appeared the book-length *Need for Roots,* with an introduction by no less a figure than T. S. Eliot. By this time Eliot had taught his audience to read him carefully, but his cautions and his concerns that readers *pay attention* to the complexities and the contradictions of Simone Weil went unnoticed. These writings and the ones that would appear—selections from her notebooks entitled *Gravity and Grace,* the *Notebooks* themselves in two thick volumes in 1956, supplemented by a third in 1970, and a second collection of essays on scientific and religious subjects in 1968, *On Science, Necessity, and the Love of God*—defied a principle of order. Her religious thought was scattered through the essays, journal entries, and a small group of letters, several of them quite long, sent to a priest friend explaining why she could not become a Catholic. All were provisional, scrappy, the record of a particular state of mind. Only in the essays did there appear any logical progression, and even there, it was brief and tentative. Very slowly readers perceived key themes that emerged from the pages, especially those written in the last two years of her life, and when they were finally recognized for what they were, radical, penetrating, and disquieting, only then did the shock, and, after it, the reaction, set in.

For far from finding any peace in the assurance she received of Christ's eternal love, the record shows that Simone Weil was driven on an intellectual and personal quest that became an ordeal for its witnesses; a trial that culminated in her death through self-starvation in August 1943, when she was only thirty-four. She was in London at the time, working for the Free French, having come from New York, where she lived briefly with her parents after they had escaped from France. Isolated from her family, her country, and all familiar surroundings, Simone nevertheless devoted herself to France and to returning to France, whatever the risks. She repeatedly begged to be parachuted to resistance groups inside the country, but the Free French leaders were more impervious to her appeals than the Spanish Loyalists had been, refusing on the grounds that her appearance and—although they did not say this—her lack of prudence would endanger her contacts. Instead, she was given the make-work assignment of preparing a paper of prescriptions for the restoration of French political and social health.

We cannot be certain how her leaders regarded this assignment, but it was work she engaged in with the utmost seriousness. She spent days reading and writing furiously, developing the ideas about French capitulation to the Nazis and French collaboration with the Nazis, the plight of the workers and the separation of groups, one from the other, of justice and *spiritual* health, subjects she had tackled piecemeal in earlier periodical articles. In perspective and at length, these questions became *The Need for Roots.* What is surprising is that although this manuscript would appear to have required the complete energies of a mind, her journals during this same period reveal other complex questions being considered, another story. In time we cannot imagine her having, she painted the image of a tormented soul, driven to ransacking world mythology in support of her belief that Christ had existed in other avatars in other times; of a relentless intellect determined to prove that the Jews had no part in Christianity, that it was all fathered by her beloved Greeks, especially Plato;

of a woman whose obsessions with food and the evil of matter
were more and more dominating her personality.

There are more questions than answers here, and speculators
must tread lightly. Nevertheless, the persistence of food imagery
throughout her work is significant in light of her anorexia, and
her growing hatred of the body must be examined in the context
of her conscious transformation from an attractive girl into an
ugly woman imprisoned in a clumsy body. Her notorious dislike
of personal contact, her repulsion if she were kissed, and her
total sexlessness, all point to personal phobias that were conquer-
ing the overworked, ill, and lonely woman. Because of her training in classical thought, she felt the need to rationalize these
phobias and make them a part of her religious development. Her
love of Romanesque art had led her to the civilization of the
Languedoc in southern France and that, in turn, had made her
conscious of the Cathars, a Gnostic religion that flourished in
the eleventh and twelfth centuries in Provence until the Albigensian Crusade ordered by Pope Innocent III and captained by the
cruel Simon de Montfort, had wiped out all traces of the culture
of the troubadours.

Under the influence of her love for the Cathars and driven by
her need to make sense of her hunger for decreation, she devoted
herself more and more to Gnostic thought and moved further
away from orthodox Christianity of any persuasion—something
few of her admirers recognize or accept. She refused baptism in
the Catholic Church, as mentioned, ostensibly because she would
not enter when so many others were left out, or accept a community that anathematized the beliefs of others. By this time she
had come to believe in a syncretism that sent her ranging from
the Egyptian Book of the Dead to Polynesian creation myths to
support her ideas. There is also the question of whether, with
her distaste for the existence of matter and her anorexia, she could
ever have received the Eucharist and accepted Christ as present
in the substance of bread.

By the spring of 1943, then, Simone Weil was eating less and
less. As a sign of solidarity with her countrymen under the occupation, she would eat only what was available to French on the
official ration. Later, she ate even less, believing that what she

did not eat would somehow go to the French in France. She continued working, however, until her starvation was well advanced; when she was removed, first to a hospital, then to a sanatorium in the Kentish countryside, she could no longer eat and was diagnosed as suffering from tuberculosis as well. At the inquest after her death, it was ruled that she had committed suicide by starving herself "while the balance of her mind was disturbed."

At the time of her death, few had heard of her beyond the narrow circle of those who knew her periodical writings in France, and even many of them did not take her seriously. After the war her religious writings were edited and published by her friend, the Catholic philosopher, Gustave Thibon, and it was the book he assembled—*Gravity and Grace*—that brought her to the attention of a wider audience.

That audience, as I have suggested, has been both attracted to and repelled by Simone Weil. Initially, my own reactions depended not entirely upon myself but rather on what I was reading. The mixture struck me as inexplicable. When I read the following in a brief essay by nonspecialist and nonacademic Kenneth Rexroth, I was inclined to assent to it: "Simone Weil was one of the most remarkable women of the twentieth, or indeed of any other century. I have great sympathy for her, but sympathy is not necessarily congeniality. It would be easier to write of her if I liked what she had to say, which I strongly do not." And his conclusion is: "Simone Weil assaulted the Garden of Gethsemane, and as is so often the case, was broken on the gate. At least she speaks, again and again, of her absolutely sure sense of the suddenly descending, all-suffusing presence of God. So we know that somewhere, somehow, in all her agony, she did find some center of peace, a peace which, unless we happen to believe in God, we may find hard to explain."

Rexroth writes from the position of a Christian humanism that rejoices more in the things of this world than Simone Weil ever could, and what he sees, he sees from where he stands. Her books remain, mocking us, and there is her life itself, so exemplary of the modern urge for a transcendence that denies the existence of any goal even while insisting that there is nothing to life but the struggle to the goal. Simone Weil, demi-Christian mystic, shares more than is apparent at first with Jean-Paul Sartre, who practiced as the high priest of a religion of literature well developed in nineteenth-century France by Baudelaire and Mallarme.

Years have passed from that religious revival in the 1950s, and interest in Simone Weil, as in the issues and ideas she engaged, has fallen into the black hole of pastness which has swallowed up so much else—and that is a pity, for the best work remains as powerful today as it was twenty-five years ago—and the principles on which the loose and inchoate movement was based seem not discredited so much as simply forgotten. Forgotten, that is, until the present, when, in the wake of the political and social movements of the 1960s, it took on new significance, for Simone Weil had done much earlier what so many young people were doing twenty years after her death. She too had tried to abandon bourgeois comfort for the life of a worker, she too joined enthusiastically in the causes of the downtrodden, she too had traveled as simply as possible, knapsack on back, thirsting for beauty and freedom. And she found it insufficient, turning at the end to belief in a religion that was a syncretist melange of Gnosticism, Christianity, Hinduism, and Greek speculation, surely a mixture every bit as odd as any being concocted in our time. And yet, the questions she raised and the life she lived remain as essential, and as exemplary, now as then.

Simone Weil's Mind

〰

ROBERT COLES

The approximations and categorizations come a little too easily—
and for one who died at thirty-four. Simone Weil was a moral
and political philosopher; a cultural critic; a schoolteacher; a
social activist, determined to involve herself in the important
struggles of her time—poverty and unemployment in the 1930s,
the rise of Fascism; a woman in search of God, and a woman
who, perhaps, met His Gracious Presence, yet found herself unable to find Him with the regularity, the conventional acquies-
cence others (seemingly) do; a person of Jewish ancestry and
Christian sensibility; a profoundly skeptical person, who questioned dozens of pieties, dogmas, received truths; and, not least,
an intellectual who had (and was prepared to express) the grav-
est doubts about her own kind—and so, like others (James Agee,
George Orwell, Georges Bernanos, Flannery O'Connor) risk the
designation of "anti-intellectual."

She wrote brilliant, polemical essays, many published only
posthumously, but she also put her body on the line—a worker
in three factories, a harvester on two farms. She resisted dozens of
all-too-faddish cultural temptations or compulsions—noteworthy
among them that mix of Marx and Freud which became for other
radical activists a virtual sectarian religion. She possessed a fiercely
logical, analytical mind, yet in her last years, especially, became
an emotional, even mystical writer. The contraries she harbored
are horns of our own various dilemmas—ambiguities we contend
with, polarities we try to understand, or with desperate effort, to
reconcile: faith and doubt; scholarly pursuits against the demands
of the political arena; idealism in contrast to the requirement of
practicality; the obligations of a particular life—and with them,
the inevitable self-centeredness—against the larger requirements

of a given world; an inclination toward generosity, which has to contend against, even in saints, the mean-spirited, wrong-headed, or punitively moralistic inclinations "civilized" people so often have as an emotional inheritance.

Simone Weil's relationship to the dominant intellectual influences of the 1930s tells a lot about her irregular, idiosyncratic, stubborn, willful spirit; and, maybe, helps us understand ourselves—because her struggle is ours: how to preserve political liberty, yet enable a radically larger degree of social and economic equity; how to find something more credible than today's fads; how to understand one's nature, one's requirements as a person struggling for some decent, reasonable measure of "moral character"? She saw early, very early, the monstrous nature of Stalinism. She gave the back of her hand to some of the psychoanalytic thinking of her time with a stunning remark that is worth a volume of appraisal: "The whole of the Freudian doctrine is saturated with the very prejudice which he makes it his mission to combat, namely, that everything that is sexual is base." She was an atheist who moved to the very edge of the communion rail at the foot of the Catholic Church's altar, only to hold back, sometimes with an all-too-critical series of reservations, or as some would have it, prideful quibbles. The direction of her thinking was cranky, mystical—especially so for someone able to be, also, a rational egalitarian; that is, one interested in getting to the roots of our social, economic, political, and spiritual malaise.

She had, in fact, made her diagnosis of that "malaise" before she herself took ill; she had turned her powerful mind toward God. She was hungry for evidence of His grace. She knew well her own pride—a companion to the brilliance of her mind, and a companion to her feverish efforts to find, to achieve humility. When she went to work in those three Parisian factories, when she worked as a harvester on those two farms, she had no illusion that her freely adopted working-class life (which she knew she could abandon any moment it pleased her to do so) would be of any help to anyone except—and this held no guarantee—herself. She wanted very much to understand how others live, but she was not a sociologist, an anthropologist, a "participant observer." Nor was she a labor organizer, anxious to exhort anyone to the liberal or Marxist gospel. The "roots" she wrote about are radical in a spiritual sense—though, God knows, she had contempt for capitalists as well as Stalinists, and she certainly drove Trotsky to full exasperation. She keeps referring to the "soul," not the "mind," and certainly not the "personality." One minute a shrewd and agile critic of capitalism, she quickly turns on an exaggerated collectivism—an issue that socialists and communists are obliged to acknowledge: who is to hold the keys of the state, be the planners, the successors to previous political or economic entrepreneurs? She opposed what she called "large factories," and she wanted a system of checks and balances that allowed no group hegemony. Her critique was essentially that of a utopian who was, at the same time, a pessimist.

In *Gravity and Grace,* words like "decreation," "self-effacement" and "renunciation" startle the contemporary reader. For all the decent, good-hearted, somewhat grandiose and unrealistic dreams for a postwar world she sketched out in *The Need For Roots,* her analysis of man's situation was that of the Christian who cannot forget Christ on the cross, His last words and what they mean for us. Christ's loneliness was hers: his last statement was that of a truly rootless person—not a Roman, not a Jew, and, obviously, not a Christian. One of his disciples had denied him three times. The others were confused, discouraged. Simone Weil lived at a time when the world seemed headed for Armageddon. Her naturally dramatic mind—only somewhat constrained by a severe rationality, and prone to the mythic—had in the reality of the decade of the 1930s a perfect foil. Her exaggerations and sometimes apocalyptic prophecies, her outrageous, unqualified generalizations—about Rome, about the Jews of Old Testament times—seem at least understandable in the context of a world almost ready to destroy itself, hence in need of a thoroughly radical penetration of intellect.

She wished for an end to the nation-state's fate as we know it; she wished for communities of people in closer touch than they now are—and all of them under a hierarchy of sorts. Not the social and economic and political hierarchies we are used to. She had her own dreams of people looking up to others, who in turn looked *up* to them! When, on this earth, such a state of affairs would be realized, she did not specify. Popes or Cardinals do wash the feet of beggars—a minute or two, alas, out of the year's accumulation of time. Like Georges Bernanos, to whom she wrote, and whose *Diary of A Country Priest* she admired enormously, she loved the poor and loved Christ and the saints who have come after Him—and had contempt for much of the Church, which she believed constantly betrayed Christ. She loved the *idea* of the Church; but it is doubtful that any institution would for long be spared her critical mind (harsh and loving, both).

For intellectuals she had strong words of disapproval: "A condition of working-class culture is the mingling of what are called 'intellectuals'—an awful name, but at present they scarcely deserve a better one—with the workers." One needn't turn on her with the familiar psychiatric weapons of this century to link such a remark with her desperate effort, expressed as an ideal in *Gravity and Grace,* for "self-effacement." Nowhere is her essentially Christian nature more evident than in her kind of anti-intellectualism—not a cheap, vulgar excess, calculated to curry the favor of ignorant, mean-spirited people, but a sincere acknowledgment on her part that the sin of pride is an especially formidable opponent for some of us. She was, perhaps, impossibly inconsistent—one moment on the Left, the next a stern, moralistic conservative—because she would not trust the intentions of her pride. The torment one senses in her is the awareness of an intellectual's *hauteur* coming up against a penitent Christian's recognition that humility is hard to achieve, even in small amounts. She was not averse to "punishment"; she recognized it as one of the soul's "needs." Perhaps she overdid the self-punishment her mind and body experienced—and, thereby, added to the very pride she hoped to diminish. But she knew the extraordinary appetites of an especially forceful, hungry, and restless mind. Saints, Dorothy Day has told us, have a special struggle with Satan. They are not at all angels; and but for God's grace and their own painful exertions, they have spent their lives seeing Hell as a certain destination.

Simone Weil's last trial has captured the interest of my ilk—so hungry for sickness. It was almost as if her mind and body

were, finally, given over to a feverish, concrete realization of
Kierkegaard's "sickness unto death." She flirted, it can be argued,
with the early Christian heresies. She condemned the flesh too
strenuously. She wanted to spring Christ loose from the Jews,
from the tradition of the Old Testament. She granted her own
evil all too much authority. (She could, of course, be wonderfully
admiring of others—thereby, ironically, denying them their due,
because evil is either everywhere, in all of us, or there is no point
to Christian faith.) Still, what are we to make of her suffering,
which preceded (it must be added) the publication of most of
her writing, and certainly, her international reputation as a
thinker whose unusual life straddled a sainthood of a secular and
religious mix?

She defies the familiar, psychological approximations of this
century—and not only because she was a gifted writer, ironist,
thinker. Even on its own turf, psychiatry is disarmed by her. She
held down her food intake to a certain level—arbitrary all right,
but pegged to the suffering reality of countless Europeans, and
especially her beloved French compatriots under the Nazis. She
was no narcissist at the edge of psychosis, hallucinating reasons
to justify *anorexia nervosa.* A steely mind was at work to the end,
gripping tenaciously that "reality" held so dear by alienists (the
irony of that word, in view of how instrumental psychiatrists have
become in giving sanction to the status quo, the utterly conventional!). She had become, in her last years, in her last sickness,
united not with madness, but with the quite widespread condition
of millions of others, including those near at hand, in blitzed,
half-destroyed London. She had also managed to put her body on
the line—struggled hard to ask for herself no more than that
which others could take for granted. Moreover, her writings for
years had shown her in search of the transcendent, and the last
months of a brief, hectic, passionate life were just that—beyond
anyone's understanding, her family's, her doctors', her own.

Her mind was lucid, increasingly mystical, in the wartime
years. She wanted desperately to be flown over France, to be re-
leased by parachute. She would, she envisioned, be a nurse to the
brave men and women of the underground. She would heal the
injured. She would scrounge food for the hungry. She would share

the terrible moments of those who dared live as she felt it fitting
to live—a suicidal wish, by the standards of the majority. But her
wish was not to be granted. A strong, haunting, fussy, provoca-
tive, truculent, gentle, giving spirit, she was herself unable to
prevail with the military authorities, who found her an odd one,
to say the least: *she,* to be dropped onto Nazi-occupied France!
Disappointed, saddened, perhaps bitterly annoyed, she turned to
intense volunteer work for the Free French in London. But her
frail body could take no more, and her powerful and undimin-
ished mind had other things to contemplate than the caloric requirements needed in a struggle with the tubercle bacillus. She
was immersed in the metaphysical poets, George Herbert especially; her mind's agony, correspondingly, ought to be regarded
meta-psychologically. Anyway, soon enough the God she loved
so long and hard—against the high odds of cultural background,
a wide-ranging, skeptical, pointedly logical mind, the place and
time on earth she was destined to occupy—the God whom she
felt in touch with for several years, finally claimed her. One dares
think that she got at least some of her wish. She would never be
flown across the English Channel, but she did cross a barrier; and
she was carried up—taken from England, only to be held, closely
held: her lifetime wish granted at last.

The Life and Death of
Simone Weil

◟

J . M . C A M E R O N

On September 3, 1943, the following headline appeared in a local English newspaper, *The Kent Messenger:* DEATH FROM STARVATION: FRENCH PROFESSOR'S CURIOUS SACRIFICE. The reference was to the death of Simone Weil, then attached to the Free French forces, on August 24, in an Ashford nursing home. The verdict of the Coroner's Court was "that the deceased did kill and slay herself by refusing to eat whilst the balance of her mind was disturbed." As her friend and biographer Simone Petrement is able to show, the truth is more complicated than that; indeed, everything connected with Simone Weil, her life of study and teaching and political agitation, her beliefs in religion, philosophy, and politics, her mysticism, and the claim made, not unreasonably, by many for her sanctity, is enormously complicated and often hard to put together in a consistent way. In death as in her life her personality is enigmatic. We are not ignorant of what she thought: the abundance of her writings and of her reported sayings and actions provides rich material for study; but at the end we are left with many questions difficult to answer.

Simone Petrement has in her fine biography, *Simone Weil: A Life* (1977), given us a great amount of information, much of it new, some of it the precious testimony of friends and witnesses (among them the biographer). With the study by the late Richard Rees, *Simone Weil: A Sketch for a Portrait* (1966), and the happy republishing of her *Notebooks* (1976), and, we must hope, of such other important works as *The Need for Roots, Gravity and Grace,* and (perhaps the most revealing clue to her spiritual character) *Waiting for God,* and now Madame Petrement's testimony, we have in English perhaps enough material on which to found a judgment of her thought. There can be no question of a definitive judgment. She is too great (though the claim for greatness would be part of a disputable judgment) for this, and perhaps the inner conflicts of her thought and character cannot be systematically presented; and no matter how well one may know France and the French there remains something hard to come to terms with about the side of her which is so much a pupil of Alain at the Lycée Henri IV and a product of the Ecole Normale.

Simone Weil was born the daughter of nonreligious Jewish parents. (She never sympathized with Judaism, did not much care for Jews, was ignorant of Jewish practice and belief, and entered a synagogue—an Ethiopian synagogue in New York—only once in her life. It is this attitude toward Judaism that, I shall argue later, is the real obstacle to her conversion to Christianity.) She was, with her brother (a young Pascal in his mathematical talent), intellectually precocious, and was early encouraged by her mother to prefer intellectual tasks to playing with dolls. From her childhood she showed sympathy to the poor. When she was eleven years old she was missed in the house; she had gone to a meeting of the unemployed. She had, as it were, a talent for affliction from an early age; for most of her life she was racked by atrocious headaches, but she never ceased to seek out external causes of suffering. It was not that she wanted to suffer but that the tasks she set herself in the world and the obligations she imposed upon herself were causes of bodily affliction and spiritual desolation.

Perhaps the most curious thing about her youth is that people were inclined to say that she was "a saint." Sometimes this was said by pious people—an old nurse is noted as having said it when Simone was eight—but not always. This went on all her life. She was not in the least a "good" little girl. She was imperious, self-willed, extravagant; she ruffled the susceptibilities of others and hurt their feelings by assuming they were made of the same hard metal as she was. She did not in her early childhood, adolescence, or early womanhood raise for herself, at least not with any seriousness, religious as distinct from philosophical questions about God; and she did not pray.

She was one of Alain's most brilliant pupils at Henri IV. We are given an account of one of her essays for him. The subject is "The Fairy Tale of the Six Swans in Grimm." The story is of the sister of six brothers turned into swans who must make six night-shirts out of anemones and in this six-year task she must never break silence. Simone's comment is: "To act is never difficult; we always act too much and scatter ourselves ceaselessly in disorderly deeds. To make six shirts from anemones and to keep silent; this is our only way of acquiring power. . . . The sole strength and sole virtue is to cease from acting." It seems she is arguing that it was the sister's silence, not the making of the shirts, that saved her brothers. This essay and others are remarkable pieces of writing for a girl of sixteen. Some of the ideas and ways of treating them are no doubt breathed into her by her teacher, but there seems to be a vein of originality. Her diploma dissertation was on "Science and Perception in Descartes." It is highly original if slightly perverse—it looks as though the actual Cartesian text did not trouble her too much—but it seems not to have pleased her director, the great Brunschvicg, who gave it the lowest possible passing mark.

By the time she went as professor to the lycée at Le Puy, her first post after her *agregation,* the external features of her character, of what had been made out of her temperamental endowment, are evident and do not change much for the rest of her life. First, there is the will to live in poverty. At Le Puy she had the salary of a full professor but decided to use only the money she would have received had she been an inferior teacher without the *agregation.* This is a pattern throughout her life. For a year, during 1934 and 1935, she did hard factory work, often to the point of utter exhaustion. In the last months of her life she tried to live on what she would have eaten had she lived under the German occupation—this was the (somewhat inadequate) ground for the coroner's verdict.

Next, there is a physical fastidiousness that made her shrink from bodily contact, even with close relatives. Sometimes she impulsively kissed her friends and this for them was always memorable. She was fiercely virginal, yet fond of men's company; this made for amusing mistakes on the part of men, who thought they could advance from *bon comarade* to something else. But she was no prude, admired the memoirs of the Cardinel de Retz, and the man too, though he was scarcely remarkable for the virtue of chastity. When a German girl asked her if she had a "friend," she was amused and not at all offended.

She wasn't self-consciously Bohemian in her way of life, but she looked Bohemian and shabby, often untidy; and she was like this always because she was totally devoted to whatever it was in social life that preoccupied her at a given time, the condition of the unemployed, the Spanish Civil War, the work in a factory; and underneath the passionate commitment, often a commitment without hope—for she was too shrewd to suppose that the goals men in politics set themselves are ever reached—there was the growing awareness that she was fearfully and unutterably connected with that which is beyond the world: that she had the vocation of a mystic.

Her full conviction that this was her vocation did not perhaps come until 1938, when, as she told Father Perrin, the Dominican priest who became her friend, Christ came and took possession of her. She wrote: "in this sudden possession of me by Christ, neither my senses nor my imagination had any part; I only felt in the midst of my suffering the presence of love, like that which one can read in the smile on a beloved face." She was greatly astonished by this happening. "I had never read the mystics," she wrote, ". . . God in his mercy had prevented me from reading the mystics, so that it should be evident to me that I had not invented this absolutely unexpected contact."

One of the many moving photographs in the Petrement biography is of a poem by George Herbert ("Love bade me welcome; yet my soul drew back / Guiltie of dust and sin") copied out by Simone Weil. It is neat, clear, without affectation, not at all emancipated from the bad handwriting models of the nineteenth century; there is no hint of the great models of European handwriting, Carolingian minuscule or the Italian chancery hand; but it is moving, in and through its limitations. There is the absence of aestheticism: it is plain that in copying out the text she is concerned only with the poem, anxious that it be easily read, that nothing come between the reader and Christ's invitation to the sinner ("You must sit down, says Love, and taste my meat. / So I did sit and eat") to the heavenly banquet. It is the hand of a conscientious French schoolmistress, a patient teacher, concerned not with herself but with what she has to communicate, without vanity but with a just confidence in herself as the custodian of a message committed to her.

She was a fine teacher, rigorous but kind, intensely concerned with the best possible standards in literature and philosophy, above all free of the aridity of the pedant. Her pupils protected her when she needed it from the attention of the school authorities. She was much loved by the children. She taught moral and political philosophy, not so much through the classical texts (though Plato was always there; Aristotle she detested and never did justice to) as through works of literature (the *Antigone* of Sophocles, "The Death of Ivan Ilyich," *Middlemarch, The Brothers Karamazov*), for she believed that to go deeply into problems involved living with concrete examples; in this she is indeed Platonic, or rather Socratic, though she would not, I think, have been happy with this distinction. She was superbly educated in the French fashion and was familiar with the body of Greek and Latin literature, with the entire canon of French literature, was well read in ancient philosophy and in European philosophy from Descartes to Kant, knew English and German literature well. This command of inner riches gives what she writes, and no doubt gave what she said, an extraordinary force and authority, even when her words are exaggerated or false.

It is harder to divest oneself of inner riches than of outward possessions; the rich man can sell all he has and give it to the poor. Those who find inner riches an obstruction to the growth of the spirit have the harder task of divesting the soul of all that makes it interesting and fetching to their fellows, of going away from the warm, rough world into other regions, into fire, or ice, or darkness. That she set herself this task from time to time is certain; and yet there is an obstinate fidelity to her vocation as teacher, both in practice—she was always teaching even when she had ceased to be a professional teacher, and she loved to teach workmen and neglected children—and in meditation; one of the most beautiful of her writings is a piece she wrote for the Catholic students at Montpellier: "Reflections on the Right Use of School Studies with a View to the Love of God."

Simone Petrement's biography has much to say about Simone Weil's life and ideas in the period when political and social action filled most of her time, about her reflections on factory work, on Germany just before Hitler came to power (these are extraordinary and in a different class from anything else written from the Left at that time), on the role of the trade unions. Boris Souvarine, one of her greatest friends in the 1930s and a man for whom she had a deep affection, said of her: "She is the only brain the working-class movement has produced in many years."

In the early 1930s almost no one distinguished Marx from Engels and Lenin. But she wrote that "Marx's entire work is permeated with the spirit incompatible with the vulgar materialism of Engels and Lenin." Such thoughts did not make the communists love her, and in return they had her contempt. She hated their idolatry of the Soviet Union, their strong-arm tactics against other parties on the Left, the theatrical methods used to transform public meetings into orgiastic assemblies chanting the praises of Stalin and Thorez. She was, therefore, not surprised, as were the fellow travelers, by the great change of line after the German-Soviet pact in 1939. At a time when it was unfashionable she told all who were prepared to listen (not many) that "the writers in Russia who refuse to lie are sent to Siberia where one leaves them—let us be clear about this—they and their families, without *any* resources to live on."

She hated capitalism, but she thought it better than a totalitarian socialism. Her great hope was that in the crisis of the thirties and the forties the colonial peoples would free themselves from European control. For her the important thing in politics was to limit those evils that are not inseparable from the human condition. She thought there are many evils that are simply a part of the order of the world. But what seemed a brutal pessimism repelled many. In an article in *Revolution proletarienne* in 1933 she wrote: "There is no difficulty whatever, once one has decided to act, in maintaining intact on the plane of action those very hopes that a critical examination has shown to be well-nigh un-

founded; in that lies the very essence of courage." Understand-
ably, her comrades did not find this enlivening.

The nature of Simone Weil's political commitment is brought
out by the brief episode in the Spanish Civil War during which
she served with Anarchist troops. She had no doubt about the
general justice of the Republican cause but was skeptical about
its purity and its prospects. Consequences did not matter to her:
the moral imperative of the situation was all. On the front in
Aragon, with the Durruti column, she wrote: "If they [i.e., the
Franco troops] capture me, they will kill me. . . . But it is what
we deserve. Our troops have shed a lot of blood. I am morally
an accomplice." An anecdote told her by the militia explains her
sense that death would not have been undeserved. Durruti had
lectured for an hour to a fifteen-year-old Falangist who had fallen
into the hands of the militia. He expounded the beauties of Anarchism and offered to spare the boy's life if he would join the
militia. The boy refused and so Durruti had him shot. Simone
Weil comments: "Yet Durruti was in some ways an admirable
man . . . [but] the death of this little hero never ceased to
weigh on my conscience."

A great puzzle over Simone Weil has always been, ever since
her mystical writings and her correspondence with Father Perrin
and Father Couturier were published, why she did not become a
Christian. A part of this problem for her was the way in which
Christianity was presented as a development of Judaism, whereas
she saw it as—an absurd thesis in fact—purely a development of
the Greek spirit. All the other reasons against baptism she
brought up from time to time—that Catholicism (this was the
only church she ever considered) was involved in the idolatry of
an institution, that the traditional *Anathema sit* delivered against
the heretic limited intellectual freedom—are important enough.
But for her they are always secondary to this enormous obstacle:
the insistence that the Old Testament and the New are organ-
ically one. (It is a piece of beautiful historical irony that this was
precisely the difficulty Charles Maurras had, though his preferred
model of Catholicism was Roman and legal, rather than Greek.)

It is interesting to note how she tries to skirt around this ob-

stacle, even, as it were, to talk through it. She sympathizes with
the Gnostics, she anxiously inquires how far the second-century
heretic Marcion, who thought the Old Testament had been fabri-
cated by the dark rulers of the present age and that the New
Testament had been polluted by the same daemotic forces, could
be regarded as a permissible interpreter of the Christian theme.
She is besotted with the Cathars, who have as well for her the
irresistible charm of a minority defeated by the cruel world of
the majority. It is extraordinary that Father Perrin should ever
have considered her a suitable candidate for baptism. Later, Father Perrin, with Gustave Thibon, the French farmer and Catholic
writer with whose family she lived for a time while she was working in the fields, saw what the problem was: "At the center of all
her oppositions was her attitude toward Israel, it was the key to
all her resistance."

She claimed to believe in the divinity of Christ and in his
presence in the Eucharist; at the same time, she professed to hate
that Judaism in which Jesus was immersed. Yet in all the Synop-
tic Gospels it is understood that his preaching is the Word of
God to Abraham and his posterity; and that only as the Word
of God to Israel in the first place has it any claim to be the Word
of God to men. This is in fact clear enough in the fourth Gospel,
the one Simone loved because she thought it the most "Greek."
The Johannine writer, although his language has caused some to
suspect affinities with Gnosticism, is in fact conducting a polemic
against that Gnosticism which denied, as virtually all the schools
of Christian Gnosticism did, the goodness of the physical world
and the full humanity of Jesus.

Her chief charge against the Old Testament is that in its earlier
parts Yahweh is shown as ordering the massacres of the inhabit-
ants of Palestine displaced by the Jews and that the God of the
Jews continued to be identified with this God of battles. She does
not seem ever to consider that there is here a soluble problem of
exegesis and historical criticism. There the words are on the page;
and they are abominable. She seems insensitive to the ethical content of the Torah and does not come to see, as she might very
well have done had she devoted as much time to the study of
the Old Testament as she did to the writings of the Greeks, that

the moral ideas of Christianity, above all the two great command-
ments of the law—love of God and love of neighbor—come from
the Torah.

It is no wonder that she resisted baptism. Paul argues that the
Gentiles may be likened to a wild olive shoot grafted onto the
rich olive tree of Israel and nourished therefore by the tree's
root (Romans 11:17–24). The background and foundation of
the New Testament is Jewish; the Greek elements are few—
perhaps the Logos doctrine in the fourth Gospel, though this may
have come from the Hellenized Judaism of Egypt, from the circles that produced Philo; the spirit of Luke's gospel is perhaps
touched with the Greek spirit, as compared with those of Mark
and Matthew. About these points there is a sufficient scholarly
consensus to make it quite certain that Simone Weil is wrong
when she writes that "the Gospels are the last marvelous expression of the Greek genius." She reads the Gospels, especially the
accounts of the Passion, as though she were reading the *Iliad*. She
never gave to the Bible the passionate attention she gave to other
works, to Homer, or to Thucydides' history, or to the Bhagavad-
Gita. This last she loved greatly, sometimes seeming to identify
Krishna with Christ.

Simone Weil was so wonderfully intelligent that there is a
puzzle here. Madame Petrement in her biography does not try to
solve it, for she so closely identifies with her subject that she does
not see, or does not bring out, that a puzzle exists. My own suggestion, though it may be quite wrong, is as follows.

Her education with Alain and at the Ecole Normale was one
which was preoccupied with *texts*—Plato, Descartes, Racine,
Kant et al. There they lie in front of one, complex, finely articu-
lated, but in the end available to the attentive reader, especially
one who has mastered that great French discipline, *explication
de texte*. They are not looked at historically and they are not seen
to have many layers of meaning, layers that are not perhaps so
logically harmonious as the surface suggests. For example, Simone Weil, like virtually all the educated French of that period,
looked upon Descartes as a philosopher with a clear doctrine.
There is no evidence that she had profited from Gilson's detailed
study of the text, a study which had shown how scholastic in its

roots the work, for all its originality, is. Historical study gives us a different Descartes from the pellucid genius who has fascinated so many generations of French. He is a more interesting thinker when historical study has worked him over, but also a more crabbed and confused one.

(In justice to her, one ought to add that Simone Weil had a marvellous sense of historical development. She was able, for example, to see with great precision the worlds of Homer and of Thucydides and to link them with the successor worlds of the Macedonian and Roman empires. Perhaps her historical sense is excessively dramatic: she hates the late Roman Republic and the Empire just as though they were contemporary tyrannies. Her moral judgments are as timeless and inflexible as Lord Acton's.)

Simone Weil even found the most difficult and uncertain of the Greek texts, the Pythagorean fragments, understandable. She was very positive about what they meant, and even argued that what they meant was essentially the same as what Plato, the Greek Stoics, the Upanishads, the Bhagavad-Gita, Saint John of the Cross, and the Cathars also meant. There is no agreement among scholars on what Pythagoras (about whom almost nothing is known for certain) and his followers maintained; and the suggestion that there is a single "truth" in the doctrines of all these individuals and schools is pure fantasy. Her view of Gnosticism is equally strange. If one compares what she has to say with what is established about the Gnostics in such a standard work as that of Hans Jonas's *The Gnostic Religion,* it is clear that the complex phenomenon of Gnosticism simply escaped her.

The case of the Cathars is the most puzzling of all. Most of what we know about them we know through the reports of the Inquisition which, with the help of the secular arm, destroyed them. But it does seem plain that they held, with the Manichaeans and some of the Gnostics (Marcion, for instance, if we count him a Gnostic), that the world of nature was not God's creation, that sexual love ought to be avoided, that the life of the body was an obstacle to spiritual perfection, and that the faithful were divided between the Perfect who eschewed sexual activity and the rest, the latter forming, as it were, the proletariat of the Cathar church.

Simone Weil may at times have felt vague sympathies with some of these beliefs but she held none of them. Her feeling of solidarity with the Cathars seems to have been prompted not by intellectual sympathy but by her emotional sympathy with the victims of the cruel Albigensian crusade, an event that was indeed like the slaughter of the indigenous peoples of Palestine recounted in the earlier books of the Bible.

What was it, then, that drew her in the later part of her short life to the Catholic Church, though she never crossed the threshold? It seems that it was the liturgy, above all plainsong, which seemed to her so beautiful that it was almost a showing of the divine glory in this world; it was the liturgy, the sacramental system, the saints, and those religious men and women—Perrin, Thibon, and others—who seemed in their characters also to have a scintilla of the divine glory. She did not see that what she took for the whole was a fragment, and that, taken to be a whole, this fragment was another religion. What brought the fragment into the genuine whole was precisely faithfulness to that biblical tradition she never understood or came to love.

It has seemed right to criticize one side of her thought in harsh terms, for writers who have interpreted her life and work have tended to avoid the hard questions about the consistency and truth of her ideas. She is so attractive, her literary gifts are so stunning, her mystical vocation so evident, that it may have seemed churlish to pay too much attention to what is extravagant in her. But when all this has been said, there remains one of the most remarkable women of our time, one who can be placed with Teresa of Avila and with the two Catherines, of Genoa and of Siena. Toward the end of her life, in New York, on the eve of her departure to England where her Passion was consummated, she wrote down what Madame Petrement rightly calls "the terrible prayer":

May all this [i.e., sensibility and intelligence, love as *her* love] be stripped away from me, devoured by God, transformed into Christ's substance, and given for food to afflicted men whose body and soul lack every kind of nourishment. And let me be a paralytic—blind, deaf, witless, and utterly decrepit. . . . Father, since thou art the

Good and I am mediocrity, rend this body and soul away from me to make them into things for your use, and let nothing remain of me, forever, except this rending itself, or else nothingness.

Either this is madness or it is obedience to a vocation few are called to. Simone Weil's life and death compel us to face or to hide from such ultimate questions.

Simone Weil: Last Things

~

MICHELE MURRAY
Time leads us—always—
whither we do not wish to go.
—Simone Weil

The angular, nervous young woman smokes too many cigarettes.
Her thin fingers are stained yellow from nicotine; ashes and dis-
carded matches litter her room. It's a cold room, colder than it
need be, and she coughs far too much in the damp English winter, a deep bronchial cough. She keeps smoking. The room is a
typical English terrace house with a garden visible from the back
window, her window. Downstairs her English landlady lives with
her two young sons and soon the woman will go down and play
with the children, talk to them and teach them with a patience
that is striking in someone so nervous and preoccupied.

She is not an attractive woman, this thin Frenchwoman with
flyaway curly hair, sharp features, thick glasses, an insistently
harsh voice, and awkward gestures. Her clothes are ill-fitting, a
great loose cape, a beret jammed on the dark hair, clumsy shoes.
But the dark eyes are unexpectedly warm and a rare smile makes
the face youthful and charming.

But the attractive child who was once inside her skin has been
destroyed. And now she is in the process of destroying even more
of herself. Some nights she does not come home at all, sleeping
in her office if she works late and the trains are no longer running. Even when she does return through the oddly long twilights
of wartime, she can be heard moving around and typing for
many hours; her light is on most of the night.

What is she doing? Does she look down at the garden as dawn
lights it up? Does she notice it at all? The evidence has vanished
just as she has, just as that time has, London in 1943, London

during World War II, the London in which Simone Weil lived
for the last eight months of her life.

Even if the records poured forth from some impossible cornu-
copia of documentation, what would we know of the particular
quality of those years? And further, what of this very singular
woman who stayed up late, pacing her room, smoking and coughing, to write in her journal and to read? What we have are the
letters she wrote and the journal, and from these we must recon-
struct as best we can the sense and the atmosphere of a past that
does not stay to repeat itself to us.

She told her parents that she was in love with London, in love
with England. One such letter said, "In one sense, both things
and people here seem to me exactly as I think I expected them
to be, and in another sense perhaps better. . . . People here do
not scream at one another as they do on the Continent . . . here
people's nerves are strained but they control them from self-
respect and from a true generosity toward others. It may be that
the war has a good deal to do with all this. People here have
suffered just enough for it to be a tonic which stimulates dormant
virtues. They have not been stunned as in France. Nevertheless,
all things considered, it seems to me certain that at this moment
of history they are worth more than us."

That last generous sentence was typical of Simone Weil's spirit
at its best. It means even more when set against the background
of her life when she was writing, a life focused on two central
concerns—God and the Free French. All of her desire was to
return to France and work with the Resistance; her activities in
London were centered around the Free French, her work was for
them—her only full-length book, *The Need for Roots,* was the
product of this work—and all her thirst was for martyrdom in
the cause of liberty. Whatever she thought of the English, they
were supernumeraries in her drama. Yet she had to be both
generous and just in her appraisal of them, and her shrewd eye
missed very little in those first months before illness over-
whelmed her.

She cultivated her illness. There is no other way to put it, given
the circumstances of her life in London. She was living in a city
deep into its fourth year of war—strict rationing, black-out, wea-

riness and malaise in the civilian population (so many others were off fighting), a damp and chill climate through the winter and early spring. It was a city of ruins; the damage of the Blitz of 1940–41 had not been repaired and would not be until the end of the war in 1945. Not all the fireweed and woodbine growing in the rubble could do much to soften the ruins or cheer those Londoners who had remained in their battered city or had returned from their evacuation billets when the raids ended.

It was a city of cold houses and cold rooms. Traditionally, English people have scorned central heating and been content with open fires to take the chill off their stone and brick houses. Icy bedrooms and cold baths were seen as steps to health and even to moral courage. Chilblains were a national affliction. And wartime fuel rationing insured that the long months of wet and windy winters would also be a time of bronchitis, influenza, and perpetually cold hands and feet.

Simone Weil believed fervently in asceticism, not only as a doctrine helpful to others, but also and especially as a command applying to herself. And she interpreted it strictly to mean denial of all bodily pleasures, not as an act good in itself (the Puritan belief) but because only in that way could the human being, whose very creation stamped him indelibly with the mark of sin, redeem himself and return to God. She accepted bodily suffering both as a visible sign of her faith in God and as a mark of solidarity with those who were poorer than she was. In the 1930s she had lived with the utmost simplicity in bare rooms and shapeless clothes, distributing most of her salary to striking French workers.

Now all her passion was focused on her compatriots under German occupation. She would allow herself no more than the official ration of food and fuel. Paris was cold? Very well, she would have no fire in her room. The French food ration would be hers as well—and without any recourse to the black market which sustained many Frenchmen and women. When Simone Weil made a bargain with herself, she did not cheat. It is the *why* of this particular bargain that is so troubling, and in time her reasons will be questioned and examined.

She seemed to believe that if she ate less, the French would eat more. Witnesses at the inquest held after her death on August

24, 1943 were quoted as saying, "She kept repeating that her food was to be sent to the French prisoners of war," and " 'I cannot eat when I think of all my people starving in France.' "

Such behavior—willful starvation—has a medical name, *Anorexia nervosa,* and it is not uncommon, especially among young women, although more often the result of diets pushed for fleshly vanity than for spiritual pride. Indeed, the verdict of the inquest was "suicide while the balance of the mind was disturbed." She had been suffering from tuberculosis, true, but the cause of death was starvation, self-starvation.

Immediately, we are confronted with one of those paradoxes that so marks the life and thought of Simone Weil. If she was indeed "disturbed in her mind," insane, as it were, how can we explain the long letters written to her parents immediately before her brief hospitalization that gave absolutely no clue to her illness? Even after she was moved from her room to a hospital and then to the sanatorium in Kent, in southeast England, where she died, she wrote her parents as if she were healthy and at home, warm and charming letters that indicate a close and loving relationship between parents and child. Her letters did not bear the return addresses of either hospital or sanatorium and the pretense collapsed only with her last note, written eight days before she died, when she was already severely weakened by starvation and pulmonary tuberculosis.

"Very little time or inspiration for letters now," she wrote in her neat, clear hand. "They will be short, erratic, and far between. . . . Heaps and heaps of love."

It could be argued that she was cruel in not preparing her parents for her death, but the carefulness of her planning that is revealed in her letters indicates lucidity rather than madness, and the caring tone shows that she had not cut any of her ties to this healthy relationship with loved parents.

There is more. During these months of 1943—first the damp winter months, then the glorious early spring which was one of the finest in memory, sending Londoners pouring out to what undamaged parks remained and softening the ruins with growths of flowering weeds—Simone Weil was working on the manuscript that became after her death the book-length *L'Enracine-*

ment, translated into English as *The Need for Roots.* She had worn herself out begging the Free French in London to allow her to parachute into France as an agent, a contact person, an intellectual liaison between the Resistance and the world outside. And she could not understand their refusal. She did not regard her poor health, blinding headaches, and physical fragility as any handicap in such a mission. And she did not grasp the point that, whatever she believed, to Vichy and the Germans she was Jewish and as such liable to instant deportation and death.

What is more, her appearance—by this time almost a caricature of the image of the "Jewish female intellectual" carried by too many people in the privacy of their heads, with her untidy curly hair, thick glasses, rumpled clothes, and nicotine-stained fingers—would place in extreme danger any resistance groups she might contact. She yearned only for sacrifice and martyrdom with the persistence and intransigence common to many who do indeed suffer martyrdom in the cause they have chosen, and she seemed quite unconscious of the others who would, willy-nilly, go along with her to martyrdoms they possibly did not want.

Absorbed in tasks more important than the pacifying of this one woman, leaders of the French forces in London assigned her intellectual work, imagining, no doubt, that she would then sit quietly at her desk and prepare some paper or other. Instead, she worked day and night on her plans for the spiritual and material future of France after the liberation, and produced what she called a "Prelude to a Declaration of Duties Towards Mankind." More than anything else, this formidable document testifies to the thoroughgoing rationalism and abstraction that are so much a part of the French intellectual and educational system that one thus trained cannot abandon a certain method of thought, regardless of what else is given up in a flight toward God or death.

The study she made mixes the profound and the brilliant with the recondite and the silly. But it is hardly the work of a person who is losing her sanity.

At the same time that she was writing *The Need for Roots,* she was continuing her private studies in comparative mythology, her journal entries, and her spiritual practices, which centered on

COLLEGE OF THE SEQUOIAS
LIBRARY

reciting the Lord's Prayer in Greek, slowly, focusing on each word with perfect attention. If her attention slipped in the slightest degree, she would begin over.

"There is something mysterious in the universe which is in complicity with those who love nothing but the good. . . . God is the sole good. All the goods contained in things have their equivalent in God. God is the sole measure of value. . . . This universe is a snare for capturing souls, in order to deliver them, with their consent, to God. It is the eternal model for punishment."

Paradoxical thoughts, to be sure—Simone Weil proceeds by paradox—and extreme in their absoluteness; yet not mad, unless all mystics are by definition mad, for she uses the language of mysticism—which is a language like any other—rather than the private speech of those locked into madness.

Her thought is lucid.

Her actions are illogical, even self-destructive.

Is the suicide always mad? Do we look for reasons for suicide so that we can link an irrational act firmly to the bounds of the rational? What if the suicide is the rational person and the one who continues to live is actually the prisoner of fantasy?

Does the instinct for life in fact override all others? In his later work, Freud postulated a powerful death wish, and in *his* late essays, a terribly disillusioned Henry Adams intimated that the power of inertia would finally overcome any countervailing force. Simone Weil herself opposes the concept of grace to that of gravity, which otherwise controls all that is material in this world.

Should the instinct for life always dominate? If the person who dies for an ideal or a nation is a hero, if the person who dies for religion is a martyr, what are the man and woman who die to the world and to themselves for a personal vision which, whatever we call it, draws them out of the common world into the isolation of death?

So, what did Simone Weil die for? Did she herself know? She has left no direct answer. But there is the increasingly desperate intelligence of *The Need for Roots,* which begins as a sober study of the possibilities for rejuvenation of the French nation and concludes with religious speculations that would strike the majority of her countrymen as, at best, unacceptable, and, at worst, quite mad. What could a nation so shaped by the pattern of Rome make of Simone Weil's fanatical hatred of Rome? What would they have made of her praise of the correct relationship between subjects and legitimate sovereignty as "an unconditional allegiance, but an allegiance paid solely to an hereditary authority, without the slightest regard either for power or possibilities of prosperity or adversity, reward or punishment"? For that matter, what do we make of it?

Her brilliance—in which she did not believe—placed her apart from all but the handful of the people whose lives she tried to enter. They knew it, even if she would not. Her waiting for God drew her into spiritual isolation that was far deeper. Her pride, which she would not yield even for the fulfillment of her desire—annihilation in God—was a prickly hedge no one could cross to kiss her with the kiss that would awaken the sleeping woman. And her serious psychological difficulties, whatever their causes, her clumsiness that came from her strangeness to her own body, her repression of feminity and sexuality, her deliberate creation of personal ugliness where none existed before—all isolated her in an airless world, the world of the poet Sylvia Plath's bell jar.

Had she lost faith in her own rightness? Had she come to the end of a carefully planned journey that took her, not where she imagined it would lead, but to a blank wall? In the face of such disappointment, no outside achievement could weigh in the balance. Think of F. O. Matthiessen plunging from the window in a seedy Boston hotel in 1950, still young, a full professor at Harvard University whose students were devoted to him, author of the brilliant *American Renaissance,* prince of critics, unable any longer to face his fear, not only of McCarthyism, but also of the collapse of his illusions about Communism, unable to face the confrontation of his Christian beliefs with his homosexuality. Everything fell away from him in his terrible isolation, and then he fell away from himself, the brilliance and the stature no help at all.

Perhaps if Simone Weil were less brilliant, less able to feed off her own mind, less able to disguise rationalizations with the

lustre of so much thought and scholarship, her friends and those
who loved her even at her most difficult would have been able to
break through and save her. Perhaps not, as with Matthiessen or
Ernest Hemingway. The mind has its own exigencies, against
which the body cannot stand, and the isolated will often shape
all happenings so that they confirm him in the isolation that he
has chosen under the impression that it is a vocation, a gift, or a
sign of election. Suicide has its own laws. "The directions that
destiny can take are not subject to variation," Cesare Pavese wrote
eight months before his own suicide.

But it is a mistake to see in her death no more than the evidence of a temporarily unbalanced mind. No doubt her sanity
was impaired by systematic starvation by the time she was taken
to the sanatorium in Kent where she died. But earlier, when she
embarked on her course, surely understanding that, with her poor
health and tendency to tuberculosis, she was giving herself over
to death, she made a decision that was the logical outcome of the
religious beliefs she had shaped for herself and which possessed
not only her mind but also her body and will.

In the notebooks written while she was in New York City in
1942 she put down a prayer that is, quite truly, terrible; that is,
it inspires terror:

Father, in the name of Christ grant me this:
That I may be unable to will any bodily movement, or even any
attempt at movement, like a total paralytic. That I may be incapable
of receiving any sensation, like someone who is completely blind,
deaf and deprived of all the senses. That I may be unable to make
the slightest connection between two thoughts, even the simplest, like
one of those total idiots who not only cannot count or read but have
never even learnt to speak. That I may be insensible to every kind of
grief and joy, and incapable of any love for any being or thing, and
not even for myself, like old people in the last stage of decrepitude.
Father, in the name of Christ grant me all this in reality.
May this body move or be still, with perfect suppleness or rigidity,
in continuous conformity to thy will. May my faculties of hearing,
sight, taste, smell and touch register the perfectly accurate impress of
thy creation. May this mind, in fullest lucidity, connect all ideas in
perfect conformity with thy truth. May this sensibility experience, in

their greatest possible intensity and in all their purity, all the nuances
of grief and joy. May this love be an absolutely devouring flame of
love of God for God. May all this be stripped away from me, devoured by God, transformed into Christ's substance, and given for
food to afflicted men whose body and soul lack every kind of nourishment. And let me be a paralytic—blind, deaf, witless and utterly
decrepit.

Father, effect this transformation now, in the name of Christ; and
although I ask it with imperfect faith, grant this request as if it were
made with perfect faith.

Father, since thou art the Good and I am mediocrity, rend this
body and soul away from me to make them into things for your use,
and let nothing remain of me, for ever, except this rending itself, or
else nothingness.

The terror comes from perceiving two things—Simone Weil's
sublime pride, like that of Milton's Lucifer; and the degree of
discontinuity between this prayer and the Christianity of the New
Testament, in which she professes to believe.

Not that others have not done much the same—read in the
Gospels a life-denying text and given a meaning to "supernatural"
that was against nature rather than fulfilling nature. The Augustinian tradition in Christianity, with its branches spreading from
Calvin's Geneva to Irish Catholicism, from Counter-Reformation
Rome to American Protestantism, is no appendage to the Christian stream, it is part of the main channel itself. Not Augustine
himself, however, could so forget his earlier joys of the flesh as
to pray for such annihilation.

The extremity of Simone Weil's prayer and the passion that
floods the simplest words are beyond the boundaries of the Christianity on which she most depends—that which united Greek
thought with a reading of Christ's message to produce as its
monument, first the Gospel of St. John, then the writings of
Dionysus the Areopagite and Plotinus. While this is a Christianity of mysticism and disembodiment, a Christianity reluctant to
accept the full humanity and suffering of Christ, preferring to see
in it only a symbolic act of the spirit, it is also a Christianity permeated with the sweet reasonableness and passion for limits that
marks classical Greek thought.

Nor is this the only striking mention of her desire, not merely for death (although that would be the result) but rather for decreation. In the same notebook that carried the text of her prayer, she put down random thoughts on the "Our Father": "The Incarnation is simply a figure of the Creation. God abdicated by giving us existence. By refusing it we abdicate and become, in that way, similar to God. God created us in his image, that is to say he gave us the power to abdicate in his favor, just as he abdicated for us."

And in the last pages of her London notebook, written shortly before her death, she spells out more clearly the consequences of her belief that creation is a blot on God: "Pleasure is the illusion that there is some good attached to one's own existence. It is a permanent illusion, and even sorrow is mixed with some pleasure. But at certain moments, brought on by an excess of physical suffering, the illusion disappears completely. One then sees one's existence naked, as a mere fact in which there is no good whatsoever. That is frightful. And that is the truth."

But is it indeed the truth? Whose truth and brought from where?

I think there are two likely ways—not explaining, certainly not that, not bringing a mystery down to some pencil marks that can be erased, as if a human person were no more than a blank sheet of paper—of pointing the way to some understanding of why that thin and nervous woman looking down into a garden from the window of her London room became, in a few months during an exquisite spring and summer, a skeletal, coughing figure lying in bed in an English nursing home.

The first, given the tenor of our age, is the psychological, especially as there is ample reason for invoking it. Simone Weil will certainly yield some portion of her mystery to Freud's language of eros and thanatos and of the return of the repressed, while Jung would have much to say of her playing with archetypes, as she does in her various notebooks, as expressive of her longing for dissolution into the final Oneness of the universe. There is sexual repression, too, and more, much more, enough so that the psychological tone will persist. Not with any claims to truth; simply because it is useful and illuminating.

The second explanation is perhaps less congenial to the temper of the times. It is a purely religious one that asks us to take seriously a set of religious beliefs, Gnosticism, especially as realized in Catharism, the religion that flourished in the Languedoc in southern France during the high Middle Ages. The civilization built by the Cathars, apparently admirable in almost all respects (as described by sympathizer Zoe Oldenbourg in *Massacre at Montsegur*) was defeated by the forces of Pope Innocent and the King of France under the command of the notorious Simon de Montfort. The ostensible reason was to wipe out religious heresy; the king's reason was to bring the rich territory of Provence, Poitou, and Anjou under the control of the crown. So the beautiful Mediterranean culture of the troubadours and the Provencal language was destroyed forever after a generation of warfare in 1209, after which the remnant of the Cathars who were not killed, imprisoned, exiled, or forcibly converted, fled to the Pyrenees and their influence vanished.

"Why does everyone go on repeating that commonplace about the impossibility of spiritual values being destroyed by brute force? It destroys them very quickly and very easily. People point to those nationalities which have survived centuries of oppression; but there are a great many more which did not survive . . . how many religions, too, have been annihilated by force, so that even the memory of them hardly survives!" ("The Romanesque Renaissance," in *Selected Essays,* ed. Richard Rees [London: Oxford University Press, 1962], p. 79).

Simone Weil admired the Cathars. In the months after she left Paris—removed from the civil-service rolls by the Vichy laws because of her Jewish ancestry, and in danger of deportation and death from the German conquerors—she lived in the Midi, sometimes in Marseilles, and sometimes on the farm of Gustave Thibon at Saint-Marcel in the Ardeche region, where she helped with the grape harvest and tried to teach the Greek version of the "Our Father" to the vineyard workers. During that time, when personal survival was the chief, if not the only concern of those around her, she wrote two essays for a special issue of the *Cahiers de Sud,* a journal published in Marseilles that specialized in the culture of Mediterranean France. In them she expressed her admiration for the Cathars even while admitting to insufficient knowledge of their closed and largely secret society.

She responded to their teachings, which drew on Platonic thought and the Greek mysteries and which emphasized the primacy of the Gospels to such an extent that the Jewish background of Christianity was erased. Given her own predispositions and her emphatic labeling of the ancient Hebrews (along with the Romans) as examples of the Great Beast, Simone Weil found in the remnants of the Cathar tradition ideas and values that were immediately sympathetic. Like the Cathars, she translated the words of the "Our Father" as "Give us this day our *supersubstantial* bread" rather than our "daily" bread (in accordance with Cathar doctrine that the material was itself evil and only the spiritual, good). She applauded the Cathar concept of total obedience to a leader not as a leader but as a man from the community who represented each member, she praised their nonviolence, and she responded with positive vigor to their belief that everything carnal was evil.

The Gnostic tradition is a long one, surfacing from time to time, as it did with the Cathars, the Bogomils of the Balkans, the Skoptsky of the Danube River Delta, and most notably, in Persian Zoroastrianism; at other times, it is an underground stream, never quite absent from human thought, yet shyly withdrawing from sunlight and persecution. Since I am hardly equipped to write a history of Gnosticism, I will limit myself to the single point that unites the various Gnostic movements—their belief in absolute dualism. It is an attempt to reconcile God's existence with the problem of evil in the world, a problem that plagued Simone Weil throughout her life, as shown by her numerous journal entries on the subject. This is not a trivial problem at any time, surely not in our times. Dostoevsky's Ivan Karamazov wrestles with it to no avail in *The Brothers Karamazov,* and Elie Wiesel, standing in the shadow of the chimneys of Auschwitz, asks himself the same question: How has God permitted this? Or does He not exist at all?

Gnosticism proposes to solve the problem by postulating the realm of spirit, which is pure good and which is God's, and the realm of matter, which is totally evil and belongs to the devil,

the "prince of this world." Death, which is the shedding of the
corrupt body so that the liberated spirit may finally rejoin God,
is the glory of life, and life itself is seen as punishment. "My existence," Simone Weil wrote, "is a diminution of God's glory.
God gives me it so that I may desire to lose it." Put this way,
Gnosticism has some elements in common with Hinduism and
Buddhism except that in the Oriental religions there is a belief in
the ultimate Oneness of everything that contradicts the strict
dualism of Gnostic teachings.

The Gnostics, it should be added, did not believe that Jesus
was actually born in the flesh, for that would have involved God
in an impossible alliance with the Devil. No, He merely took on
the *appearance* of flesh the better to reach corrupt man. Early
Christianity was prone to this heresy once substantial numbers of
converts from the Greek world joined the Jewish-oriented Christian communities, and it is to these Gnostic elements that Paul
addressed many of his most ringing affirmations of Christ Jesus
as true God *and* true man. The Church Fathers in the East and
the West struggled repeatedly with this heresy in its many forms,
anathematizing and excommunicating one sect after another for
denying the true corporeality of Jesus.

The Fathers drove the Gnostic current underground. But they
did not choke it off completely. And this constituted a threat to the
Church until the Cathars were so decisively and brutally wiped
out. As Steven Runciman wrote in *The Medieval Manichees:*

The Gnostics included a large proportion of the Early Christian
Church. But it could not be Christianity. To accept it, Christians must
abandon their Jewish past. Jesus must come to destroy not to fulfill
the promises of the Old Testament; nor could He atone by His death
for the Fall of Man if man had always been bad and never fallen.
Inevitably the vital importance of Jesus must fade in the Gnostic cos-
mology, and Christianity loses its essential doctrine. Unless Christians were prepared to make this sacrifice of the Atonement, they
must reject Gnosticism from the Church.

Simone Weil welcomed any attempt to separate the Jewish
past of Christianity from what she conceived to be its single and
proper ancestor—Greek thought—although she saw Christian

figurae and avatars in religious traditions of all times and places. But she clung to the figure of Jesus as the central element of the religion, the redeemer king who sacrificed himself for others. More than that, she identified so strongly with Jesus that she herself was impelled to do, as far as it resided in her power, the very same thing. Her death would be a sacrificial offering for her countrymen, not because they deserved it—she had few illusions about the causes and meaning of the French defeat by the Germans in 1940—but because they needed it.

Perhaps she had reached a dead end in her thinking as she confronted the impossibility of either doing without Jesus or allowing for his existence in a Christianity that, as her later notebooks show, was becoming for her progressively more disembodied and syncretistic. Almost frantically, she ransacked the myths of other religions and cultures, called on the witness of the Egyptian Book of the Dead, Gilgamish, the Norse Eddas, her beloved Bhagavad-Gita and Plato, Neo-Platonic thought, the wisdom of the Pythagoreans, and even the creation myths of primitive peoples from Australia to Africa, to satisfy herself that Christ was but one avatar of God, supreme perhaps, yet not unique.

The speculation is problematical. Her actions are not. Deprived of the chance to sacrifice herself for her countrymen by parachuting into France and joining the Resistance, Simone Weil chose her death from the model proposed by those Cathari who had achieved the highest mystical experience and passed the most secret initiation tests to become Perfecta, the leaders of the community. Steven Runciman explained: "There was one other ceremony or rather practice in which the Perfect indulged, though its importance and frequency has probably been exaggerated by horrified Orthodox writers. This was the Endura. Certain of the Perfect carried out their doctrines to their logical end and deliberately committed suicide by self-starvation. The whole process was undertaken with the observance of a ritual, and the actual deathbed was the scene of rejoicing amongst the sectaries, the dying man or woman being regarded with deep reverential admiration."

Was this in fact her model? Simone Weil did not commit herself in print. But there are tantalizing clues in her notes that indicate the direction of her thought. She spent some time reading the Tibetan holy books, attracted by the figure of Milarepa—the great religious teacher and holy man of early Tibetan history—and one of her meditations on this subject reads: "Milarepa and food. After having destroyed to the utmost the reality of the universe, he finally reached its irreducible point, the point where the very mind which conceives finds itself degraded to being one out of the number of appearances. . . . Food constitutes this point. Food is the irreducible element. . . . Fasting constitutes an experimental knowledge of the irreducible character of food, and hence of the reality of the sensible universe."

It all came together—her religious beliefs, her solitude, her neuroses, the circumstances—and so she died, the brilliant student and teacher, the factory worker and radical, the pacifist and patriot, the philosopher and political theorist, the Greek scholar and farm laborer, and the lover of Plato, poetry, Gregorian chant, Romanesque churches, and the Italian countryside. It seems so much to have finally ended in such a small space—the hospital bed, the inflexible will, the bodily shrinking into death by subtraction. I do not think I—or anyone—knows exactly how it happened, but there are clues; there are stages that led Simone Weil, by apparent logic, to her end.

Simone Weil's *Iliad*

〜

MICHAEL K. FERBER

Our first impression of Simone Weil's essay, "The *Iliad,* or, The Poem of Force," is that of a clear, cold, dry wind that stings us awake and drives the mist away from our eyes.[1] A world of harsh, solid truth comes into sharp focus; we seem to see for the first time, in James Agee's great phrase, "the cruel radiance of what is." This impact is due in large part to the transparency of her prose. Her sentences are usually short, nearly always simple and lucid. Her critical terms could hardly be less esoteric: force, soul, thing, death. Her tone is an austere and distant sadness, though she departs from it now and then and draws nearer her subject, as in her sigh over Hector, who lay dead far from the hot bath Andromache was even then preparing for him. "Far from hot baths he was indeed, poor man. And not he alone. Nearly all the *Iliad* takes place far from hot baths." Yet these departures do not detract from, they even contribute to, our impression of severe impartiality and bitterness. It is the same voice that she ascribes to Homer himself.

The strong effect of the essay also comes from the thoroughness with which Weil turns over her few and simple subjects. At times there is sheer repetition, as in the opening paragraph, where "force" occurs nine times. "Force employed by man, force that enslaves man, force before which man's flesh shrinks away."

1. This essay is available in French as "L'*Iliade,* ou le Poème de la Force," in *La Source Greque* (Paris: Gallimard, 1953). It has been translated as "The *Iliad,* or the Poem of Force" by Mary McCarthy (*Politics* [November 1945]), and reprinted with the same title as a Pendle Hill Pamphlet (Wallingford, Pa.: Pendle Hill, 1956); it is also available in *Intimations of Christianity among the Ancient Greeks,* trans. Elisabeth Chase Geissbuhler (Boston: Beacon, 1958), as "The *Iliad,* or The Poem of Might."

Usually she repeats her sentence structure while enumerating examples. "We see their sword bury itself in the breast of a disarmed enemy who is in the very act of pleading at their knees. We see them triumph over a dying man by describing to him the outrages his corpse will endure. We see Achilles cut the throats of twelve Trojan boys on the funeral pyre of Patroclus as naturally as we cut flowers for a grave." The result is a relentless drumming into our minds, into our souls, of the reality of violence in the *Iliad* and in life. We may have been half asleep as we began the essay, but unless we turned away from squeamishness before suffering, we have been awakened and brought to attention.

"Attention," in fact, is the right word here. In her remarkable essay on the "Right Use of School Studies with a View to the Love of God," Simone Weil claims that the only serious purpose of academic study is to develop our powers of attention. Attention is the greatest of all efforts, and it must be slowly and painfully learned. The purpose of attention, in turn, is not to give us more powerful intellects, minds capable of taking up any matter and penetrating to its essence, but rather to prepare us for genuine prayer. "Attention," she writes, "consists of suspending our thought, leaving it detached, empty, and ready to be penetrated by the object," passive, not active and meddlesome, and the supreme object of attention is God. Genuine prayer is pure attentiveness directed toward God. "Above all," she adds, "our thought should be empty, waiting, not seeking anything."[2] "To wait" in French is *attendre*, whose connection with *attention* cannot be caught in modern English, for our word "attend" has lost most of its original meaning.[3] Our mind, cleared and focused by intellectual discipline, gives attention to God and "attends" his coming.

2. Simone Weil, *Waiting for God,* introduction by Leslie Fiedler, trans. Emma Craufurd (1951; reprint ed., New York: Capricorn, 1959), pp. 111, 112. Contains "Reflections on the Right Use of School Studies with a View to the Love of God." Subsequent references will be noted in the text as WG.
3. I owe to Elizabeth Young-Bruehl the suggestion that Weil also had in mind the Latin *animum attendere,* to direct or apply the mind.

The essay on the *Iliad,* one could argue, is a vehicle for an act of attention, and, if we discount its last few pages, which take up more general subjects, all her considerable rhetorical powers are aimed at making us "attend." We are to attend to her essay, of course, and to the *Iliad* itself, but more important, we are to attend to the truths the *Iliad* shares with the real world. Even that is not the goal, for ultimately we are to attend to God. If we reply that God is conspicuously absent from the *Iliad* we pose no problem for her argument, because in her view God is also conspicuously absent from the world.

No doubt it would be best if we could combine the discipline of our faculty of attention with an openness to the message of the poem by learning Greek and studying the original text, as she did, but the value of the *Iliad,* which it shares with a very small number of literary works, is that it is a peculiarly excellent means of access to some basic truths of the world. It is their "purest and loveliest" reflection. "Nearly all the *Iliad* takes place far from hot baths. Nearly all of human life, then and now, takes place far from hot baths." Her discussion passes easily from the poem to the real world, and she dwells as long on the exact nature of a thing or process in real life—the effects of war on the soldier, for example—as she does on its presence in the *Iliad.* Very interested in the mentality of the slave, she fills in the brief accounts of Briseis' grief over Patroclus and of Hector's premonitions of Andromache's fate with ideas drawn from her own meditations and not, I think, derivable from the text. It matters little. Homer, she believed, understood the affliction of the slave's soul, and if we understand it too we will see how profoundly right he is. After fifteen pages on the operations of force inside and outside the *Iliad,* to take a final example, she can sum up the matter with the sentence, "Such is the nature of force." We are not to ask whether she means force in Homer or force in life. Homer is life.

She is not the first, of course, to see Homer as life, or reality, or nature. When Pope, in his *Essay on Criticism,* had Virgil discover that "Nature and Homer were . . . the same," he was formulating an extreme version of an ancient, if not universal, veneration. Since ancient times Virgil and the Bible have acquired a similar authority—it is Virgil, not Homer, who guides Dante to the very edge of Paradise—but it is only the *Iliad* and a few other works, certainly not Virgil or the Old Testament, that hold this special rank for Simone Weil.

She is also not the only French writer of her generation to turn to the *Iliad* for insight into reality. Albert Camus turned to it, and to the Greeks generally, to define the ideals of beauty, limit, and contemplation of the natural world that he set against the modern idolatry of totality, history, and the manmade environment (see, for example, "Helen's Exile" in *The Myth of Sisyphus*). In 1943 Rachel Bespaloff wrote a book called *On the Iliad* to which Simone Weil's friend Jean Wahl wrote a preface.[4] (That book, in my opinion, is a reply to Simone Weil, although she is never mentioned in it; ideas and phrases she uses find echoes in it, and most of its main topics are those that she conspicuously omits or slights: Thetis and Achilles, Helen, the comedy of the gods, Priam and Achilles.) Someone who knows French and French literature better than I do ought to look into the possibility that the *Iliad* had an important part in the social and moral revaluation that took place during the Occupation and the postwar years.[5]

It is not that the *Iliad* offered any rationale for France's ignominious collapse in 1940. Paris was not Troy, holding out heroically for ten years against an equally heroic host of besiegers. (Weil had remained in Paris longer than necessary in the vain hope that it would be defended as it had been in 1870.)[6] But perhaps the sense of even-handed disillusionment in the midst of endless days of violence that bring permanent joy to no one, this clear-eyed and bitter feeling she rightly claims we find in the *Iliad,* offered a kind of solace. If we can bear the world of Homer, even find in it moments of beauty and grace, then we can bear our world of violence and defeat.

In her claim that the *Iliad* is "the purest and loveliest of mir-

4. Bespaloff, *On the Iliad,* trans. Mary McCarthy (New York: Harper, Bollingen, 1947).

5. On this, see Gabriel Germain, *Homer,* trans. Richard Howard (New York: Grove Press, 1960), pp. 51, 114.

6. Jacques Cabaud, *Simone Weil: A Fellowship in Love* (New York: Channel Press, 1964), p. 196.

rors," Weil is of course invoking a mimetic theory of literature, or at least a mimetic theory of literary value. A work of art is good, in other words, to the extent that it reflects the way things really are. Elsewhere she defines all art, good or bad, as imitative: "Art is an attempt to transport into a limited quantity of matter, modeled by man, an image of the infinite beauty of the entire universe." She is mainly interested, however, in artistic value. "If the attempt succeeds," she goes on,

> this portion of matter should not hide the universe, but on the contrary it should reveal its reality to all around.
>
> Works of art that are neither pure and true reflections of the beauty of the world nor openings onto this beauty are not strictly speaking beautiful; their authors may be very talented but they lack real genius. (WG, pp. 168–69)

There are elements of an expressive or romantic theory here, and in her claim that "God has inspired every first-rate work of art" there is a version of expressivism as old as the opening lines of the *Iliad* itself, but her theory is essentially a mimetic one. Now it would be easy to pick apart the assumptions on which a mimetic theory of art rests, in both its descriptive and its normative aspects. It would also be easy to show the kind of things most mimetic theories leave out. She has nothing to say, for instance, about the formal qualities of the *Iliad,* its great "geometrical" symmetries, its structures of incremental repetition and variation, its patterns of imagery, its highly formulaic style. These matters are presumably mere superficialities, examples of what she calls the "luster of beauty," and not beauty itself (WG, p. 169).

But what we most want to know of any mimetic theory, including hers, if it is to be of any use to us, is just what the reality is that art is supposed to represent. Weil, to be sure, has a great deal to tell us about essential reality, but most of it, I think we must agree, is unconventional and strange, even bizarre, though some of it is also deeply traditional. This is not to say that it is wrong; it may even be true, but it is hardly obvious or unproblematic.

As it happens, most of the more striking of her beliefs are left out of the essay, no doubt because of her sense of decorum and perhaps also because of her purpose in writing it, which was more to bring us to an understanding of reality than to illuminate Homer, though for her they are ultimately the same. Some of those she does include—such as her comments on slavery—I do not find objectionable in themselves, though they are debatable, and others are full of insight. Yet since we are told that the *Iliad* reflects the world of force and is great because it reflects it perfectly, we are allowed to ask what this world of force is, and if it is true.

To put it too simply, the world we inhabit, unless one is a truly spiritual soul, is a world of necessity or "gravity." It is a world from which God is voluntarily absent, though he exists; indeed he created the world by contracting his powers and presence. He only approaches in rare moments of grace when our souls empty themselves of self and turn toward God in pure attentiveness. In this we are following God's example, for he emptied himself when he became Christ (the doctrine of *kenosis*) and voluntarily suffered the purest affliction, dying as a criminal on the cross. All nature, including psychic nature when not touched by grace, obeys the severe rule of "gravity"—we are irremediably stained with sin and suffering and selfishness. Any attempt to deny our misery and construct a happy life is based on lies and delusions. Our only purpose in this life is to learn to love God, not in spite of the prevailing affliction but even because of it. "To love God through and across the destruction of Troy and Carthage—and with no consolation."[7]

We are helped in our efforts to love God by the beauty of nature. "In the beauty of the world brute necessity becomes an object of love" (WG, p. 128), for necessity is the law of God that all matter obeys. "What is more beautiful," Weil asks, "than the action of gravity on the fugitive folds of the sea waves, or on the almost eternal folds of the mountains?" (WG, pp. 128–29). That ships are wrecked by the sea and people drown only adds to its beauty. "All the horrors produced in this world are like the folds imposed upon the waves by gravity. That is why they con-

7. Simone Weil, *Gravity and Grace,* trans. Emma Craufurd (London, Routledge, Kegan & Paul, 1952). Hereafter cited in text as GG.

tain an element of beauty. Sometimes a poem, such as the *Iliad*, brings this beauty to light" (WG, p. 129). We can also learn to love God through ministering in selfless attentiveness to our fellow sufferers. They and we must come to see that true affliction is a kind of privilege, a way to the presence of God.

> The knowledge of this presence of God does not afford consolation; it takes nothing from the fearful bitterness of affliction; nor does it heal the mutilation of the soul. But we know quite certainly that God's love for us is the very substance of this bitterness and this mutilation.
>
> I should like out of gratitude to be capable of bearing witness to this.
>
> The poet of the *Iliad* loved God enough to have this capacity. This indeed is the implicit signification of the poem and the one source of its beauty. But it has scarcely been understood. (WG, pp. 89–90)

I cannot hope to do justice here to the power and scope of her vision of the universe, and even less can I hope to determine how true it is. I have many doubts, and I think much of it is undiscussible, that is, it rests on a vision or set of intuitions that are only tangentially susceptible of argument; at the end of this paper, however, I will say something about force as she sees it. Her vision is so extreme a formulation of one strand of Christianity (manifested in Jansenism and Calvinism, for example) that it must color her view of any subject she takes seriously. It is a testimony to her intellectual honesty that she saw things as clearly as she did, but it blinded her, I think, to some essential features of the *Iliad*. Insofar as her essay rests on her religious and metaphysical assumptions, insofar as she appeals, however implicitly, to our belief in them for her evaluation of the poem, the essay is a problem and, as an interpretation, a failure.

II Many who have commented on it agree that the essay, whatever power it may have, is not a satisfactory account of the *Iliad*. Leslie Fiedler calls it "splendid, though absurdly and deliberately partial" (WG, 12). There are passages in it that no one would quarrel with, like the pages on the seesaw progress of the war and the consequent brevity of all joy in victory. She is also very fine in her account of the pervading tone of "bitterness that proceeds from tenderness and that spreads over the whole human race, impartial as sunlight." In her central interpretive claims, however, she commits what Harold Bloom might call a "strong misreading" of the *Iliad*. We can see the problems most clearly in her two discussions of the encounter between Achilles and Priam.

Weil defines the suppliant as one whose life hangs entirely on the whim of another and who for that reason is no different from a thing or a corpse. She quotes passages from Lycaon's pathetic supplication of Achilles and Achilles' merciless response (21.64 ff). She then turns to Priam, another suppliant of Achilles, and likens his impression on Achilles and the Myrmidons to that made by a corpse: "a shudder seizes those who see him." This shudder or *frisson* is not in the Greek, however, and neither is the corpse. The impression Priam makes is not that of a cadaver but of an outcast and possibly dangerous stranger who has come unarmed by surprise: it is "wonder" or "amazement" that seizes Achilles.[8] Priam grasps Achilles' knees as a suppliant, kisses the hands that slew his son, and appeals to Achilles' feelings for his own father as grounds for taking pity on another father kneeling at his feet. That is just what Achilles does, and in the most poignant moment of the entire epic Priam and Achilles weep together, the one for his son, the other, who slew him, for his father far away and for his friend whom that son slew. "And their sobs resounded through the house." Weil's treatment of this profound and radiant moment is perverse. All she really wants to show is that Priam is still a mere thing of no importance to Achilles. Achilles might, she admits, be moved to tears, but he can, and does, treat Priam as if he were not there. He can "with a single movement push him to the ground" while he takes his fill of memories and tears, for Priam completely lacks the "indefinable influence that the presence of another human being has on us."

8. Weil quotes the simile about a murderer outcast from his land (24.480–84) as if it were about a corpse. The Greek noun she mistranslates as *frisson* is *thambos*, "wonder, astonishment, surprise"; the verb is *thambēsen, thambēsan*.

Now there is nothing in the original to suggest that Achilles pushes Priam to the floor. In fact the Greek says just the opposite: Achilles "took the old man's hand and pushed him / gently away,"[9] to indicate to Priam that, if anything, he should cease being a suppliant.[10] Priam has more than an indefinable influence. The ferocious warrior is moved to gentleness for the first time in the poem. And far from letting Priam lie at his feet until "chance" inspires someone to pick him up, as she goes on to say, Achilles raises him to his feet as soon as Achilles has wept his fill. If he frightens and silences Priam a few moments later, it is not that he has simply threatened him, as Weil seems to imply, but that he fears Priam may lose control if he returns to the grief he has just set aside. She also does not mention, in this first discussion, that after Achilles agrees to return the body of Hector and personally helps prepare it, he and Priam break bread and sit gazing in wonder at each other. This is the climactic moment of the *Iliad,* and it casts its poignant grace over all the fury and the mire that came before.[11]

As if she recognizes she has not done justice to this scene, Weil takes it up briefly again toward the end of her essay where she discusses the rare moments of love or friendship that relieve the monotonous horror of war and death. "But the purest triumph of love, the crowning grace of war, is the friendship that floods the hearts of mortal enemies. Before it a murdered son or a murdered friend no longer cries out for vengeance. Before it—even more miraculous—the distance between benefactor and suppliant,

9. *The Iliad of Homer,* trans. Richmond Lattimore (Chicago: University of Chicago Press, 1951), 24.508–9. In this essay I refer to this translation and to that by Robert Fitzgerald (Garden City, N.Y.: Doubleday, Anchor Press, 1974).

10. The Greek for "gently" (*ēka*) Weil translates weakly as "un peu." McCarthy unfairly omits it, as if she goes along with her harsh misreading. Geissbuhler restores "gently" and thus somewhat misrepresents the French. For "Achille a d'un geste poussé à terre le vieillard" there is no warrant in the Greek. McCarthy inexplicably softens the French by translating it as "push away."

11. Gabriel Germain relies on this scene to reply, very briefly, to Weil. She forgets, he says, that "the anger of Achilles [is] both satisfied and *surmounted*" (p. 51).

between victor and vanished, shrinks to nothing[.]" She then quotes the passage she omitted in her earlier account, where Priam and Achilles eat and gaze at one another. Her words here contradict what she said there; there the whole point was that, despite the shared tears, Priam remains a thing, or nothing, and the distance between him and Achilles remains infinite. Yet even this reconsideration leaves their encounter as only the most notable of exceptional luminous moments whose function is "to make us feel with sharp regret what it is that violence has killed and will kill again." She does not do it justice.

In misconstruing this scene as she does, Weil also fails to notice some of its other important features. Priam is not a suppliant like his son Lycaon, whose miserable death she recounts just before turning to the father. Lycaon is defeated in battle, and by the rules he can expect only death or slavery. But Priam comes voluntarily to the camp of his most hated enemy, and though he is still a suppliant he is also a marvel, a man to be admired. He is not a metaphorical corpse. As far as that goes, even the real corpse in this scene is not just a corpse, for it is that corpse that brings Priam at such great risk to Achilles and occasions their hour of grieving communion. It was another corpse, too, that drove Achilles to slay Hector, not just to satisfy the vengeance of the survivors but to propitiate the spirit of the dead.

For the dead have spirits. Every passage Weil cites in her long litany of slaughter we could match with a passage of furious and foolhardy attempts by the comrades of the slaughtered one to pull him back behind the lines. The rites of the dead—sacrifices, games, and cremation—are religiously performed, and every hero fears the desecration of his body by dogs and birds more than death itself. Honor and shame, the great norms of the heroic code, are more important than life and death. Weil seems blind to this crucial dimension of the Homeric universe; she would have it that "no comforting fiction intervenes; no consoling prospect of immortality; and on the hero's head no washed-out halo of patriotism descends." In saying this she is seriously wrong.

Now it can be argued that, despite the recurrence of rites of the dead and despite the purpose of Priam's climactic mission to Achilles, the prospect of personal immortality does not much mitigate the evil of death as Homer presents it.[12] The immortal part of Achilles himself, after all, finds no compensation in his afterlife. In the *Odyssey* Achilles' shade tells Odysseus, "Better, I say, to break sod as a farm hand / for some poor country man, on iron rations, / than lord it over the exhausted dead"[13] (11.489–91). But the other kind of immortality we mentioned provides not only a comfort in defeat or death but the great spur for all heroic action: glory, *klea andrōn,* the fame of men. Odysseus is too tactful to remind Achilles' complaining shade that he is in Hades in the first place because he chose a short life of glory over a long life of obscurity, but it is true. Nearly every hero of the *Iliad* makes the same choice, though they are sometimes tempted to renounce glory for what we would take to be a more rational or prudent course. Hector in his final hour, when he sees Deiphobus is no longer with him, turns to face Achilles alone rather than resume his flight around the walls of Troy. He knows the gods have abandoned him and he must die. "Still, I would not / die without delivering a stroke, / or die ingloriously, but in some action / memorable to men in days to come" (Fitzgerald, 22.304–5). Of course these words and countless others to the same purpose are assigned to characters by an author whose profession is to do just that—make memorable actions—but even if the bard's professional rationale has colored the *Iliad* (and more obviously the *Odyssey*), it is Homer's imaginative world of which Weil is speaking, and there we do find a "consoling prospect of immortality."

The possibility of fame that long outlives one's death, whether it is preserved by bards whose muses are the daughters of memory or told by wise Nestors well instructed in the chronicles, holds power over the heroes of Homer because it is a part of a social system in which the central values in this life are honor and prestige. Greek aristocrats scramble incessantly for rank. Every deed, every speech, every exchange of gifts is tinged by consciousness of its efficacy in promoting one's social status. The *Iliad* itself,

12. Bespaloff goes so far as to say that the cult of the dead "has no influence whatever on the poet's philosophical thought" (p. 88).

13. *The Odyssey,* trans. Robert Fitzgerald (1961; reprint ed., Garden City, N.Y.: Anchor, 1963).

though set in the final years of the Trojan War, is about a point of honor between two Greeks; the wrath of Achilles announced in the opening line is not directed at Hector or Priam but at Agamemnon. Homeric society is a shame-culture, according to E. R. Dodds,[14] as opposed to a guilt-culture; the highest good for Homeric man is not a quiet conscience or obedience to a god as it supposedly is for us, but the enjoyment of public esteem and the avoidance of shame or public disapproval. Putting aside the pleas of his father and mother that he remain inside the walls, Hector tells them he will fight Achilles out of shame before his fellow Trojans (22.105). Homeric man is an extrovert and a creature of his fellows; he lacks our modern sense of responsibility for unseen deeds, let alone for private thoughts and wishes.

The Homeric man's sense of self or identity, then, is very different from ours. He not only takes his definition from his social environment to a greater extent than we think we do, but his primary social bonds differ from ours in emphasis and intensity. We may think of ourselves as a teacher or plumber or a Sylvania employee, a husband or wife, a parent, an American, perhaps a Harvard man, perhaps a tennis buff, in more or less that order; a Greek is always the son of someone. (Odysseus is occasionally, and touchingly, the father of someone.) Patronymics are interchangeable with "first" names, and sometimes we even have "grand-patronymics," if that is a word. When two warriors meet and exchange boasts before they exchange spearcasts they usually include their genealogies; such a habit even leads to a truce once, when it turns out two of their grandfathers were friends. These are not just decorous courtesies. The hero is a member of a lineage; more than that, he is the lineage itself reincarnate. His highest calling, and fullest act of self-expression are to add his glorious deeds to the record of the glorious deeds of his ancestors. Whether he dies in the process or not is of lesser importance, as long as a son survives him and bards take note. In a famous passage the son of Hippolochus beautifully expresses this outlook to the son of Tydeus:

14. Dodds, *The Greeks and the Irrational* (Berkeley and Los Angeles: University of California Press, 1951), chapter two.

As is the generation of leaves, so is that of humanity.
The wind scatters the leaves on the ground, but the live timber
burgeons with leaves again in the season of spring returning.
So one generation of men will grow while another dies.
(Lattimore, 6.146–50)

To a Homeric hero leaves are of no importance; what counts is
the family tree.

So when Priam comes to claim the body of his son it is not just
a manner of speaking to say he is claiming a part of himself.
What gives Priam the courage to come to Achilles, what lends
him dignity in voluntary supplication, is that in a more than
metaphorical sense Priam is more fully Priam, King of Troy,
there with his son's remains in the tent of his enemy than he was
back home on his Trojan throne.

I have dwelled on Homeric culture to this extent in order to
show what Simone Weil leaves out of her study of the *Iliad*. Of
course it is only a brief study, but nonetheless I think her approach is to dismiss the particulars that I have stressed because
they are incidental to the timeless truths the *Iliad* perfectly mir-
rors. Hers is a version of what C. S. Lewis has called the doctrine
of the Unchanging Human Heart, the belief that what is of value
in any work of literature is what it shares with our age and with
all ages. She does not, of course, say that we already know what
the *Iliad* teaches, but rather that what the *Iliad* teaches is true
now and always has been, that it is essential that we learn it, and
that the *Iliad* gives us a clear and beautiful means of discovering
it. I do not question that the *Iliad* holds unchanging truths, or
that it can show us a world enough like ours to be a vehicle of
moral or religious instruction: it is still recognizably the *Iliad*
that Weil interprets. But the world of the *Iliad* is richly and
strangely different from ours, and these differences are not only
central to the shape and meaning of the poem but they can teach
us moral lessons as well.

Let me take one example from basic Homeric vocabulary.
Whether or not we are Christian we nearly all think in the dualistic terminology of body and soul. We may deny the soul's immortality, we may read philosophical refutations of its very existence, but the dichotomy between body and soul, or body and

mind, or whatever other variants we invent, continues unconsciously to structure our thought. Such a dualism, severe, exacting,
and with its implications deeply thought out, governs Simone
Weil's religious and moral thought. No such dualism, however, is
to be found in the *Iliad:* Homer had no words for either "body"
or "soul."[15] He would not have understood most of his twentieth-
century interpreter's points—that the soul lives in a house, for example, and becomes cramped and bent if the house becomes a
thing. Homer of course has some terms that overlap ours, but
their central meanings are different; the difference is bound up
with the different sense of identity that we have been discussing.
If Simone Weil's eyes had been less tutored by her assumptions,
the shock of unrecognition in her beloved *Iliad* might have led
her to question those assumptions. If she had wavered in her beliefs about body and soul she might never have written *Waiting
for God* or *Gravity and Grace,* but she might also still be alive.

III   Toward the end of the essay on the *Iliad,* Weil offers us a
fine piece of historical imagination. The "extraordinary sense of
equity" in the *Iliad,* our feeling that its author was neither Greek
nor Trojan, may be due to the history of the Achaeans. They who
conquered Troy were themselves conquered by the Dorians only
two or three generations later, so when they looked back on the
Trojan War they could see it with the eyes of conquerors and
conquered simultaneously. This is mere fancy, she says, and so it
is, but I find it intriguing and attractive. She is certainly right to
lay stress on the tone of impartiality that pervades the poem. As
Northrop Frye says, "It is hardly possible to overestimate the importance for Western literature of the *Iliad's* demonstration that
the fall of an enemy, no less than of a friend or leader, is tragic
and not comic. With the *Iliad,* once for all, an objective and disinterested element enters into the poet's vision of human life."[16]

15. See Bruno Snell, *The Discovery of the Mind,* trans. T. G. Rosen-
meyer (1953; reprint ed., New York: Harper Torchbooks, 1960),
chapter one.
16. Frye, *Anatomy of Criticism: Four Essays* (Princeton: Princeton
University Press, 1957), p. 319.

Yet Weil in her notebooks offers a very different sort of explanation for this disinterested empathy: "It is impossible to understand and love at the same time both the victors and the vanquished, as the *Iliad* does, except from the place, outside the
world, where God's Wisdom dwells." Homer "knew and loved
God." "Only a just man made perfect could have written the
Iliad."[17]

With these ideas, only implicit in the *Iliad* essay, we have returned to her religious beliefs. Among those I summarized earlier
I would like to stress the verticality of her thought, implicit in
her terms "gravity" and "grace" and explicit in her frequent use
of phrases like "here below," in her stress on yearning and waiting, eyes turned upward, and in her claim that "we are incapable
of progressing vertically" (WG, p. 133; see Fiedler in WG, pp. 36–
37). God is absolutely transcendent. Now it seems to me that the
world of the *Iliad* is one of the most horizontal worlds imaginable.
Homer is everywhere lovingly attentive to details of things and
events: to the tides of battle, the techniques of sailing and slaugh-
tering, the skills of the heroes at wrestling and foot racing. What
could be more horizontal than the catalog of ships? Even the
Olympian gods do not represent true transcendence or verticality;
they at best represent another horizontal plane, higher in rank and
power but lower in moral and even spiritual status than the humans
in whose affairs they are continually meddling. It would be reasonable to expect then that for Weil the *Iliad* would be incomplete,
a world conspicuously lacking the one thing needful, an Old
Testament crying out for a New. She does indeed seem to treat
the *Iliad* and certain other ancient works as a kind of Old Testament. The real Old Testament, though its God is transcendent
enough, she largely rejects as "a tissue of horrors":[18] "I know
that the author of the *Iliad* knew and loved God and the author
of the Book of Joshua did not" (FLN, p. 145).[19] Moreover she

17. Weil, *First and Last Notebooks,* trans. Richard Rees (New York:
Oxford University Press, 1970), pp. 148, 145, 336. Hereafter cited in
the text as FLN.

18. Weil, *Seventy Letters,* trans. Richard Rees (London: Oxford University Press, 1965), p. 160. Hereafter cited as L.

19. "Her Bible . . . would presumably have consisted of the New

can say that the *Iliad* "draws a picture of God's absence."[20]

We must remember, however, that for Simone Weil God is indeed absent "here below." The coming of Christ does not seem to have changed the world, and the New Testament simply presents with a unique focus and unusual clarity the same eternal truths about suffering and necessity that we find, in fact, in the *Iliad:* "all the *Iliad* is bathed in Christian light" (WG, p. 70). So the thrust of this-worldly horizontality that we find in Homer is illusory: the real message of the poem, and the faith of its poet, depend upon the felt absence of an absolutely transcendent God. As for all those gods and goddesses, she suggests in a notebook, they are demons; only Zeus is God, and his golden balance is necessity (NSW, p. 455). The *Iliad* has been rotated ninety degrees.

IV Weil, as I said, places the *Iliad* in a small group of great literary works. Most of them, as we might expect, are tragedies: the *Iliad* itself, Aeschylus, Sophocles, Shakespeare's *King Lear,* Racine's *Phèdre. King Lear* and *Phèdre,* in fact, are singled out as the only great works by their authors,[21] and though she does not say this, it seems no accident that they are usually felt to be the most harrowing of their author's tragedies, the ones offering the least consolation or compensation. Among other writers she mentions Villon, Cervantes, and Molière, not, to be sure, because of

---

Testament preceded by Plato and the Bhagavad-Gita" (E. W. F. Tomlin, *Simone Weil* [New Haven: Yale University Press, 1954] pp. 38–39). The *Iliad* would seem even more important than these. Compare Goethe: "Had we never come to know the melancholy of the Orient, had Homer remained our Bible, how different a form would mankind have achieved!" (cited in Karl Löwith, *From Hegel to Nietzsche,* trans. David Grene [1964; reprint ed., Garden City, N.Y.: Anchor, 1967] p. 21).

20. *The Notebooks of Simone Weil,* trans. Arthur Wills, 2 vols. (New York: Putnam, 1956), p. 405. Hereafter cited in the text as NSW.

21. GG, p. 136; also in Weil, *On Science, Necessity, and the Love of God,* ed. and trans. Richard Rees (London: Oxford University Press, 1968), p. 162. *On Science* contains "Morality and Literature." Hereafter cited in the text as SN.

their humor, but because in their fundamental seriousness they convey the cruelty of society or the sadness of life. The *Odyssey* and the *Aeneid* are not on the list. They and nearly everything else are dismissed as "fictions" that deceive us about fundamental moral and metaphysical truths. The great works are not really fictions, for they "give us, in the guise of fiction, something equivalent to the actual density of the real, that density which life offers us every day but which we are unable to grasp because we are amusing ourselves with lies" (SN, p. 162). That density, properly seen, is beautiful and lends its beauty to the works that make us see it.

The passage I have just quoted is from a fascinating but difficult little essay called "Morality and Literature." She begins it, as she begins the *Iliad* essay and many others, with a breath-taking claim:

Nothing is so beautiful and wonderful, nothing is so continually fresh and surprising, so full of sweet and perpetual ecstasy, as the good. No desert is so dreary, monotonous, and boring as evil. This is the truth about authentic good and evil. With fictional good and evil it is the other way round. Fictional good is boring and flat, while fictional evil is varied and intriguing, attractive, profound, and full of charm.

She illustrates this claim by comparing the passionate interest we would feel in watching a man walk in air or walk with ease over red-hot coals in real life with our boredom with such things in literature. In literature that would be just plain walking, because the air and hot coals are easily conjured fictions; of greater interest would be the sight of people leaping madly about as if on hot coals, for then the variety of forms would attract us. Goodness is simple, like walking; evil is various, like leaping about.

I find this argument, which I have somewhat abbreviated, very confusing. She seems first to be saying something that I think we have all felt about the attractions of evil in literature. It may partly account for the absence of Dante from her select canon, for most readers seem to find the *Inferno* the most interesting of the three parts of the *Divine Comedy*. Many readers prefer Milton's Satan to his God for similar reasons. This fact of experience,

if it is one, is an important matter to pursue, but to get to the
bottom of it, it seems to me, we must deal with the fact that evil
also holds its attractions in real life. As long as we are at a safe
distance, aesthetic or otherwise, we are fascinated by sin, by horrible crimes, monsters, earthquakes, and gas chambers. Weil herself seems to evoke the old tradition that evil is multiple and
goodness is simple or singular, and if that is true it would follow
that evil is more interesting wherever it occurs. We might just
have to face that fact; it makes goodness no less good, after all, to
say it is uninteresting. Yet we naturally do not want to leave it at
that, for like good post-Homeric Greeks we would like to think
that the good, the beautiful, and the true are all one, and all
forms of the One, and we are uncomfortable at seeing the evil
sidle over to the beautiful.

Weil wants to insist, however, that in real life the opposite is
the case: the real good is "an unfathomable marvel." But the
problem with her argument is that it rests on an equivocation.
Words like "interesting" and "monotonous" are not just aesthetic
categories but are hybrid terms that cover the good and the true
as well as the beautiful (and their opposites). Simone Weil finds
the truth very interesting in part because it is true. Real goodness,
in turn, is interesting not only because it is really good, but—and
this compounds the problem—because it is rare, and rarity is
partly an aesthetic category. A rare thing interests us because of
its variety: it is different from most other things.[22]

I may have added puzzles of my own to the puzzles in her
essay, but two things seem to emerge clearly enough. One is that
we can see another reason for her love of the *Iliad,* for the most
obvious and palpable of evils in the *Iliad* is not very interesting
or marvelous, and that is the death of an individual warrior. According to one count, 243 named warriors meet their doom
(Germain, p. 180), and while it may be interesting to learn how
many ways a man may be done in by different weapons, such an
interest is of a minute and morbid sort and no answer to the

22. Elizabeth Young-Bruehl has reminded me that truly Christian virtue is supposed to be invisible to mortals. To the extent that virtue tri-
umphs, or even displays itself, it is tarnished. The consequences of this
doctrine for literature are drastic.

cumulative weight of death upon death. Perhaps Homer's original audience took delight in all the names and details, but it is hard to believe that they too did not feel the tedious burden of it all. The second point has to do with Weil's moralism. I may be mistaken that the rarity of goodness, which she does not explicitly argue here, underlies her argument, but there is no doubt from her other writings that she believed it. So tainted are we by sin, by necessity, by gravity, that a genuinely good act is a miracle. Everything that we usually call good is illusory, a flabby fiction that only prevents us from doing genuine good. This bleak and uncompromising moral standpoint we must keep in mind as we turn once more to "The Poem of Force."

V In criticizing Simone Weil's reading of the *Iliad* I do not mean to suggest that mimetic criteria or moral standards are invalid and irrelevant in literary criticism. They bring problems with them and can lead one astray if they are invoked too early in the process of understanding and judging. After the current fad of French structuralism, however, according to which reality is an asymptote of language, it would be a relief to find serious and thoughtful critics asking old-fashioned questions again, like "Is this true?" and "Does this help us do right in the world?" rather than "How intricately and cleverly is this put together?" I admire her attempt to bring "nonliterary" values to bear on the *Iliad,* even if they overwhelm it at times, and I can only hope that I will have the courage to follow her example in the face of contrary trends.

Whatever their bearing on the *Iliad,* Weil makes a number of important and thoughtful claims about the nature of force, and in taking these up I feel very tentative and deferential. These are matters of such importance that there can be no expertise about them, only wisdom, and I am too young to have much yet. Simone Weil was also young, but she meditated longer and more intensely than most thinkers twice her age, and she saw her country fall into a greater catastrophe than an American can easily imagine. For what it is worth, then, my opinion is divided over her theory of force.

"Force," she says, "is as pitiless to the man who possesses it, or thinks he does, as it is to its victims; the second it crushes, the first it intoxicates. The truth is, nobody really possesses it." It changes hands so easily that it begins to seem independent, a blind, automatic justice that kills those who kill. This seems to me a fundamental insight, a truth proverbial in ancient times but forgotten so often that it must be restated freshly again and again. If we take this insight seriously and follow its implications we can begin to make judgments of political and social events free of certain illusions. She herself brings it to bear on the Russian Revolution, for example, in an early essay on "the causes of liberty and social oppression" that was the most brilliant piece she ever wrote, in my opinion:

The powerful means are oppressive, the non-powerful means remain inoperative. Each time that the oppressed have tried to set up groups able to exercise a real influence, such groups, whether they went by the name of parties or unions, have reproduced in full within themselves all the vices of the system which they claimed to reform or abolish, namely, bureaucratic organization, reversal of the relationship between means and ends, contempt for the individual, separation between thought and action, the mechanization of thought itself, the exploitation of stupidity and lies as means of propaganda, and so on.[23]

From this analysis free of illusions, however, as we can see from this passage, she draws only disillusionment. About all she can hope for is a certain amount of clear thinking (see OL, pp. 23, 124) and resolute commitment to struggle no matter what the odds. In the *Iliad* essay she goes even further, if that is possible, by means of a metaphysical extension of the idea of force:

In any case, this poem is a miracle. Its bitterness is the only justifiable bitterness, for it springs from the subjections of the human spirit to force, that is, in the last analysis, to matter. This subjection is the common lot, although each spirit will bear it differently, in proportion to its own virtue. No one in the *Iliad* is spared by it, as no one on earth is.

23. Weil, *Oppression and Liberty,* trans. Arthur Wills and John Petrie (Amherst: University of Massachusetts Press, 1973), p. 120. Hereafter cited as OL.

Serious thought about the automatism of force, however, might lead in another direction. We might try to imagine a way of organizing a movement for social change that does not rely upon it, or makes a different use of it. To carry out this hard task we must think our way out of the definition of "force" Weil imposes on us, for after a certain point it seems to baffle all thought with its global range of meanings. She does not distinguish between violence and other kinds of force; indeed she cannot do so because she conceives of force, as she says in the passage I have just quoted, as ultimately a kind of matter. "All forms of force are material," she says in her essay on oppression and liberty; "the expression 'spiritual force' is essentially contradictory" (OL, p. 98). Such a view of force, deriving it seems from her passionate admiration of geometry and physics, has an aura of French logic and clarity about it, but it is also a misplaced concretion, a metaphysical spectre that benumbs thought. It has the same hard-nosed no-nonsense impact as Chairman Mao's dictum that "All power grows out of the barrel of a gun," which is equally mistaken, as Mao knew very well.

Let me set against Weil's idea of force Hannah Arendt's account of forgiveness, in which she also speaks of the automatism of violence:

. . . [F]orgiveness is the exact opposite of vengeance, which acts in the form of re-acting against an original trespassing, whereby far from putting an end to the consequences of the first misdeed, everybody remains bound to the process, permitting the chain reaction contained in every action to take its unhindered course. In contrast to revenge, which is the natural, automatic reaction to transgression and which because of the irreversibility of the action process can be expected and even calculated, the act of forgiving can never be predicted; it is the only reaction that acts in an unexpected way and thus retains, though being a reaction, something of the original character of action. Forgiving, in other words, is the only reaction which does not merely re-act but acts anew and unexpectedly, unconditioned by the act which provoked it and therefore freeing from its consequences both the one who forgives and the one who is forgiven. The freedom contained in Jesus' teachings of forgiveness is the freedom from vengeance, which encloses both doer and sufferer in the relentless automatism of the action process, which by itself need never come to an end.[24]

Is forgiveness a negligible force? Is it just a piece of wishful thinking that it could have any effect on social change? Let me put it in a more hard-nosed way. Can we not work out a strategy for social change that would incorporate a refusal to react in kind as one of its tactics? Not necessarily to forgive in a Christian sense but to throw the enemy off balance, make him do things he would rather not, draw support away from him, without violence? Weil would call Martin Luther King's "soul force" a contradiction in terms, but it seems to me he accomplished something. So did Gandhi with his "truth-grasping." So have millions of workers and citizens by strikes and boycotts. So, I am proud to say, did the antiwar movement in the 1960s and early 1970s, and not by the bombings (which the FBI not only welcomed but helped carry out), but by massive demonstrations and by draft resistance: by hanging in, paying a price, and refusing to conform to the image the government wanted to impose on us.

These, it might be said, are modest achievements, born of exceptional circumstances, and not really a test of the force of nonviolence.[25] I disagree, but then perhaps I am only pitting my optimism against Simone Weil's pessimism, my revolutionary duty to hope against the reasons and experiences behind her despair. I believe there is some evidence that nonviolent social movements can succeed and it is of the greatest importance to understand them. Simone Weil's "force" stands in the way.[26]

24. Arendt, *The Human Condition* (Chicago: University of Chicago Press, 1958), pp. 240–41.
25. We might also mention the traditions of anarcho-syndicalism and council communism, to which Weil was attracted, as forces never "successful" but far from dead in Europe, as May 1968 proved. They are essentially unviolent, if not nonviolent, and they explicitly resist the bureaucratization and reversal of means and ends that she laments.
26. For two of many efforts to draw the distinctions necessary to think fruitfully about violence, see Arendt, *On Violence* (New York: Harcourt, Brace & World, 1970), with its definitions of violence, power, and force; and Anthony Arblaster, "What is Violence?", in *The Socialist Register,* ed. Ralph Miliband and John Saville (London: Nevlin, 1975), which sympathizes with Weil's usage but finally rejects it.

Yet we need her vision. It will help keep us from the illusions that easily beset social reformers and revolutionaries. Her critique of Marx and Lenin is a bracing wind that blows cobwebs from the mind. Her vision of war's effects on man in the *Iliad* essay, and of the automatism of violence, if not of all force, is an essential contribution to our moral literature. Once the shooting starts outside the windows the world may well become the one she paints, where the people who possess force walk through the human substance around them as through a nonresistant medium. But until that time there are forces of resistance that we can learn to wield, forces that might stave off such a time, and such a world. Perhaps there is no reason to be optimistic, but there is no necessity to despair.

Notes on
Simone Weil's *Iliad*

⌒

JOSEPH H. SUMMERS

A number of readers have remarked that Simone Weil's "The *Iliad,* or the Poem of Force" distorts many of the values of the Greek epic. Ever since I first read Mary McCarthy's translation of that brilliant essay in Dwight Macdonald's magazine *Politics* in 1945, however, rather than thinking of it as primarily "about" the *Iliad* (or even about the nature of reality), I have thought of it as primarily a document of its time: an extraordinary response to the war with Hitler and the fall of France, written by a Frenchwoman primarily for her compatriots in both occupied and unoccupied France in the early 1940s. Its original publication under the acronym of "Emile Novis" in the *Cahiers du Sud* of December 1940 and January 1941 seemed to signal the fact that, like other works of that time and place, it contained a secret and dangerous message about the present under the guise of a study or "adaptation" of a work from the past. But unlike Anouilh's *Antigone,* which I thought simplified and to some degree cheapened the Greek text that it pretended to translate or adapt, Weil's "L'*Iliade,* ou le Poème de la Force," even in its distortions, struck me as moving and ennobling—not merely in its anguished response to the defeated and the enslaved, but particularly in its perception of the dehumanization, the reciprocal enslavement of the victors and the defeated in a total war. The paradigm was of a world engaged in what seemed an endless war. That anyone of left sympathies could see anything pitiable in the triumphant German armies of Hitler was remarkable enough; that a Frenchwoman and a Jew who passionately identified with the defeated and the oppressed could do so struck me as miraculous.

Any number of the remarkable formulations in her essay that

are presented as observations on the *Iliad* or as universal truths seem to me to possess an odd and touching resonance when one thinks of them as written in 1940 and presented anonymously to the French people:

Whoever, within his own soul and in human relations, escapes the dominion of force is loved but loved sorrowfully because of the threat of destruction that constantly hangs over him.

Only he who has measured the dominion of force, and knows how not to respect it, is capable of love and justice.

But nothing the peoples of Europe have produced is worth the first known poem that appeared among them. Perhaps they will yet rediscover the epic genius, when they learn that there is no refuge from fate, learn not to admire force, not to hate the enemy, nor to scorn the unfortunate. How soon this will happen is another question.[1]

The surfaces here are literary and philosophical, but the passionate quality of the perception is, I think, both political and religious, and very much "engaged." Weil seems to have felt that the paralyzing danger for her and for other French intellectuals of the time was that they might devote their energies and imaginations so completely to hating the evil enemy and to scorning the defeated (particularly those in both occupied and Vichy France) that the forces of "right" might become as committed to destruction and death and dehumanization as the forces of evil they wished to destroy.

If it did not quite come to that in World War II (although Simone Weil had serious doubts about some of the developments among the Free French, and we may be permitted to have them about both our treatment of the Japanese within the United States and our dropping of the atomic bombs on Hiroshima and Nagasaki), we can surely recognize that the dangers were real by analogy to what happened to the forces of the United States and to a large part of the American people during the later war in Indochina. Weil was ineradicably French, and she was a patriot of a peculiarly conscientious sort. She remarked somewhere, "I

1. I quote from Mary McCarthy's translation in *The Mint* 2(1948): 84–111.

have been much more wounded by the things done by my country than by those done to it." If by a notable stretch of the imagination one can imagine her as being German, I think one must recognize that a German Simone Weil's reading of the *Iliad*—or at least her presentation of her reading to others in 1940—would have turned out very differently. The essay we have is a meditation on a hideous war primarily from the point of view of the conquered. If she had been a compatriot of the still aggressive conquerors, she would surely have emphasized more clearly the injustice and stupidity of the aggressors rather than her attempt to understand and to endure the defeat with a minimal loss of humanity. (Of course, a German Simone Weil might very well have devoted all her energies to doing whatever was possible—or impossible—to end the carnage rather than to writing an essay on the *Iliad* at all.)

Some readers have labeled both the *Iliad* essay and a number of Weil's other writings as Jansenist. Almost every reader thinks of her in relation to Pascal, the Pascal of the *Provinciales* as well as the *Pensées*. The contemporary writer who seems to me in some ways spiritually closest to her was the Bernanos of *The Diary of a Country Priest, Les Grands Cimetières sous la lune,* and the dramatization that Poulenc adapted for the libretto of *The Dialogues of the Carmelites.* Still, I feel uncomfortable with generalizations concerning Weil's dualism of body and soul. Of course such a dualism (as I understand it, a predominantly un-Christian one) is embedded in our language and thought, and it is almost impossible for any European or American to be unaffected by it. And many of Weil's writings ("La Pesanteur et la Grace," for example) often seem to push dualism to extremes. But a number of her formulations seem related more closely to her habit of juxtaposing diametrically opposed aphoristic "truths" as the beginning of "thought" or meditation than to her final philosophical commitments. One can find examples of the habit throughout her writings, but here is a good one in the notebooks where, in a meditation on violence and nonviolence, she places the opposing aphorisms in brackets:

$\Big\{$ Nothing ineffective has value.
$\Big\}$ The seduction of force is base.
 A terrible difficulty there.[2]

It seems to me that in the *Iliad* essay she is often rejecting an easy Platonism that imagines the triumph of the soul apart from the body, and is insisting rather that the suffering and mechanization of the body, whether inflicted by a military conqueror, a slave master, or the very experience of war itself (in other essays the agent is the factory system) *do* inevitably mark the soul—and that all souls are, to some extent, so marked.

Certainly Weil was often concerned with precisely the notion of "pure action" as a commitment of the whole being, body and soul marvelously united. Again, some passages from the notebooks explore the concept and the difficulties:

All one can say is that the intention, in the strongest sense, is to do the least harm possible, everything considered, and the necessities taken account of. An evil that I can't keep from doing without doing another even greater one—it isn't I who do it, it is necessity. [To do good isn't given to man, only to avert evil.] . . .

The golden scales of Zeus, a symbol with two meanings. Symbol of blind necessity, symbol of the decision of the just. The union of those two symbols, a mystery.

Spirit of mind [*L'esprit*] in its highest degree imitates in some manner matter; absent from its thoughts and its works. Supreme mystery.

Purity in action and time—the moment. To infix the point of action into the course of time.

Example of *good* action. Browning and Elisabeth. The true difficulty, not to do what is good when one has seen it, but to see so intensely that thought passes into action, as when one reads music, and the notes that enter through the eyes come out in sound at the finger tips—as when one sees a football, and one has it in one's arms. Not to glance aside from the thought, although the risk—the risk that one may be mistaken—may be infinite.

What if Elisabeth had died?

2. *Cahiers* (Paris, 1951), 1:154. I give my own translations for the notebook citations.

If, contemplating the thing which appears good and contemplating no less fixedly the infinite risk, one acts—isn't the action good?[3]

Her examples of those who have truly united thought and action include, as one might expect, Sophocles' Orestes, Antigone, Eteocles.

In her essay on the *Iliad,* as in much of her other writing, Simone Weil was concerned with problems of power and force, individual and collective. She saw as essentially miraculous the ability of some individuals to "absorb" violence by refusing to take revenge. Weil considered the problems of nonviolence and pacifism on a number of occasions:

Nonviolence is good only if it is effective. Thus, the question of the young man to Gandhi concerning his sister. The response ought to be: use force, at least until you are someone who can defend her, with some probability of success, without violence. At least until you possess a radiant force of which the energy (that is to say its possible efficiency, in the most material sense) may be equal to that contained in your muscles.

There have been such people. St. Francis.

To strive to become someone who can be nonviolent.

That depends, *too,* on the adversary.

To strive to substitute, *more and more,* in the world, *effective* non-violence for violence.[4]

Simone Weil thought of herself as a pacifist for a while. She tried to engage in the Spanish struggle on the side of the Loyalists, and found herself overcome by the horrors and what she saw as the betrayals. But after Munich, she seems to have given up the notion of pacifism as a possible political option for her. When war came to France, she identified, I think, not with governments or armies but with the victims, those who suffered. After her escape from France to the United States and, later, to England, her attempts to return have been called "crackpot"; but

3. Ibid., pp. 90–91.
4. Ibid., pp. 153–54.

her brother, Andre Weil, reports that her initial idea was to work as a nurse in the front lines, as had been possible for women during World War I: it was only after she discovered that she could not do so that she tried to be parachuted into France to work with the Underground. Andre Weil has remarked about those efforts, "I don't believe she thought she could do something important. She thought she would do something useful, but most of all she wanted to share in other people's suffering. I don't think she was what some people call a dolorist—she was not looking for suffering for its own sake—but when others were suffering, she wanted to have her share of it."[5]

Although she sometimes called herself "Cassandra,"[6] the Simone Weil who wrote *The Need for Roots* was surely not committed to despair. At the time when she wrote the *Iliad* essay, a friend—the poet Jean Tortel—reports that she always carried an old copy of Théophile de Viau's *Les Amours Tragiques de Pyrame et Thisbé,* which she must have loved partly for its incendiary attacks on tyrannical royal absolutism. (When Tortel remarked that Théophile was doubtless an atheist, Weil was incensed: "How dare you pretend that the single conscience of his time could have been an atheist!")[7] Her sympathies were naturally with the Left. She was politically "active" for some years, and she inspired affection among her fellow factory workers. She continued to talk to Leftists and sometimes to help them even when she was unsure of, or disapproved of, their programs. Andre Weil gives an amusing account of how, when Trotsky came to Paris "and his friends in Paris just didn't know where they could find a sleeping place for him" (it was probably dangerous to play host to Trotsky at the time), it was Simone Weil who arranged for him to spend a few nights in her apartment:

5. Interview with Malcolm Muggeridge, in Simone Weil, *Gateway to God,* ed. David Raper (Glasgow, 1974), p. 158.
6. Jacques Cabaud, *Simone Weil: A Fellowship in Love* (New York, 1964), p. 186.
7. Simone Petrement, *La Vie de Simone Weil, II (1934–1943)* (Paris, 1973), p. 295. My translation.

They had a long conversation. Anyone who doubts about my sister's sense of humour would have had no such doubts if he had heard her tell about that conversation with Trotsky. The way that she told about political discussions, political meetings was always *very* funny. Her interview with Trotsky ended up with Trotsky saying to her: "I see you disagree with me in almost everything. Why do you put me up in your house? Do you belong to the Salvation Army?"[8]

Despite all the activism, I cannot imagine that Simone Weil was effective in organized political activity—any more than she was competent at any craft that required manual dexterity. Her gifts were different—and astonishing. Much of her writing fulfills her own exacting standard of the beautiful:

The beautiful is what one can contemplate. A statue, a picture that one can look at for some hours.
The beautiful, it is something to which one can pay attention.[9]

Beyond contemplation, some of her writings can provide both inspiration and useful warnings for those still working for peace and a world with fewer slaves.

8. *Gateway to God,* p. 154.
9. *Cahiers,* 1:129.

Patriotism and *The Need For Roots:*
The Antipolitics of Simone Weil

$\sim$

CONOR CRUISE O'BRIEN

T. S. Eliot ended his introduction to Arthur Wills's translation of
L'Enracinement (*The Need for Roots*)[1] with the words:

This book belongs in that category of prolegomena to politics which
politicians seldom read, and which most of them would be unlikely to
understand or to know how to apply. Such books do not influence the
contemporary conduct of affairs: for the men and women already engaged in this career and committed to the jargon of the market place,
they always come too late. This is one of those books which ought to
be studied by the young before their leisure has been lost and their
capacity for thought destroyed in the life of the hustings and the
legislative assembly; books the effects of which, we can only hope,
will become apparent in the attitude of mind of another generation.

These words call into question my own credentials for writing on
this subject, or indeed on any subject. In my country I am a politician. I participate in the life of the hustings and in the legislative assembly. My capacity for thought is thereby deemed to be
destroyed. The existence of this discouraging handicap is confirmed by the fact that I have considerable difficulty in understanding *The Need for Roots* and cannot claim to know how to
"apply it" or how much sense it makes even to talk about applying it.

I should perhaps end there. Certainly those who agree with
Eliot's view may logically and with propriety withdraw at this

1. *L'Enracinement* was published in Paris in 1949. The English translation *The Need for Roots* was published in New York in 1952 and,
in paperpack, in 1953. The full titles are: *L'Enracinement: Prelude à
une declaration des devoirs envers l'être humain; The Need for Roots:
Prelude to a Declaration of Duties towards Mankind.*

point. The rest of my words are for those who are prepared to entertain the hypothesis that Eliot may have been wrong, at least to some extent.

Now the concept of applying Simone Weil's thought in practical politics is I think contradictory to the main thrust of that thought itself, which is that politics—and indeed social life generally—is the domain of The Great Beast, or of the devil, something to be suffered, something to be cried out against and struck back at, not something that can be set right. She is not entirely consistent in this. In Part One of *The Need for Roots* ("The Needs of the Soul") Simone Weil sketches the kind of reconstruction of French society that the Free French might carry out after the liberation. It is a rather disconcerting sketch. A France reconstructed on Weilian lines—or as I think pseudo-Weilian lines—would have had no political parties, no trade unions, no freedom of association. It would have had a rigid, primitive, and eccentric form of censorship—one that would permit Jacques Maritain to be punished for having said something misleading about Aristotle. It would be organized on hierarchical lines, although we are not told just what these lines would be. There would be liberty, or something so described, coming second after "order" and just before "obedience" among the needs of the soul, but the guarantees of this liberty are in no way indicated. "Liberty," we are told, "consists in the ability to choose" but "when the possibilities of choice are so wide as to injure the commonweal, men cease to enjoy liberty." The text bristles with peremptory and often cryptic affirmations.

The atmosphere she evokes is that of a state governed by a spiritual and moral elite, a rule of the saints. In practice an effort by mortal and fallible men to "apply" *The Need for Roots* would probably have resulted in something quite like Vichy France— the resemblance to which she acknowledged with characteristic courage and integrity—but minus collaboration with the Nazis, and with de Gaulle at the top instead of Petain. This is the rather discouraging outcome of a hypothetical effort to apply in politics the thinking of a writer who was essentially nonpolitical, and even antipolitical.

As I have indicated, I think the programmatic parts of *The Need for Roots* are a kind of lapse; they seem to have been elicited from Simone Weil by the demands of the war effort, rather than shaped by the necessities of her own lone thinking. She herself was unable to take seriously the idea of applying them. "It is no use asking ourselves whether we are or are not capable of applying [this method of political action]. The answer would always be no!" She did think they might influence political decisions, and that their influence would be benign. As far as her "method of political action" was concerned—as distinct from more personal and profound aspects of her thought to which I come later—I think she was wrong on both counts. I think politicians made no use of her method, and if they had made any it would probably have been bad. General de Gaulle—presumably the politician most intended to be influenced—thought that she was out of her mind.[2] He was of course quite wrong, but the verdict does set rather clear limits to the possible influence of her method on the politics of post-Liberation France.[3]

Politics proceeds by associations of people, and Simone Weil had a deep-rooted aversion from such associations. This is why I call her antipolitical. On this matter the key passage is the following, from the section on "Freedom of Opinion" in "The Needs of the Soul":

2. "But she is mad," the general is said to have exclaimed on being shown her "Project for a Formation of Front-Line Nurses." See Simone Petrement, *Simone Weil: A Life* (New York: Pantheon, 1976), p. 514. Madame Petrement adds: "there is no doubt that she never spoke with de Gaulle."

3. See again Petrement, pp. 503–4, for the examination of a claim that a paper by Simone Weil, "Reflections on the Rebellion," the only paper of hers that de Gaulle could be persuaded to read from start to finish, led to the formation of the National Council of the Resistance. But Madame Petrement shows that what Weil had in mind was something quite different—an *international* European Council, not a French national one. Also the National Council was intended to serve a purpose specifically rejected by Weil—the reconstitution of political parties in France. This is the only paper of hers which it has been claimed had "practical consequences." If it did, they were certainly not consequences intended or desired by the author of the paper.

The intelligence is defeated as soon as the expression of one's thoughts is preceded, explicitly or implicitly, by the little word "we." And when the light of the intelligence grows dim, it is not very long before the love of good becomes lost.

The immediate, practical solution would be the abolition of political parties. Party strife, as it existed under the Third Republic, is intolerable. The single party, which is, moreover, its inevitable outcome, is the worst evil of all.

Elsewhere she speaks of "we" as positing an illegitimate middle term between the soul and God.

So rigorous an enemy of the first-person plural as Simone Weil is necessarily an enemy of political involvement also. And if man is a political animal, as Aristotle thought, to be rigorously antipolitical is to be antihuman as well.

And indeed I think she *is* antihuman in the sense in which Swift, and to a lesser extent Albert Schweitzer, were antihuman—combining great compassion for the suffering with a settled contempt for those of us who are up and around, but not up to much. Note her trust in intelligence and distrust of friendship.[4] What she says, though acute and interesting, and no doubt true for herself, is not necessarily true for other people. Does the love of good

4. "Distrust," not "dislike." A school classmate of hers, Suzanne Aron, wrote of her, "She had a desperate desire for tenderness, communion, friendship, and she didn't always discover the secret of how to obtain what she desired so deeply" (Petrement, p. 23). It was perhaps not so much a matter of inability to make friends, as Aron suggests, as of her settled attitude of self-denial, pushed to its final logical consequences in the form of her death. Compare her reasons for refusing baptism, as given in a letter to the Dominican Father Perrin, in 1942. "There is a Catholic circle ready to give an eager welcome to whoever enters it. Well I don't want to be adopted into a circle. . . . In saying I don't want this, I am expressing myself badly, for I should like it very much; I should find it all delightful. But I feel that it is not permissible for me. I feel that it is necessary and ordained that I should be alone, a stranger and an exile in relation to every human circle without exception. . . ." The full text of this letter, in English, is available in the collection of letters and essays under the title *Waiting for God* (New York: Harper Colophon, 1973), pp. 52–57. See also the section on friendship in the same volume, a notably abstract and exalted view of the subject.

depend on the light of the intelligence? It hardly seems so; we can all think of rather stupid people who are kind and honest, and of quite intelligent people who are mean and treacherous.[5] Might not friendship conceivably be a more likely channel for the love of good than intelligence? And might not the impairment of friendship by the demands of intelligence be a greater evil than the impairment of the expression of intelligence by the demands of friendship?

Certainly a *political* mind has to work quite differently from this, and reverse the value system. Consider for example Edmund Burke, a man whose capacity for thought not even the life of the hustings and the legislative assembly could altogether destroy. Burke set a high value on friendship, and his conception of a group of friends working in concert for political ends was a stage in the development of the modern political party—and even though modern parties are not uniquely composed of friends, friendships still play quite an important part in them.

It was of intelligence, rather than friendship, that Burke was suspicious, and he was particularly sour about the loftier pretensions of intelligence, the flights of those who in his time were called philosophers—very much the same as what we mean now by intellectuals. "Bears," he wrote, "lick, cuddle and cherish their young but bears are not philosophers." Nor did Burke regard limitations on the expression of intelligence as necessarily bad. "We practice an economy of truth," he wrote, "that we may live to tell it the longer."[6] Burke's intellectual powers are far more formidable than but a very few of those whom we class as intellectuals, but in this "economy of truth" passage he places himself firmly on the "political" side of the line that separates the politician from the pure intellectual. Simone Weil stands as firmly on

5. It is fair to say that Simone Weil was consistent in her tendency to correlate decency and intelligence. Of the workers whom she met during her year of factory work she wrote, "I have always found, among these rough simple creatures, that generosity of heart and a skill with general ideas were directly proportioned to each other" (Petrement, p. 232). It may be of course that those workers who lacked "skill with general ideas" could not easily communicate with Simone Weil. Nor does her own language imply much capacity to communicate with them.
6. First of the *Letters on a Regicide Peace.*

the other side of that line: for her, Burke's economy of truth is the sin against the light.

Simone Weil, the antipolitician, is a pure intellectual. Those intellectuals who seriously engage in politics (no matter what kind of politics) are impure intellectuals, necessarily committed to the Burkian economy, and doomed, according to Simone Weil, to the dimming both of their intellectual and of their moral sense. The political intellectual—who is of course the only politician now at all likely to know or want to know about Simone Weil—will necessarily feel reluctant to accept her view about his predicament. He will wish to claim that, even though he practices an economy of truth, he still brings into circulation more truth than, without him, would be in circulation in a vital domain of social life—one that stands in need of as much truth as it can tolerate. But he will nonetheless be uncomfortably conscious of the force of Simone Weil's observations. There is a Russian fable along this line about two revolutionary intellectuals. They set out to fool the secret police by pretending to be dull, greedy, and conformist types. They are so successful in their pretence, that they end up altogether forgetting what their original intention was and become in reality dull, greedy, and conformist—and tools of the secret police in the bargain. This is the kind of rake's progress that Simone Weil seems to have in mind when she writes about the effects of the economy of truth.

But the effect in politics of the pure intellectual, such as Simone Weil, is normally exerted through the impure intellectuals, the only kind that domain will tolerate. Save in the most exceptional circumstances, the pure intellectual can only, in consequence, be a small influence, indirect, filtered, and perhaps distorted. Even so, it would often work as an antipolitical influence, dissociative rather than associative, tending at times to the liberation of the individual conscience and to the extinction of a politician who might, just possibly, have been useful in his chosen domain if he had not fallen victim to the vertigo of intellectual purity. There is, of course, the alternative possibility that he has been saved from degenerating into a tool of the secret police, and then there are the wider and more permanent aspects of her political influence, which I shall discuss later.

In relation to politics, as to so much else, Simone Weil is the outsider, the lonely stranger. Her observations are detached, aloof, unfriendly, often very penetrating, sometimes perverse. Her best political sayings are aphorisms in the classical French hit-and-run tradition. She is especially vigilant, as one would expect, on that suspect frontier between the life of the intellect and political action. In a few pithy remarks about Marx and about Lenin, she sees intellectual disasters transforming themselves into political ones: "Marx worked out the conclusions before the method. He insisted on making his method into an instrument for predicting a future in accordance with his desires."[7] As for Lenin he went in for "thinking with the object of refuting, the solution being given before the research." And even more sharply, "The stifling regime which weighs at present upon the Russian people was already implied in embryo in Lenin's attitude towards his own process of thought. Long before it robbed the whole of Russia of liberty of thought the Bolshevik party had already taken it away from their own leader."[8]

Her comments on Marx are I believe both pithy and true. Those on Lenin are brilliant, but illustrate the intellectual limitations of pure intellectuals. The *idea* that Lenin's method of thought was imposed upon him by the Bolshevik party will not stand close examination. Lenin by his technique of "split, split and split again" ensured that his party agreed with him, not vice versa.

In placing the blame on the party, Simone Weil's bias against the first-person plural is visible again; in reality, an unusually imperious first-person singular had much more to do with the matter. The concept also demonstrates the intellectual's characteristic overemphasis on the importance of thought. The nature of Russian society as it existed before the First World War, and

7. "On the Contradictions of Marxism," in *Oppression and Liberty*, trans. Arthur Wills and John Petrie (Amherst: University of Massachusetts Press, 1973). The essay itself is undated but appears to be later than the essay on Lenin referred to below.
8. "Lenin's Materialism and Empirico-criticism," in *Oppression and Liberty*. It originally appeared in the periodical *Critique Sociale*, November 1933.

the disastrous impact on that society of that war, followed by collapse and foreign intervention, did much more to produce the stifling regime than did the exiled Lenin's treatment of his thought processes.

Elsewhere, indeed, Simone Weil shows her awareness of such limitations of thought, and it would be useless to look for consistency in her writings on revolution. Immediately after the passage on Lenin, in her essay on "Lenin's Materialism and Empirico-criticism," she contrasts Lenin unfavorably with Marx. "Marx fortunately went about the process of thinking in a different way." But in the passage on Marx from which I have quoted—from an apparently later essay "On the Contradictions of Marxism"—she shows that Marx abused the process of thought in precisely the same way that Lenin did, by finding the solution first and then looking for arguments to buttress it, rather than for means of testing it. This intellectual history is continuous; it is the history of the growth of a religion, not a science—and this Simone Weil saw—and it is because it was a religion that its fanatical and ruthless leaders were capable of taking over the bankrupt and devastated Russian Empire. Lenin's attitude to his processes of thought was in fact a symptom of his capacity to fill that vacuum.

Simone Weil's dissociative bent and her exaltation of the claims of the intellect do not, then, always stand her in good stead in her consideration of political processes. It is a different matter when she deals with the basic political bonding itself—in tribe, nation, state—and what might be called the original sin of that bonding—the notion of the inherent superiority of the entity constituted by it. In her consistent witness against that concept, in all its manifestations, lies the great and permanent value of Simone Weil's political writing.

"To love the little platoon to which we belong in society," wrote Edmund Burke, "is the first, the germ as it were, of public affections." Simone Weil was conscious of a counter truth to this; that it is possible to love the little platoon too much, so much that wider or higher affections fail to germinate. Of Jewish origin herself, she was profoundly repelled by the concept of the chosen people. This repulsion is a fundamental and abiding element in her mind and character. It could both carry her to strange extremes and stop her dead in her tracks. At one time it made it possible for her to counsel the acceptance of an anti-Semitic state in France as a lesser evil than war; at another it made it impossible for her to accept baptism into the Catholic Church. Both that acceptance and that refusal are significant expressions of what I call her antipolitics; her radical rejection of all limited associations.

The "acceptance" is contained in two letters in the spring of 1938, one to Jean Posternak, the second to the writer Gaston Bergery, later a Vichy diplomat. In the letter to Posternak she wrote:

At the moment, there are two possibilities. One is war with Germany for the sake of Czechoslovakia. Public opinion is scarcely interested in that remote country, but the Quai d'Orsay resolutely prefers war to German hegemony in central Europe; and as for the Communist party, any Franco-German war suits its book. . . . What may prevent violent measures is the generally recognized weakness of the French army. The other possibility is an antidemocratic *coup d'etat* supported by Daladier and the army and accompanied by a very violent outbreak of anti-Semitism (of which there are signs everywhere), and by brutal measures against the parties and organizations of the left. Of the two possibilities I prefer the latter, since it would be less murderous of French youth as a whole.[9]

In the letter to Bergery, developing the theme of German hegemony being preferable to war, she added: "No doubt the superiority of German armed forces would lead France to adopt certain laws of exclusion, chiefly against Communists and Jews— which is, in my eyes, and probably in the eyes of the majority of Frenchmen, nearly an indifferent matter in itself. One can quite well conceive that nothing essential would be affected."[10]

Madame Petrement makes the just comment: "She continued to think nothing would be worse than a war. Moreover, her disinterestedness made her prefer, of the two evils, the one of which she personally would be the victim."

Three further points need to be made here. The first is to

9. Petrement, p. 326.
10. Ibid., p. 327.

notice the intellectual courage with which she recognizes the terrible alternatives: war or acceptance of German hegemony. Most intellectuals at the time wanted to think they could reject *both* war *and* German hegemony. The second point concerns the coldness, even the apparent callousness, with which she refers to the probable fate of a minority to which she herself belongs: it would have been impossible for Simone Weil to refer to the "exclusion" of a minority as "nearly an indifferent matter in itself" if she had not herself belonged to that minority.

The third point is that "the certain law of exclusion" which she envisaged would have most directly affected people like herself: middle-class Jewish intellectuals of left-wing views. That was the "little platoon" to which she could not help belonging, but which she tried to sacrifice, because she belonged to it, in favor of the wider loyalty to humanity as a whole. Hitler's entry into Prague appears to have convinced her, however, that sacrifices of this kind could not in fact avert the greater evil of general war. Once the war was there she wanted to take the fullest possible part in its sacrifices, and did so, to the point of self-inflicted death by hunger. (*L'Enracinement* was written shortly before her death, and after her abandonment of the "lesser evil" concept.)

While Judaism repelled her, basically because of the concept of the chosen people, Catholicism strongly attracted her, because of the proclaimed universality of its message. But those who are drawn to Catholicism by that appeal are doomed to a degree of disillusionment when they encounter actual Catholics, in their local and national groupings, no more immune than others to tribal pride and prejudice. It was with French Catholics that Simone Weil had to do, and French Catholic traditions have been among the most exuberantly jingo in the world. The God of Charles Peguy for example was not out of tune with French Catholic opinion when he made his famous declaration: *"Quand il n'y aura plus ces Français, dit Dieu, il n'y aura plus personne pour me comprendre."*

For Peguy this was in part a joke, a tender in-joke, but nonetheless to be felt as conveying a truth. Simone Weil, who was not particularly good at jokes, could see nothing but blasphemy in this kind of cozy tribal Catholicism. She had not rejected the Jews as chosen people in order to accept the French, or any others, in that capacity. That *seems* easy enough: there are plenty of people who are opposed to nationalistic hubris, or think they are. But Simone Weil's antinationalism was real, in a sense in which most people's was not, and in reality reveals itself in the thoroughness, the consistency, and intellectual daring with which it finds expression. These qualities are at their most remarkable near the end of her life, when she was working for the Free French in England. There is an apparent paradox here, but it is a superficial one. Many, probably most, of those with whom she was working—and not least their chief—were nationalists, even ultra-nationalists. But Simone Weil was not there for nationalistic reasons. On the contrary, she saw Nazi Germany as the supreme contemporary embodiment of triumphal nationalism.

That was what she was against, and if France had been the main contemporary carrier of that disease she would have been against France. To be against German nationalism meant being against French nationalism too. She argues this with great lucidity and coolness in the second part of *The Need for Roots.* On the Catholic bishops in France and Germany she writes:

Christians today don't like raising the question of the respective rights over their heart enjoyed by God and their country. The German bishops ended one of their most courageous protests by saying that they refused ever to have to make a choice between God and Germany. And why did they refuse to do this? Circumstances can always arise which make it necessary to choose between God and no matter what earthly object, and the choice must never be in doubt. But the French bishops would not have expressed themselves any differently. Joan of Arc's popularity during the past quarter of a century was not an altogether healthy business; it was a convenient way of forgetting that there is a difference between France and God. Yet this lack of inward courage to challenge the accepted notion of patriotism didn't make for greater energy in patriotic performance. Joan of Arc's statue was occupying a prominent place in every church throughout the country, all through those terrible days when Frenchmen abandoned France to her fate.

"If any man come to me, and hate not his father and mother, and wife, and children, and brethren, and sisters, yea, and his own life also, he cannot be my disciple." If it is commanded to hate all that, using the word "hate" in a certain sense, it is certainly forbidden also to love one's country, using the word "love" in a certain sense. For the proper object of love is goodness, and "God alone is good."

"Our patriotism," she wrote, "comes straight from the Romans"—a people whom she detested even to an extravagant degree. She saw them as a people who idolized themselves, adding: "It is this idolatry of self which they have bequeathed to us in the form of patriotism."

When she condemns "our patriotism" she is referring to the prevalent form of patriotism in France, derived from Rome and encouraged in the schools. The "our" should be stressed: that first-person plural again. She had her own form of patriotism; though she seldom gave it direct verbal expression, a love of France shines through many of her pages. It is rather an abstract love, of a great historic center of art and thought, more than of a lot of people; an intellectual love, something rare but real, and in her case passionate. Her greatest fear for the France she loved was of its falling victim to the form of patriotism she despised.

Her comments in *L'Enracinement* on Hitler and racism, on collaborationism, and on colonialism are evidence of the depth to which these ideas permeated her mind. Hitler she sees as simply applying something handed on to him, in the form of the Roman idea of greatness consisting in the capacity to triumph over other peoples. And "in so far as he simply reached out for the only form of greatness he had been told about," he was, she says, "a better man than any of us." Elsewhere he is seen as drawing part of his inspiration from the Old Testament: "He simply selected as his machine the notion of a chosen race, a race destined to make everything bow before it." As for his doctrines of race: "We should be strangely simple if we believed that racialism is anything at all except a more romantic version of nationalism."

Her observations on collaborators and collaboration fit exactly into the general pattern of her antinationalism, and show some of the lengths to which her intellectual courage could carry her. She saw—and it is one of her most piercing insights—how the traditional triumphant French nationalism, so prevalent among the French right and among Catholics, could turn into collaborationism in the circumstances of 1940. "If France," she wrote, "found herself on the side of the vanquished, they thought, it could only be because of some faulty deal, some mistake, some misunderstanding; her natural place was on the side of the victors; therefore, the easiest, the least arduous, least painful method of bringing about the indispensable rectification was to change sides. This state of mind was very prevalent in certain circles at Vichy in July, 1940."

She had of course clearly ranged herself on the side of the Resistance and against collaboration. But she was impatient—as she showed in America—with those who too easily condemned collaborators from a distance, and she was uneasily aware of certain possibilities in the Resistance itself. These feelings find expression in the following very remarkable passage in *L'Enracinement,* rooted in her basic horror of the idea of a chosen people:

There was once a nation which believed itself to be holy, with the direst consequences for its well-being; and in connection with this, it is strange to reflect that the Pharisees were the resisters in this nation, and the publicans the collaborators, and then to remind oneself what were Christ's relations with each of these two national groups.

This would seem to oblige us to consider that our resistance would be a spiritually dangerous, even a spiritually harmful, position, if amid the motives which inspire it we did not manage to restrain the patriotic motive within the necessary bounds. It is precisely this danger that, in the extremely clumsy phraseology of our time, is meant by those who, sincerely or not, say they are afraid this [Free French] movement may turn into something Fascist; for Fascism is always intimately connected with a certain variety of patriotic feeling.

She was acutely aware that some attitudes that were common to traditional French nationalism, and also to the ultra-patriotic elements in the Resistance, found their most characteristic expression in a domineering attitude to colonial people. She saw—and her insight here is historically as well as psychologically true— how the same word that was designated to mask *domination* in the colonies could be turned to mask *acceptance of domination* in the metropolis: "Thus it is that a number of Frenchmen, having found it perfectly natural to talk about collaboration to the oppressed natives of the French colonies, went on making use of this word without any trouble in talking with their German masters."

The hopes of the Free French, at the time she was writing, were concentrated on recovering the French Empire, and using it as a base for the liberation of France. It is understandable therefore if there is a certain degree of hesitation in her reference to relations with the empire for the duration of the war. Nonetheless, she clearly foresees that a liberated France may try to hold on to her empire and thereby bring great troubles on both France and the peoples of the empire. She saw an immediate need to head off that danger when she wrote:

It may be that France now has to choose between her attachment to her Empire and the need to have a soul of her own again; or, in more general terms, between having a soul of her own and the Roman or Corneille-esque conception of greatness.

If she chooses wrongly, if we ourselves force her to choose wrongly, which is only too likely, she will have neither the one nor the other, but only the most appalling adversity, which she will undergo with astonishment, without anybody being able to discover any reason for it. And all those who are now in a position to get up and speak or to wield a pen will be eternally responsible for having committed a crime.

There appears to be a challenge in those last words, addressed to the spokesmen of Free France including de Gaulle. As I mentioned, he thought she was mad. Yet her advice was sane and sound, her prophecy as to what would happen if it were not taken proved absolutely true, like Cassandra's.

Perhaps the greatest tragedy, in Simone Weil's life and death, is that she died, of a kind of self-inflicted wound, just as the time was coming when her spirit and her voice would be most desperately needed. Obviously no single person could have averted the French decision to reconquer Indochina, or to hold Algeria by force, or the needless horrors that followed from these decisions, or the inheritance by America of France's Indochina disaster, and the prolonged further aggravation of that disaster that followed. Yet any reader of Simone Weil knows with certainty that if she had lived, her voice would have been lifted up against these things; and that the opposition to them would thereby have gained immensely in intensity, determination, and integrity.

Her capacity for dissociation would have served her well, when what people were pressed to join was a Gadarene rush. At a time when everybody in the West was being harangued about the dangers of communism, she would have seen those dangers—as she did see them, clearly, in the thirties—but she would also have seen the dangers of *anti*communism, and stressed them not only because they were nearer, but for the fundamental reason that, for us in the West, they were the dangers *within us,* the means for the moment of exalting our triumphant group feelings, and our tendency to see evil as something external to us.

She could never have fallen in, as Albert Camus and so many other gifted intellectuals did, with the convenient localization of slavery "over there" and liberty "over here." She could not—as Solzhenitsyn to the grief of many of his admirers has done—have ever identified the "loss" of Indochina to the West with the "loss" of something called liberty to Indochina. Just possibly the fire and honesty of her witness might have helped to shorten the war, as Albert Schweitzer's, for example, probably helped to bring nuclear testing to an end. We cannot know, and she herself would have been the last to exaggerate the capacity of anyone like her to influence the action of the enormous beast, which is human society.

We are left with her example and her warnings. Few of us are likely to follow the example of this strange ascetic, and certainly no politician who claimed to follow it would be believed, and rightly so. Most of us, for obvious reasons, would sympathize with the advice given to her by her friend Dr. Louis Bercher: "The basic thing here seemed to me to be the desire for purity. It is the source of all heresies, I told her. Remember the Cathars! Man is not pure but a 'sinner.' And the sinner must stink a bit, at the least. . . . Simone didn't deny this, but she didn't give in to my point either."[11]

But one does not need to be convinced by her mystical intuitions, or propose to imitate her life, in order to see that her warn-

11. Ibid., p. 419.

ings about nationalism, in all its multiform disguises, possess not only moral force but great practical shrewdness and permanent political value. She was a true prophet who foresaw the "appalling adversity" that certain tendencies present in the movement to which she adhered were capable of bringing on her country and on others.

That is the kind of insight of which practicing politicians in every country are in most need. Simone Weil's contribution to politics is not in system or method, or even in analysis, but in her lucid sensitivity to the dangerous forces at work in all collective activities, and her refusal to localize these forces exclusively in some other nation, or among the adherents of some other faith or ideology. One may, as I do, feel that there is something inhuman about her. Yet it could be that what we feel to be inhuman in her is that which made her capable of turning away from those aspects of our all-too-human attachments that put our neighbors, our environment, our world, our children, ourselves all in deadly danger.

Marxism-Leninism and the
Language of *Politics* Magazine:
The First New Left . . . and the Third

〜

STAUGHTON LYND

Simone Weil may be viewed as a solitary seeker. She may also be viewed, and I propose to view her, as one of an international group of seekers whom I will term the first New Left.[1]

The first New Left was made up of radicals in the years 1930–1945 who broke not only from Stalinism but also from Leninism, and not only from Leninism, but also from Trotskyism, and not only from Trotskyism, but in part from Marxism itself.

In the United States many of those who should be considered members of the first New Left were associated with *Politics* magazine. Among this group were Dwight Macdonald, Conrad Lynn, William Worthy, Paul Goodman, and C. Wright Mills. It was also *Politics* that published Simone Weil for the first time in the United States. I shall return to *Politics* later.

First I want to make clear the reality of the first New Left as an international phenomenon. Then I will attempt to suggest the special contribution made to it by the lucid and thoroughgoing essays of Simone Weil. This will put us in a position to consider *Politics* in context and so come, finally, to the connection between this ancient history and where we find ourselves now.

---

1. Direct quotations in the following essay are drawn primarily from three sources. They are the collection of Simone Weil's political essays published in English as *Oppression and Liberty,* trans. Arthur Wills and John Petrie (Amherst: University of Massachusetts Press, 1973); *The Essays of A. J. Muste,* ed. Nat Hentoff (Indianapolis: Bobbs-Merrill Co., 1967); and the files of *Politics* magazine.

I   The reality of the first New Left as an international phenomenon is sufficiently demonstrated by three lives: Ignazio Silone,
A. J. Muste, and Simone Weil.

Ignazio Silone was a member of the Communist Party for ten
years. Before leaving the party in 1931, he had risen to become
a member of the Executive Committee of the Third International.
In 1936 he published the magnificent novel *Bread and Wine,*
written, so Silone states, "out of the fullness of my heart just after
the Fascist occupation of Ethiopia and during the Purge Trials
in Moscow, which had been set up by Stalin to destroy the last
remnants of the opposition. It was hard to imagine a sorrier state
of affairs. The inhuman behavior of General Graziani to Ethiopian combatants and civilians, the enthusiasm of many Italians
for the conquest of the Empire, the passivity of most of the population, and the impotence of the anti-Fascists all filled the soul
with a deep sense of shame. To this was added my horror and
disgust at having served a revolutionary ideal in my youth that,
in its Stalinist form, was turning out to be nothing but 'red
Fascism,' as I defined it at the time."

Bread and Wine concerns a Communist named Pietro Spina
who, having gone into exile after Mussolini seized power, secretly
returns to Italy and falls desperately ill. A peasant shelters him.
In his extremity, Spina adopts the vestments of a priest as a disguise. But as his clandestine existence takes him from person to
person—old comrades, a Catholic monk who was his teacher in
high school, a young woman preparing to enter a convent—the
disguise becomes something more than that. Spina comes to feel
that the Marxist abstractions he brought with him from exile do
not describe the elemental realities of peasant life in southern
Italy. He also comes to feel that Christianity, provided its tenets
are fully acted out, can give him a new place to begin.

The dominant themes of *Bread and Wine* are characteristic of
what I have called the first New Left as a whole. At one point in
the novel, Spina, despairing of finding allies anywhere, takes
charcoal and in the middle of the night writes on the whitewashed
walls of the town buildings slogans such as "Down With the
War." A girl who has befriended him is puzzled that so small an
act could give the authorities so much concern. Spina explains

that in a dictatorship the act of one person's saying "no" calls into question the whole public order. When, in 1946, Dave Dellinger and others, who had resisted World War II in prison, issued a call to a conference on nonviolent revolution, they quoted this passage from *Bread and Wine.*

A second illustrative life is that of A. J. Muste who from 1933 to 1936 belonged to a succession of Marxist parties and, in his own words, "accepted fully the Marxist-Leninist position and metaphysics." For him at the time, this commitment to Marxism-Leninism seemed the logical culmination of his long experience with the labor movement, which he began as an organizer of the Lawrence, Massachusetts Textile Strike of 1919, and continued as director of the Brookwood Labor College. Nevertheless, Muste broke with Marxism in 1936. He explained his decision in a letter to a friend:

War is the central problem for us all today. . . . International war and coercion at home will continue to exist for just so long as people regard these things as suitable, as even conceivable instruments of policy. . . . The Christian position does not mean to justify or con-done the capitalist system. Quite the contrary. It provides the one measure by which the capitalist system stands thoroughly and effec-tively condemned. It stands condemned because it makes the Chris-tian relation in its full sense, the relation of brotherhood between human beings, impossible. . . . So long, however, as the matter re-mains on the plane of economics and self-interest, no one is in a position to condemn another. When we feel indignation, as we do even in spite of ourselves, we then enter the realm of standards and values, the realm in which moral judgment is pronounced, the realm in which ethical and spiritual appeals are made . . . the realm of morality and religion.

He elaborated these thoughts in an essay of December 1936 from which I quote the following sentences, every one of which might have been written by Simone Weil.

The devoted members of any movement, among other reasons be-cause they have experience of what is fine and true in the movement, are apt to rationalize away its defeats as merely superficial and tem-porary. Personally, I have had to conclude that it is inexcusable, after all that has taken place in the labor movement since 1914, not to be willing to study the whole situation afresh, and as deeply and thoroughly as possible. . . .

If one looks squarely at [the facts] touching all organizations in the labor movement, then I think one is driven to the conclusion that the root of the difficulty is moral and spiritual, not primarily political or economic or organizational. Inextricably mingled with and in the end corrupting, thwarting, largely defeating all that is fine, idealistic, courageous, self-sacrificing in the proletarian movement is the philosophy of power, the will to power, the desire to humiliate and dominate over or destroy the opponent, the acceptance of the methods of violence and deceit, the theory that "the end justifies the means." There is a succumbing to the spirit which so largely dominates the existing social and political order and an acceptance of the methods of capitalism at its worst.

If, with Muste and Silone in mind, one turns to a third life, that of Simone Weil, the impression is overwhelming, not only that these three are brothers and sisters of the spirit, but also that from her earliest essays Simone Weil anticipated every major theme of the second New Left of the 1950s and 1960s.

Consider her essay, "Are We Heading for the Proletarian Revolution?" published in the periodical *Proletarian Revolution* in 1933. In this essay Ms. Weil asserted among other things the following ten points:

(1) In the Soviet Union, after fifteen years:

Instead of genuine freedom of the press, there is the impossibility of expressing a free opinion, whether in the form of a printed, typewritten or hand-written document, or simply by word of mouth, without running the risk of being deported; instead of the free play of parties within the framework of the soviet system, there is the cry of "one party in power, and all the rest in prison"; instead of a communist party destined to rally together, for the purposes of free cooperation, men possessing the highest degree of devotion, conscientiousness, culture, and critical aptitude, there is a mere administrative machine, a passive instrument in the hands of the Secretariat, which, as Trotsky himself admits, is a party only in name; instead of soviets, unions and co-operatives functioning democratically and directing the economic and political life of the country, there are organizations bearing, it is true, the same names, but reduced to mere administrative mechanisms; instead of the people armed and organized as a militia to ensure by itself alone defense abroad and order at home, there is a standing army, and a police freed from control and a hundred times better armed than that of the Tsar; lastly, and above all, instead of elected officials, permanently subject to control and dismissal, who were to ensure the functioning of government until such time as "every cook would learn how to rule the State," there is a professional bureaucracy, freed from responsibility, recruited by cooption and possessing, through the concentration in its hands of all economic and political power, a strength hitherto unknown in the annals of history.

Thus Weil began where Camus, C. Wright Mills, Kolakowski, and E. P. Thompson would also begin a generation later: with the understanding that the Soviet Union has not fulfilled the great dream of a society where the free development of each is the condition of the free development of all.

(2) Trotsky's view that the Soviet Union was a "workers' state" albeit with "bureaucratic deformations" obscured the reality that the oppression of the workers in the Soviet Union was not a step in the direction of socialism. One could conceptualize the Soviet Union as transitional only on the assumption that "there can at the present time be only two types of State, the capitalist State and the workers' State." The evidence, however, pointed to the conclusion that the Soviet Union was a third kind of state, unforeseen by Marx to be sure, but nevertheless there.

(3) Fascism, Weil continued, "fits no more easily into the categories of classical Marxism than does the Russian State." It was a mistake to believe that the Nazi regime was merely an instrument of German capitalism. The fact, she asserted, was that Stalinist socialism and National Socialism had much in common, and a military alliance between the two regimes was by no means excluded.

(4) However phenomena such as the Soviet Union, fascism, and the New Deal were categorized, the one movement lacking from the scene was "that very movement which, according to the forecasts, was to constitute its essential feature, namely, the struggle for economic and political emancipation of the workers." To be sure, scattered militants, little groups "divided by obscure quarrels," might be found. "But the ideal of a society governed

in the economic and political sphere by co-operation between the workers now inspires scarcely a single mass movement, whether spontaneous or organized; and that at the very moment when, on every hand, there is nothing but talk of the bankruptcy of capitalism."

(5) The oppression of working people—and here Weil came to her affirmative analysis—was an oppression exercised neither in the name of armed force nor in the name of wealth transformed into capital, rather it was oppression exercised in the name of management. That is to say—and here she strode beyond either Adolf Berle, who expressed a version of the same idea contemporaneously, or James Burnham, who echoed it superficially in his book, *The Managerial Revolution*—the oppression of working people "has become, with the advent of mechanization, a mere aspect of the relationships involved in the very technique of production." Soviet experience demonstrated that if the ownership of production was changed but the technique of production was left unchanged, the oppression of working people continued. Weil then pointed, as have David Montgomery and other labor historians in the last few years, to the skilled machine workers who until early in the twentieth century "carried out their work while using machines with as much freedom, initiative and intelligence as the craftsman who wields his tool." It was these skilled machine workers who in every advanced capitalist economy had constituted the only hope of the revolutionary movement, for it was only they "who combined thought and action in industrial work, or who took an active and vital part in the carrying on of the undertaking; the only ones capable of feeling themselves ready to take over one day the responsibility for the whole of economic and political life." But it was precisely these skilled workers—who could in some sense be viewed as embodying the new society within the womb of the old—whom capitalism had largely eliminated with the introduction of the assembly line and the breaking-down of complex jobs into small, mindless, repetitive tasks. In place of the socialist machinists described by Montgomery (and, for that matter, in place of the metal workers of Petrograd and Moscow who formed the nucleus of the soviets), rationalization has barely left more than spe-

cialized unskilled workmen, completely enslaved to the machine."

(6) "War, which perpetuates itself under the form of prepara-
tion for war, has once and for all given the State an important
role in production." As Walter Oakes would write a decade later
in *Politics* there had come into being a "permanent war economy."

(7) Modern capitalism was governed by three bureaucracies:
the industrial bureaucracy, the government bureaucracy, and the
trade union bureaucracy. C. Wright Mills would make the elabo-
ration of this insight a life's work.

(8) Left political parties cannot substitute themselves for the
working class itself. In Weil's words: "Militants cannot take the
place of the working class. The emancipation of the workers will
be carried out by the workers themselves, or it will not take place
at all." Any attempt to bring about revolution from above, by
manipulation, ran the grave risk of creating, not revolution, but
counter-revolution.

(9) Nevertheless, one should not despair. The fact that success
is less likely than had been assumed is not a reason to cease
struggling. "A man who is thrown overboard in the middle of
the ocean ought not to let himself drown, even though there is
very little chance of his reaching safety, but to go on swimming
until exhausted. And we are not really without hope. . . . The
mere fact that we exist, that we conceive and want something
different from what exists, constitutes a reason for hoping."

(10) Nor should the aforementioned analysis lead one to give
up hope in the industrial working class. "The working class still
contains, scattered here and there, to a large extent outside organized labor," working people prepared to devote themselves
"with the resolution and conscientiousness that a good workman
puts into his work" to the building of a rational society. The task
of the revolutionary was to help these potential leaders in "think-
[ing] things out," in acquiring influence in trade unions, in band-
ing together for such actions as were possible in the streets and
factories.

An effort tending towards the grouping together of all that has remained healthy at the very heart of industrial undertakings, avoiding
both the stirring up of primitive feelings of revolt and the crystalli-

zation of an administrative apparatus, may not be much, but there is nothing else. The only hope of socialism resides in those who have already brought about in themselves, as far as is possible in the society of today, that union between manual and intellectual labor which characterizes the society we are aiming at.

II   Had Simone Weil died at twenty-four, the age at which she wrote the essay just summarized, instead of at thirty-four, her achievement would have been great. Forty-three years later [1976] I can find hardly a word I would wish to change. Further, her evocation of the nature of the task of the intellectual who seeks to work with industrial workers is more sensitive and more precise than any other I know.

In fact, between 1933 and her death in 1943 Weil conducted a richly complex and wide-ranging exploration of the themes set out in this initial essay. I lack the mastery of all her writings that could do justice to it, but it is possible to try to underline three themes that she comes back to again and again.

First, New Leftists are often accused of "mindless activism" but it is not a charge that will stick against Simone Weil. What the epithet accurately describes is the fact that in breaking with the mother church of Marxism and its well-elaborated creedal language, heretics of the New Left have often proceeded largely by intuition, or to say it better, have often lacked the new language to characterize the actions they felt drawn to undertake. Hence Simone Weil's intellectual clarity is a priceless gift to the New Left tradition. So persistent, so painstaking was her effort to think things back to their beginnings that, criticizing the critics, she found Marxism to be in many of its mansions a structure built on unexamined foundations and therefore, in the worst sense of the term, in many ways a "religion" rather than a "science." She was especially critical of the notion that the development of technology under capitalism was beneficent. As she interpreted Marx, the development of "productive forces" was simply *assumed* to be a positive historical force, of its own motion bursting through the restraints imposed by "productive relations" and automatically producing something better.

Simone Weil wrote in 1934 of this Marxist concept of productive forces that "to believe that our will coincides with a mysterious will which is at work in the universe and helps us to conquer is to think religiously, to believe in Providence." The experienced reality is that assembly-line work and the specialization of tasks promoted by Taylorism destroy human dignity no matter who owns the productive forces. Instead of mass production, Weil wrote in fragments from the years 1933–1938, the need is for more flexible machines and a new science to invent them. Work, she wrote, should be coordinated by the best workers in rotation with no other reward for the responsibilities of coordination than the opportunity to comprehend the productive process as a whole. A liberated society would "individualize the machine." Unless Western civilization could "adapt itself to a decentralized world," with a material basis in cooperative production by small groups of workers using new kinds of flexible machines made possible by a science consciously directed to that end, Western civilization would collapse. Fortunately, in electricity there was available "an appropriate form of power" for a decentralized economy. It was then in no way irrational to assert that the main task of revolutionary thought was, not to promote leisure on the basis of a technology assumed to be unchanging, but "to discover how it is possible for work to be free."

Second, believing as she did that the problem of capitalist society is that human beings do not participate in the decisions that affect their work, Weil stood for the proposition that New Left values of activism and participatory decision making, far from being petty-bourgeois notions irrelevant to the world of work, are above all relevant to work and to the life of the industrial worker.

It occurs to me that a major cause of the disintegration of the movement of the 1960s was that when toward the end of the decade the movement recognized the importance of reaching out to industrial workers, it felt impotent to do so, and handed over that task to the sects. In this, our movement took its cue from Marx. Marx, as Simone Weil emphasized, described the alienation of work in a capitalist factory in words that it would be impossible to improve. We know, she wrote,

Marx's terrible utterances on this subject: "In craftsmanship and fab-
rication by hand, the worker makes use of the tool; in the factory, he
is at the service of the machine." "In the factory there exists a dead
mechanism, independent of the workers, which incorporates them as
living cogs." "It is only with mechanization that the inversion [of the
relationship between the worker and the conditions of work] becomes a reality that can be grasped in the technique itself." "The
separation of the spiritual forces of the process of production from
manual work, and the transformation of the former into forces of
oppression exercised by capital over labor, is fully accomplished . . .
in large-scale industry built up by mechanization. The detail of the
individual destiny . . . of the worker working at the machine disappears like some squalid trifle before the knowledge, the tremendous
natural forces and the collective labor which are crystallized in the
machine system and go to make up the owner's power."

But Marx wrote these phrases *about* workers rather than *to* workers. In these phrases Marx memorably characterized the collective
condition of those who worked in capitalist factories, but he did
not suggest that revolutionaries agitate among workers around
the concepts of fetishism and alienation. When it came to practical agitation, Marx assumed—in the *Communist Manifesto* for
instance—that agitation among workers would be around matters
such as the length of the work day and the level of wages, not
around the undemocratic organization of the factory, or the humiliating individual experience of work itself. Similarly, we in
the movement of the 1960s, having said to ourselves that we
should start to communicate with workers as well as students,
simply assumed that this meant abandoning the rhetoric of the
early Students for a Democratic Society's *Port Huron Statement*
and adopting a new, grim language about material deprivation.

We were wrong. We were dead wrong, and the lack of life in
the organizing that has gone on since proves this to be so. The
best statement of this conclusion is Steve Packard's article "Steel
Mill Blues" in *Liberation Magazine* (December 1975). Steve
worked in a mill for six months. When he went to work there
he was a member of a Marxist-Leninist sect, though his experiences while at work convinced him to leave it. Summing up,
Steve writes:

I think the deepest needs of my friends here, the needs that require radical changes, are those unclear things that brought me into the Movement long ago. I felt then that history was ready for the development of a whole new kind of person. Somehow things like community, art, sex roles, justice, particularly democracy, creativity—somehow things like this were almost remolded into a new vision.

Around 1970 I began to forget or abandon these politics. But that newer, free-er, wider, higher vision is what the average people need. It's the only thing that Billy and my other friends could really throw their lives into.

Simone Weil came to similar conclusions after nine months of factory work in 1934–35. The conclusions she reached then were confirmed by the French sit-down strikes of June 1936, when in her words the oppressed were "able to assert their existence for a few days and lift their heads and impose their will and obtain some advantages which they do not owe to a condescending generosity," and by the Spanish Civil War, for her "one of those extraordinary periods . . . when those who have always been subordinate assume responsibility." The earlier, personal experience of factory work was more important, however. Everyone knows that there are historical moments—as in the Paris Commune of 1871, the Russian Revolutions of 1905 and 1917, the general strikes in Minneapolis, San Francisco, and Toledo in 1934, or the General Motors sit-down strike of January 1937—when working people spontaneously demonstrate the most astounding capacity collectively to organize their affairs. Labor history can be written as a succession of such moments, like beads on a string. But that sort of history gives one no idea of what in the daily individual lives of working people acts as a source for the capacity for rebellion. In my opinion, Simone Weil's greatest single achievement as a social analyst was her insight into the oppressive character of capitalist factory work as an individual experience. It is easy to talk about socialism as the extension of democracy to the workplace. Historically and psychologically, however, the thirst for democracy requires a prior affirmation of personal, individual dignity. Only when peasants and artisans came to believe in the priesthood of all believers did they begin to think of themselves as collectively capable to govern. We must, absolutely must, find a language in which to talk with one another about the way in which we are robbed of our selfhood when we are denied the opportunity to participate as fully as we are capable of doing in decisions affecting our work. Simone Weil came closer to finding that language than anyone else to date.

She did so, for instance, in the essay "Factory Work" first published in *Politics* in December 1946.

Weil worked in a plant where she stamped out parts on a press. Some of the plant's production consisted of rush orders for armaments. There was a moving belt-line, as she called it, the speed of which according to one of her fellow workers had been doubled during the past four years.

The first point she makes about her experience of factory work is that one cannot discover workingmen's discontents simply by taking a poll. As André Gorz also has emphasized, those who have deep and painful feelings hide the feelings even from themselves. Weil writes: "The first effect of suffering is the attempt of thought to *escape*. It refuses to confront the adversity that wounds it. Thus, when workingmen speak of their lot, they repeat more often than not the catchwords coined by people who are not workingmen." Again she observes: "Humiliation always has for its effect the creation of forbidden zones where thought may not venture and which are shrouded by silence or illusion." The experience of shame at being treated as employees are treated, and underneath that, the belief that it is shameful not to have been able to escape the lot of an employee—these sentiments, so much the reverse of that brawny-armed confidence ascribed to proletarians by some Marxists, also separate workers from each other. "Each is isolated as though on an island," Weil relates. "Those who do escape from the island will not look back."

Why is work in a capitalist factory experienced as shameful? Because it is not free, answers Simone Weil. The workers are obliged to consider themselves as nothing. "What especially constrains them to this is the way in which they have to take orders." Since these orders are usually unexpected and unpredictable, the worker is unable mentally to anticipate the future, "to outline it beforehand, and in a sense, to possess it." Thought draws back from the future because the future, insofar as it is different from the present, will be so because of some arbitrary humiliating order. "This perpetual recoil upon the present produces a kind of brutish stupor."

Workers while at work are exiles, Weil comments in the language of her essay on "roots," uprooted, unable to feel at home. One cannot move freely, as is possible in a place that belongs to one. Nor can one pause and in small ways vary the rhythm of one's work.

One can actually see women waiting ten minutes outside a plant under a driving rain, across from an open door through which their bosses are passing. They are working women and they will not enter until the whistle has blown. The door is more alien to them than that of any strange house, which they would enter quite naturally if seeking cover. No intimacy binds workingmen to the places and objects amidst which their lives are used up. Wages and other social demands had less to do with the sit-down strikes of '36 than the need to feel at home in the factories at least once in their lives. Society must be corrupted to its very core when workingmen can feel at home in a plant only during a strike, and utter aliens during working hours—when by every dictate of common sense the exact opposite ought to prevail.

Summarizing Simone Weil's experience of factory work, one might say that "work should involve incentives worthier than money or survival. It should be educative, not stultifying; creative, not mechanical; self-directed, not manipulated"; and one might say that, to bring about this change, society should consider "experiments in decentralization, based on the vision of man as master of his machines and his society," because "the personal capacity to cope with life has been reduced everywhere by the introduction of technology that only minorities of men (barely) understand." It is food for thought that the words I have just used to summarize, accurately I think, Weil's reflections on factory work, are words from the now-forgotten *Port Huron Statement.*

Simone Weil left the factory, but there was a sense in which for the remainder of her life she had won through to a sense of genuine identity with working people, exchanging it for her identification with the class into which she was born. I am not thinking of her later insistence on doing agricultural work, nor of her decision to eat no more as an exile in London than was permitted to civilians in occupied France. I am thinking of certain passages in a fragment she wrote entitled "On the Contradictions of Marxism." Therein she said:

I do not think the workers' movement in this country will become something living again until it seeks, I will not say doctrines, but a source of inspiration, in what Marx and Marxists have fought against and very foolishly despised: in Proudhon, in the workers' groups of 1848, in the trade-union tradition, in the anarchist spirit.

—that is to say, I think, in a tradition of common struggle and utopian hope created by workers *themselves*. Marx, she went on, was cruelly abstract in believing, on the one hand, that violent revolution "is in reality the crowning point of a transformation that is already more than half accomplished, and brings to power a category of men who already more than half possessed that power," and on the other hand, that the capitalist proletariat, dehumanized by oppressive conditions of work, was prepared to assume command of the capitalist economy. Working people are not, Weil held, ready to run the workplace. The analogy to the medieval bourgeoisie, which in fact created a new society of cities within feudal society, is false. To propagate the hope of an imminent blessed catastrophe, which would miraculously make the last first, and the first last, is to stir working people into actions that would benefit, not themselves, but their managers.

In what sense then can one rationally project a working-class revolution? Perhaps, Weil wrote,

being a revolutionary means calling forth by one's wishes and helping by one's acts everything which can, directly or indirectly, alleviate or lift the weight that presses on the mass of men, break the chains that degrade labor, reject the lies by means of which it is sought to disguise or excuse the systematic humiliation of the majority.

If this is revolution, she continued, it is a revolution as old as oppression, a spirit of revolt that quickened the Roman plebeians, and at the end of the Middle Ages, the wool workers of Florence, the English peasantry, and the artisans of Ghent; it is the struggle of those who obey against those who command, which will continue as long as there are societies in which some have more power than others.

In Weil's view Marxism had in some respects seriously debased this permanent spirit of revolution. Writing, as it were, from the standpoint of a worker misled by middle-class revolutionaries, she charged Marxism with "flashy pseudo-scientific trimmings, a messianic eloquence, an unfettering of appetites that have disfigured" the working-class tradition. "Nothing entitles one to assure the workers that science is on their side," she wrote. Further, nothing entitles one to assure the workers that it is up to them to save the world. This, she insisted, was the attitude of one who regards the working class as an instrumentality. Workers, she said, "are unhappy, unjustly so; it is well that they defend themselves; it would be better if they could liberate themselves; and that is all that can be said about it."

From this perspective two corollaries followed. First, hostility to the Leninist project of substituting the party for the action of the working class itself. Weil, as already indicated, had set forth this position in her first writing on the subject. Later she added the perception that Marx, who was "struck by the fact that social groups manufacture moralities for their own use, thanks to which the specific activity of each one is placed outside the reach of evil," ironically "arrived at a morality which placed the social category to which he belonged—that of professional revolutionaries—above sin." Unlike Rosa Luxemburg, therefore, Simone Weil could not appeal from Leninist vanguardism to a Marxist model. In Ms. Weil's view, Marx himself had projected the concept of a party making use of the working class to achieve goals entertained not by workers but by the party in their name.

A second corollary, which for Simone Weil followed from the axiom of genuine identification with the working class, was that, if the workers seemed unrevolutionary, one did not casually abandon them in search of a functional equivalent, say in the Third World. Rather, if the workers seemed unrevolutionary, one took a second look at reform. Simone Weil came very close to the thesis of André Gorz in *Strategy for Labor,* that there are two kinds of reform: quantitative reforms, which lead to cooptation by the system as it is; and qualitative reforms, whereby the op-

pressed take partial control over decision making, which whets
their appetite for more control and therefore leads to revolution.
The antiwar movement of the 1960s developed a similar concept
of "resistance," a form of struggle intermediate between reform
and revolution. Simone Weil expressly conceptualized the possibility of nonviolent mass action. "Antiquity," she wrote in one of
her fragments,

has not only bequeathed us the story of the interminable and point-
less massacres around Troy, but also the story of the energetic and
pacific action by which the Roman plebeians, without spilling a drop
of blood, emerged from a condition bordering on slavery and obtained, as the guarantee of their newly-won rights, the institution of
the tribunate. It was in precisely the same way that the French workers, by their pacific occupation of the factories [in June 1936], imposed paid holidays, guaranteed wages and workers' delegates.

I have emphasized two recurrent ideas in the social thinking
of Simone Weil: in contrast to the common criticism of the New
Left as mindless activism, this member of the first New Left
rigorously explained her postulates, and indeed turned the tables
by accusing Marxism itself of logic repeatedly anchored in mere
assumption. Thus Simone Weil exemplified the possibility of a
rational New Left. Second, she demonstrated the fruitfulness of
New Left categories such as participatory democracy in understanding the concrete individual experience of factory workers
under capitalism. She showed that those seeking a more humane
and democratic socialism need not draw back in fear, and abandon all that they have theretofore learned, in confronting the
experience of industrial work. My own conversations with working people during the past six years are in accord. I think that all
across the country there is a discussion not happening between
former student radicals who think that they must use the language of Marxism-Leninism in order to communicate with workers, and puzzled workers who would like to talk about the lives
they are leading and the decisions affecting those lives.

So third, I want to say that Weil offers one final theme or
image which in a degree knits together her criticism of Marxism
as unscientific, and her concern with the actual experience of

oppressed individuals. Marx, she said, thought he was using the method of Darwin but was actually using the method of Lamarck. By this she meant that Marx, like Lamarck, assumed that the environment miraculously produced an adaptation of organisms to its requirements—as in the Lamarckian explanation that baby giraffes were born with longer necks because of their parents' attempts to reach bananas; so in Marxism, because capitalism was ripe for change the proletariat was thought ready to change it. In either its Lamarckian or Marxist version, in this theory the environment was the protagonist of change.

A truly Darwinian social science would emphasize the ceaseless small initiatives whereby individuals seek to change the world around them. To be sure, such initiatives are selectively reinforced or destroyed by the social environment, just as are biological mutations by nature. The Marx who wrote that men make their own history, but that they make it under certain conditions, was absolutely right and consistent with Darwinian biology, so Weil believed. She often emphasized the many-sided, uneven, and ambiguous character of Marx's work; and if one prefers, one may see her, not as a critic of Marxism, but as a champion of the activist Marx against the Marx who, after the failure of the 1843 revolutions, and especially in old age, increasingly emphasized the impact of circumstances on man.

III　Having charted, to some degree, the first New Left and Simone Weil's place within it, I want to look more closely at the principal American embodiment of the first New Left, the magazine *Politics*.

Politics has a special place in the hearts and minds of its admirers. To read it, former s.d.s. president Todd Gitlin wrote me recently, is like sipping rare old wine. To some of us it seems that there was more good sense and fresh thinking in this one magazine during the three or four years of its active existence than in all the pages of all the left journals from that day to this. (Personally, one of the things I did when most disoriented by the events of the late 1960s was to read through *Politics* again from the first issue to the last.)

If there is such a thing as a review of a periodical, let me briefly try to write it. The first issue of *Politics* appeared in February 1944. The lead editorial by Dwight Macdonald stated:

The next few decades require not an "oasis psychology" among left intellectuals, but rather a more conscious, active intervention in the historical process. It will be a period of tremendous suffering, tremendous revolutionary *possibilities,* in Europe and in the colonial countries. One's endeavor should be not to withdraw into illusory "oases" but rather to go out into the desert, share the common experience, and try to find a road out of the wilderness.

Already in this first issue there was evidence of the effort to find a new language for the new realities of the mid-twentieth century. The system exemplified by both the Soviet Union and Nazi Germany, which Simone Weil had identified without naming, was termed "bureaucratic collectivism." Simone Weil's perception that henceforth capitalist economies would be symbiotically linked to war was developed, as I noted, by Walter Oakes who, coining the term "permanent war economy," wrote: "The fact is that the capitalist system cannot stand the strain of another siege of unemployment comparable to 1930–1940. . . . The traditional methods . . . will not be followed." Paul Goodman contributed a piece on "The Attempt To Invent An American Style."

Politics followed with particular attention the growing movement for racial equality, exemplified by agitation in the army and by so-called riots in Harlem, which the magazine defended. Race, an editorial observed in August 1944, "is the one issue which really cuts to the bottom of things and so has an intrinsically revolutionary dynamic."

Also fully reported in *Politics* was the resistance movement in Federal prisons by objectors to World War II. A single issue told of a work strike at Danbury against segregation, a hunger strike at Lewisburg over censorship of the mail, and the continuing noncooperation of Louis Taylor and Stanley Murphy, who, having fasted eighty-two days at Danbury, had been transferred to Springfield, Missouri, where they continued their protest. Commenting, Dwight Macdonald wrote of the conscientious objector:

In a period like the present in this country, when there is no immediate prospect of effective political action to realize ultimate principles,
there is something very attractive about the C.O.'s kind of individual
moral stand. His day-to-day actions and long-range convictions, if
they do not wholly coincide, are at least on speaking terms with each
other. One of the psychologically dessicating qualities of Trotskyist
political behavior, in my experience, was the gross failure of the co-
incidence. As an individual, the Trotskyist in a non-revolutionary
period conforms outwardly to the left around him: he pays taxes, he
does what the boss tells him to, he refrains from assaulting bourgeois
politicians or blowing up banks, and in time of war he performs the
ultimate act of outward conformity: he enters the Army if drafted.
The political logic of his behavior is perfect: he does all this pro-
visionally, as it were, because he believes he can thus better prepare
an organization which can act in some future crisis; the less energies
he dissipates in premature individualistic gestures of rebellion, the
more he distinguishes himself in everyday behavior from the mass of
people, the more effectively he can get into contact with them to influence them on basic issues. And yet, and yet . . . the years go by,
the grand political end is still far off, and he is in danger of either
dropping out of the revolutionary movement and accepting the dominant values of this society (a transition eased by his years of outward
conformity), or else, if he remains faithful, of becoming deadened,
routinized by years of frustration which is doubly severe because it
exists on the level of personal behavior as well as politics. The C.O.,
like the European anarchist or our own old-time Wobblies, at least
reacts spontaneously, immediately against the evils he fights, and
shapes his everyday behavior to fit his principles. This is a great
thing.

Thus the as-yet unnamed New Left began to identify its parentage
and to define its views.

Looking abroad, *Politics* saw most hope in the resistance movements of Europe on the verge of liberation. An article on "Dual
Power in France" reported that the resistance committees saw
themselves as continuing after the war and as constituting a new
Estates General. Furiously *Politics* excoriated the *New Leader*
magazine for withholding support from the Resistance because
of Communist involvement in it. "This writer [Macdonald] is as

much opposed to Stalinism as any of the *New Leader* experts, but he submits that 'to tell progress from reaction' is a somewhat more difficult job than just to look where the Communist Party has some influence and then throw one's weight into the other camp. . . . It is in the French popular liberation committees, in the *FFI* and in the workers' militia that democratic socialist elements are to be found, and not among the Paris ministerial bureaucracy or in the ranks of over-aged former parliamentarians." Still listening for new language and assisting in its invention, *Politics* declared in March 1945:

Two new terms have emerged in this concluding phase of the war which are not [as yet] devalued, which retain all their sharpness and moral purity: "collaboration" and "resistance." I think it deeply significant that these are becoming the great political watchwords in Europe today, since they indicate no specific, positive ideology, no aspiring faith, but simply the fact that people either "go along" or that they "resist." . . . To resist, to reject simply—this is the first condition for the human spirit's survival in the face of the increasingly tighter organization of state power everywhere. That this is not a sufficient condition is true—only a general, positive faith and system of ideas can save us in the long run. Such a faith and system are no longer held by significant numbers of people. But they will only develop, if they do, from the seeds of "resistance." . . .

It was all the more disappointing to read this and in the spring of 1946 to read that *Politics* was obliged to present an analysis of "Why the Resistance Failed."

Politics was not without its humor. The high point, for this reader, was a pyrotechnical exchange between Paul Goodman and C. Wright Mills concerning modern psychology. According to Mills, Goodman preached a "gonad theory of revolution." If anything, revolutionaries were sexual ascetics, Mills went on. He concluded: "Leave Mr. Goodman with his revolution in the bedroom. We have still to search out the barricades of our freedom." Goodman replied with dignity. When sexuality is free, he wrote, "it is only one among several productive forces"; when repressed, it is "the most important destructive influence that there is." The political energies of sexual ascetics "are precisely the energies that we see in the sadism and masochism of monolithic parties and in

transitional dictatorships that become permanent." Marx, Goodman went on, appeals to human nature against the alienation
produced by "the collective conditions of work which exist under
capitalism and which will continue to exist in any modern industrial society."

These last words of Paul Goodman repeated the fundamental
message of Simone Weil. She appeared as a contributor in *Politics*
in February 1945, as a posthumous contributor to a symposium
on "War As An Institution." In her piece, entitled "Reflections
on War," she stated: "One point was common to all the Marxist
trends: the explicit refusal to condemn war as such." Further,
she asserted: "Armies wielded by the apparatus of the sovereign
State cannot bring liberty to anybody."

With the advent of the atom bomb, war became *Politics'* preoccupation, and Simone Weil its patron saint. It was in this period that her essay on the *Iliad* was published, announced on the
cover by the picture of a splendid Greek helmet with horsehair
crest and nosepiece all but hiding the eyes. It was in this period
also that Macdonald wrote the essays for which the magazine is
best remembered: "The Responsibility of Peoples" and "The
Root is Man." I shall not attempt to summarize them. They are
part of a living tradition, as suggested by Professor Chomsky's
citation of them in his writings against the Vietnam War.

Rather, I want to call attention to the dramatic absence in
Politics of that which was so crucial for Simone Weil: systematic
attention to the particular experience of working people. To be
sure, there were occasional articles on strikes. What there was
not was that which illuminated *Politics'* reporting of the black,
pacifist, and European resistance movements: letters from participant observers, individual accounts of little-known skirmishes,
in short, the reporting in depth that can happen only when people who are publishing a magazine are personally in touch with
people taking part in a certain form of struggle. *Politics* was not
in touch. Its failure to include in its developing articulation of
New Left ideology the experiences and insights of contemporary
working-class struggle, a failure inherited by our movement of
the 1960s, was a principal cause of its demise and ours. And this
is why, the richness and vitality of *Politics* notwithstanding, today

as we make a new beginning we appropriately look back over its head to Simone Weil, who in her incipient New Leftism found the working class to be absolutely central.

There was much in American working-class life that *Politics* might have reported.

During World War II itself there took place a rash of wildcat strikes in defiance of the no-strike policy of the union leadership. In 1944, the year in which *Politics* began publication, more workers went on strike than in 1937, the year of the General Motors and Little Steel strikes. In 1944, also, the United Automobile Workers (UAW) national convention very nearly repudiated the no-strike policy in the midst of war. As a statistical phenomenon the World War II strike wave is well known. Its causes are much less clear, though worth serious attention. The financial status of the average worker was better than before the war. Women, blacks, and Southern whites moved into industry in large numbers during the war, and the role of each of these groups in the strike movement is uncertain. Nor is it clear to what extent the rank-and-file workers who went on strike despite the no-strike policy would have responded to the idea of a *labor* party, endorsed by the Michigan state CIO Convention in 1943. On the whole, the wildcat strikes appear usually to have been catalyzed by just that sort of arbitrary discipline that was so offensive to Simone Weil. In March 1944, for example, two war veterans working at the massive Ford River Rouge plant were caught smoking and fired. Two hundred and fifty of their fellow-workers hurried to the labor relations office to protest. When a plant protection guard attempted to intervene, they physically attacked him and, breaking into the labor relations office, spent two hours knocking over desks, destroying documents, emptying files, and breaking windows. The two discharged workers were quoted as saying that they "would just as soon be in a prison camp as work under the conditions imposed by the labor relations division at the Ford plant."

Politics might also have reported local experiments such as the formation of the United Labor Party in Akron and nearby cities in 1946. I have told this story in *Liberation* (December 1973). What especially leaves one with a sense of lost possibilities is that the rank-and-file workers, former Trotskyists and former Wobblies who tried to create a labor party in northeastern Ohio, had so much the same sense of making a New Left beginning expressed by Dwight Macdonald and *Politics.* The United Labor Party deliberately broke with both the Social Democratic and Bolshevik models of a radical party. They opposed the use of party pseudonyms as a conspiratorial practice inappropriate in America. They prided themselves on their comradely and libertarian practices; a member recalls that the United Labor Party said it was the only left party that treated members as well as nonmembers, and that it was the only group to which he ever belonged in which everyone seemed to trust each other. There was a strong Wobbly-like emphasis on *doing* rather than *talking.* Indeed, in the spring of 1947 United Labor Party members joined Dwight Macdonald, A. J. Muste, and Dave Dellinger in a national "Break with Conscription" action by publicly mailing their draft cards to President Truman.

One would have liked to see in the pages of *Politics,* rather than in a less accessible publication, the following description of the United Labor Party by two of its members:

What marks the ULP most of all, is the basic work it has done in mobilizing and articulating a folk culture in politics. It does not possess, nor does it hanker after, a unique gobbledegook "party environment" separate from all else. It wants to encompass everything that is common to plebeian culture. . . . For those who have waited and wondered what an American party might look like, it is something to ponder.

To do this, it has first of all renounced the precious cannibalism of the orthodox Left. . . . It dos not regard itself, and does not operate, as a competitor to other minority parties. . . . It aims at the untouched workingclass for its recruits (welcoming all others, of course). It reserves its offensive artillery for the major parties, who deserve the maximum fire-power. It refuses to hang about its neck the stinking albatross of being "The Chosen Party."

Such a description of a political style on the left was presumably as refreshing a quarter of a century ago as it would still be, alas, today.

The point, in sum, is that the New Left as it first manifested itself in the United States was brilliant, but one-sided. Many of the persons associated with *Politics* were to play central roles in the creation of a second New Left in this country. The failure of our first New Left to incorporate within itself a language descriptive of the day-to-day experiences of working people has accordingly continued to cripple the effort to move beyond orthodox Marxism without losing what remains valuable and essential in its teaching.

It may be objected that neither Marxism nor Simone Weil provides proof as to why any special importance should be attached to the experience of work, and to working people. This is a legitimate objection to which there may be more than one solution. Marxism, I take it, holds that in the last analysis working people are important because they and they alone have in their hands the power to overthrow capitalism and so usher mankind from the realm of necessity to the realm of freedom. If I read Simone Weil correctly, her feeling was that working people are important because they are oppressed and need help, and because, also, work provides human beings a unique opportunity to come into contact with the order of the world outside themselves. Affirming all these sentiments, I would emphasize another: that the dependence and relative helplessness of employees oblige them to turn to one another for mutual aid, in strikes and trade unions. No matter how bureaucratized trade unions may become, it remains true for working people as for no other group in capitalist society that "an injury to one is an injury to all." In this sense, perhaps, industrial life does create a new society or at least a seed of it within the shell of the old.

IV   Although the connection between this ancient history and where we find ourselves now may be clearer, perhaps I should underscore what I perceive as most important.

One comes away from encounter with Simone Weil refreshed in the belief that a small piece of *good work,* for instance, a single life well lived, makes a difference. It is so in the life of the spirit; and it is also so in science, where progress may wait on a particular experiment, an individual discovery. Perhaps in the small-scale organizing that many of us have been doing since the disintegration of S.D.S. we have been thus experimenting. Perhaps, if none of our experiments have yet been successful, one day soon it will be otherwise. At that point a new movement—a third New Left —will regroup around that solitary advance.

In the life of the spirit, too, small things may count for much. In her later writings Simone Weil spoke of seeds, of catalysts, of points of gravity: physical small things to show how it is that the spirit may part waves and move mountains.

Simone Weil teaches that the first step in advancing toward our end is to desire it greatly. "The first condition for moving in this direction is to let one's thoughts dwell on it. It is not one of those things that can be obtained by accident. Maybe one can receive it after desiring it long and persistently."

Simone Weil's Work Experiences:
From Wigan Pier to Chrystie Street

$\sim$

GEORGE ABBOTT WHITE
for William J. Surrock and Joseph F. White

Why did she work? Or at least, why did Simone Weil do the kind
of work she did—manual labor—and long hours at it in factory
and field?[1]

From her earliest years she was trained, after all, to work with
her mind. No one proceeds from the lycée Henri IV to the Ecole
Normale without having learned how to read carefully and
think critically, without having learned skillfully to manipulate
concepts and ideas in conversation and in writing. And she was
not only trained to be an intellectual to the highest degree, as her
brother—himself a distinguished mathematician—was also the
first to insist, but she pursued this training and practiced what she
learned with an intensity and a diligence that put her contemporaries to shame. She did think and teach and write; she wrote
more, and more of value, in her thirty-four years, than all but a
few write in a lifetime. She was an intellectual who worked ex-
traordinarily hard with her mind. Yet why was this not enough?

Simone Weil's work experiences become somewhat more understandable if we recall the work experiences of the American
New Left. Beginning in the early 1960s, thousands of young men
and women left their colleges and universities to work with
Blacks in the South, poor whites in Appalachia, Chicanos and In-
dians in the Southwest and on the West Coast, unemployed
Blacks and whites in the devastated centers of Los Angeles,

1. Earlier versions of this essay were given at The Catholic Worker
(Friday Evening discussion), New York City, and the Yale University
School of Management. Annie-Marie Fraser and Robert Ellsberg were
generous hosts at the former and John Dorfman at the latter; each assisted in what Peter Maurin called "the clarification of thought."

Chicago, Cleveland, Philadelphia and Boston. Having struggled with working people and the dispossessed around Civil Rights, antiwar, economic, educational and social service issues, many of these students then returned to their studies and completed their degrees, including advanced or professional degrees. Others remained as unskilled workers (or trained as skilled or semi-skilled workers, but remained) in order to organize within existing unions or remained, as most recently is the case with several small left groups, to create revolutionary cadre among the workers, in classic Marxist-Leninist fashion.

This New Left did political work as it observed working people work, or itself performed manual labor in homes, workshops, factories, and farms. In any event, what was achieved by those who left was for some a form of paying one's "dues," an alleviation of what was called "white guilt" or "white-skin privilege," whereas for others, it was the tangible and intangible sense of what, in America, constituted the true structure of social class and the nature of privilege. And there had been concrete achievements: here a stoplight installed at a threatening intersection, there a racist social worker removed, a worksite opened to minorities, abortions made available at a local health center. But because of those who both stayed and left, higher education had been changed. Less central for political and intellectual certification, less mystifying and less controlling as an institution, still others could now leave American colleges and universities not only without a stint with the workers, but without excessive feelings of guilt, shame, or incompetence. Deeply involved with drugs or experiments in sexuality, a few of these "dropouts" plummeted down the American class ladder, straight off the bottom, it seemed, into marginal existence in urban collectives or on rural communes. Others turned their intelligence and considerable adaptive abilities to a growing crafts (as distinct from "counter") culture, and turning back the clock and the productive process— or so they believed—physicists became potters; English majors, weavers; microbiologists, cabinet makers; sociologists, silversmiths. These latter turned to manual labor more as a means of organizing themselves than other workers, except by the indirect example of lovely things well made.

Points of tangency with Simone Weil's work experiences will become obvious later, but useful as this analogy with the New Left may be, changed assumptions and shifting contexts should alert us, now, to its limitations when pressed into service across the decades. Whatever her work experiences may have meant, it is unlikely their meaning will be known only by assessment against our present, or even our most recent past. But fortunately, Simone Weil was not alone in whatever it was that impelled her to turn from the safe trajectory others of her class and training were on to a direct encounter with working people's lives and manual labor. With George Orwell and Dorothy Day she had, in Robert Coles's phrase, "spiritual kin"; companions, in a sense, who had their roots in the twenties and thirties and who, although separated from her in many ways, nevertheless were themselves dissatisfied with their intellectual "accomplishments," uneasy with the "aspirations" of their contemporaries, puzzled by the contradictions between what they had read and been taught, and what they had glimpsed with their own eyes or had chanced to overhear from those who had also, perhaps, begun to question and search.

Simone Weil took a job in a factory in the "Red belt" that rings Paris in December 1934. In 1928, a graduate of Eton had arrived after a frustrating five years with the Imperial Police in Burma. Eric Blair (as he then called himself) took a room in a cheap hotel in a working-class district of the city in order to think and write, but a year later when his writings had generated no income he found himself, in his words, "almost penniless and in urgent need of work."[2] The "work" Blair/Orwell found in the wretched kitchens of Paris in 1929, while millions of his countrymen were unemployed across the Channel, would make its way into *Down and Out in Paris and London* (1933), just as his experiences with tramps, hop-pickers, prostitutes, drunks, petty criminals and unemployed miners in the next few years would make their way into uncomfortable essays, and an even more un-

2. It often has been pointed out that Orwell had an aunt in Paris at the time to whom he could have appealed for help. This situation has its parallels to various of Simone Weil's tests, and of course the appeal was never made.

comfortable book, *The Road to Wigan Pier* (1937).[3] With his journey to Wigan Pier, George Orwell would find England's North Country more foreign to him, significantly, than England's Burma, just as Simone Weil would find herself a "foreigner" in greater Paris simply by virtue of having shared the life of French rural and industrial workers.

During these same early thirties, a journalist of the American Left would stop writing imaginative fiction and quit the company of poets, dramatists and Left intellectuals, have a daughter, convert to Roman Catholicism, separate from her common-law husband, and found the Catholic Worker Movement in New York City with an older man, a French peasant and moral philosopher named Peter Maurin. Dorothy Day would continue as a journalist, writing essays and editorials that condemned a system where the very few had so much and the many had so very little. She would continue this work, as well as the considerable manual labor required to provide caretaking of the poor, unemployed, and disoriented, until her death almost half a century later, but she would not leave the Lower East Side, nor the wretchedly poor and utterly dispossessed she had come to know and to love and to work with—a lumpenproletariat who collected there like human sludge at the bottom of an enormous, wealthy machine of a city.[4]

3. As a dishwasher, garbage hauler, general cleaning aide and food preparer, Orwell's experiences behind the swinging doors of haute cuisine restaurants were only a prelude to the manual labor he performed back in England. While a tramp, Orwell picked hops and other farm produce south of London and, while not actually mining coal to the North, he came to know the physical cost involved by observing closely alongside those who did. As a result, it could be said that he amassed considerable knowledge of a wide range of manual labor practiced by working people.

4. Although Dorothy Day was not a manual laborer to the extent that Simone Weil was, nor the kind of "participant-observer" Orwell became, she nonetheless experienced the necessity pressed upon people by physical labor in her day-and-night capacity of caretaker. In addition— and not dissimilar from the principled behavior of Simone Weil or George Orwell—Dorothy Day personally participated in the grinding work the production of a large newspaper involves; unwilling to relegate "lesser" tasks to others, she sorted, addressed, labeled and mailed what she also wrote and edited and proofed.

With these people she would practice what the Gospel calls the works of mercy, working longer hours under worse physical and emotional conditions than the vast majority of the 100,000 subscribers to the monthly newspaper of the movement, *The Catholic Worker*. Come March and October a letter would issue from Chrystie Street,[5] and Dorothy Day would beg from her readers, sometimes reminding them that she was, in turn, "reminding the young people who come to work with us that they are not citizens [in the country of the poor]. They cannot get away from their privileged backgrounds." And in the same letter, sometimes in the same paragraph, she would begin celebrating the beauty and the joy that could always be found in even that country—in a cup of hot tea, in some bright flowers growing in a pot on a nearby tenement window sill, or observing that "Arthur Sullivan just baked seventeen loaves of whole wheat bread . . . this evening before supper someone brought in some apple pies and fresh tomatoes."

George Orwell may be said to have been obsessed by class differences to the extent that Dorothy Day may be said to have been haunted by God. Neither is the half that, taken together, adds up to the "whole" of Simone Weil. (Who was certainly obsessed and haunted, both by class differences and God, and a great many *other* concerns as well.) Manual labor was a central value for each, however, and once Simone Weil's work experiences are laid out separately, and then set alongside those of the other two, a just estimate of all three becomes slightly more possible. Indeed, something curious occurs, for no matter how bizarre, willful, awkward, and driven their efforts at manual labor may have appeared to their contemporaries, taken in retrospect and seen as a shared response to a common crisis, the bizarre becomes ordinary, the willful, natural, the awkward, understood (even heroic, when the

5. The Catholic Worker may be said to have begun in Dorothy Day's two-room apartment at East Fifteenth Street and Avenue A. But landlords, crowding, urban removal, and the like forced it to move to Mott Street in the 1940s, Chrystie Street during the 1950s and 1960s, and in the 1970s to its present location, 36 East First Street; all Lower East Side, New York City. The author's point of entry was the Chrystie Street location, hence, the essay's title.

odds are fairly considered), and what drove them must be appreciated, by even their most stern and cynical critics, as something close to a calling. And who would not respond, if the voice that spoke to one was as direct and as compelling a voice as the voice that must have spoken to those three?

II   In May 1929, the Weil family moved to 3 rue Auguste-Compte, their home for as long as they lived in Paris. Simone Petrement in her biography of Simone Weil has detailed the splendid view

that spreads out below from these rooms on the sixth and seventh floors in a rather high section of town. . . . Standing there one can see across the way the Sacre Coeur in Montmartre, which appears to be on the same level, but from which one is separated by the whole center of Paris, which extends lower down in a broad valley and then climbs in a gentle slope toward the two heights. From the terrace [of their apartment] one can see on the left the Eiffel Tower, the Chaillot Palace, the dome of the Invalides, the top of the Arc de Triomphe, Sainte-Clotilde, the towers of Saint-Sulspice, the roof of the Opera, and the roofs of the Louvre; and on the right the steeple of Sainte-Chapelle, the Saint-Jacques du Haut-Pas.

Andre Weil has remarked that his father was happiest when he was working, but it should be noted that to maintain the relative comfort the Weils enjoyed in their apartment at the northeast corner of the attractive Luxembourg Gardens, Dr. Weil, a general practitioner, had to work very hard.[6] Perhaps her father's at-

6. All doctors are assumed to be rich. But as Dr. John D. Stoeckle has noted in the course of his research into doctors and patients in the 1930s, in America this was only the case for a very small number of primarily urban physicians with either privileged clientele ("the carriage trade") or inherited wealth of their own. Given the fact that few prepaid health-care plans existed (meaning the absence of third-party payments so much a part of our present health-care system), and that people were unaccustomed to seeing the doctor at anything like our current rate, doctors had to see a great many patients to make a living—though this was somewhat less the case with urban physicians than with those practicing in rural areas. (Conversations with John D. Stoeckle, M.D., and Jacqueline E. Chevalley, M.D.) See also "A Brief

tentiveness made an impression, perhaps her very natural competitiveness with her older brother (whose intellectual precocity and productiveness is well known) made her more active, yet whatever her feelings toward professional or intellectual work, from the time she was a child she also thought about manual labor, wanted to do manual labor, did as much of that kind of work as she was able, well before she began teaching in her early twenties.

Not surprisingly, her first published piece, written while she was still at the Ecole Normale, was on the nature of manual labor, and in it she asserted that the problem of perception was closely bound to what she considered to be the problem of work. Closely reasoned and insightful, Simone Weil knew, as did others, the essay was too abstract and formal; it lacked contact with everyday experience. Perhaps the remedy was teaching, in the late twenties, at a school for railway workers a short distance from her home. Her first biographer, Jacques Cabaud, says that the school's purpose was to enable the men "to graduate from manual labor to white-collar work." He adds that the teacher-organizers also "hoped to provide for the proletariat a grounding in cultural subjects," and that for Simone Weil, "It is hardly possible to exaggerate the importance of the contacts made while [there]."[7] One might question a venture that saw movement from manual to white-collar work as a "graduation," or the characterization of the activity as "benevolent teaching," but the words are Cabaud's and we question, only because Simone Weil and others have taught us to be skeptical about such middle class projects on behalf of workers. We do know, however, that the

Note on Medical Economics" and "Medical Lessons from History," in Lewis Thomas, M.D., *The Medusa and the Snail* (New York: Bantam Books, 1979).

7. Jacques Cabaud, *Simone Weil: A Fellowship in Love* (New York: Channel Press, 1964), p. 39. This furnishes a good example of how it is biographers differ in their handling of information and its subsequent interpretation. Simone Petrement, keenly aware of the importance of Simone Weil's work experiences, describes this school for workers at 3 rue Falguiere very briefly, and makes nothing like Cabaud's claim for its importance. See Simone Petrement, *Simone Weil: A Life* (New York: Pantheon Books, 1976), pp. 57–58.

men responded to her teaching, seriously discussed social and political theory, and that one man in particular convinced his teacher that "he had been reading Plato and Descartes," and had, moreover, "acquired a very sound grasp of their meaning." That the classics could successfully be shared with workers confirmed the validity of her work as well as her teacher Alain's insistence upon the importance of contact with working people.

During the summer of 1929, Simone Weil stayed with an aunt in Normandy and worked ten hours a day digging potatoes. Earlier, she had visited the mother of a friend at St. Malo de la Lande, near the western coast of Normandy, where for two summers she had worked almost nonstop during the six weeks of the wheat harvest. A story is told that while working there one day, she came across great heaps of thistles that had been separated from the wheat. Without a moment's thought she scooped them up with her hands and dumped them to the side of the fields, like the men would do.[8]

After receiving her diploma from the Ecole in 1931, she left for the coastal town of Reville, in the northeast of the Normandy peninsula. Now it was the lives of fishermen she wanted to know. "But her reputation as a Communist had preceded her," writes Cabaud, "she had the air of the lone wolf and the introvert; and her large hood and spectacles were regarded with suspicion and something akin to fear." One captain was not put off, and before

8. In her pursuit of necessary work experiences, Simone Weil went where other women did not. Of this, Simone Petrement has said, ". . . her whole conception of what she wanted to do with her life, it was—as she herself said later—a great misfortune to have been born a female. So she had decided to reduce this obstacle as much as possible by disregarding it, that is to say, by giving up any desire to think of herself as a woman or to be regarded as such by others, at least for a set period of time." Although "her family would chafe her affectionately about her wish to be treated as a boy," they also strongly supported her general aspirations in many areas. Her mother "tried to develop masculine virtues in her daughter instead of a feminine personality." Setting this into a feminist context, one would be encouraged by Simone Petrement's quotation of a letter from Mme. Weil to a friend, ". . . I do my best to encourage in Simone not the simpering graces of a little girl but the forthrightness of a boy, even if this must at times seem rude" (Petrement, pp. 27–28).

long Marcel Lecarpentier and his brother had made Simone Weil feel welcome aboard their thirty-foot boat. Along with another man, they would often set out at night ("people thereabouts were scandalized," writes Petrement), after first wading in icy water up to their waists, catching bait with handnets along the shoreline. Three hours of baiting, the boat made for deeper waters, then dropping the nets, hauling them in after a time, dropping the nets, hauling them in. The hours were long and the order of work inflexible; once down, the nets could only be hauled up in sequence, no matter what the weather or need. One chilly evening, Simone Weil, along with the rest of the crew, sailed back into port soaked to the skin by a storm that had blown up while they were out.

Doing work, she also observed workers; she visited Berlin in the summer of 1932 for this purpose when Hitler was, in Joachim Fest's phrase, "at the gates of power." The ancient Hindenberg had won a majority in the recent election, although Hitler had registered substantial gains, and in any event his Nazis continued the plan of terror in the streets.[9] Simone Weil had wanted to observe the overall political situation, especially its effect upon unions and the Left, but was immediately struck by the fierce sectarian struggles between the German Socialists and the German Communists. Like George Orwell, she was alternately amused and furious with a spectacle in which partisans of the Left fought one another, while the unaligned workers watched, baffled, from the sidelines. Closer in spirit to the Soviet Union than she would be again, still, she had nevertheless come to feel that the greatest danger to a workers' movement was for it to be put into the hands of a Russian bureaucracy, no matter what its

9. Pappen made a conciliatory gesture toward Hitler, in Fest's account, but Hitler put him off. "Thereupon," Fest writes, "the conditions of virtual civil war, with wild clashes reached their climax. In the five weeks up to July 20 there were nearly 500 such clashes in Prussia alone, with a toll of 99 dead and 1,125 wounded. Throughout the Reich seventeen persons were killed on July 10; in many places the army had to intervene in the furious street battles." "Ernest Thalmann, the Communist leader," Fest underscores, "rightly defined the lifting of the ban on the SA as an open invitation to murder" (Joachim C. Fest, *Hitler* [New York: Harcourt, Brace and Jovanovich, 1974], p. 338).

professed sympathies. Later that summer she pressed on with her critique of Lenin. His destruction of the soviets and what she now read of his admiration of Taylorism made her contemptuous.[10] She embarked on a devastating analysis of "state socialism" and its analogues with Hitler's National Socialism that would become a keystone, years after her death, for Hannah Arendt and other theorists of totalitarianism.[11]

In the autumn of 1932, Simone Weil was teaching in Auxerre where she purchased a small printing press for her students' use. It was unpopular with them, however, and they told her that they did not wish to "dirty" their hands learning how to operate it. Their teacher had no such qualms and found farms in the area of

10. The appropriateness of Taylorism as social engineering was perhaps on his mind when W. H. G. Armytage wrote, "Taylorism's most distinguished convert was to apply it to building not a business but a state. On 28 April 1918, Lenin, in an article in *Pravda* on 'The Urgent Problems of Soviet Rule,' urged 'We should try out every scientific and progressive suggestion of the Taylor system . . . we must introduce in Russia the study and teachings of the new Taylor system and its systematic trial and adaptation' " (W. H. G. Armytage, *A Social History of Engineering* [Cambridge, Mass.: The MIT Press, 1961], p. 281). Simone Weil likely had this and other quotations in mind as she rethought Lenin in the late 1920s and early 1930s. Her own pungent remarks on Lenin, Leninism and Marxism-Leninism can be found throughout the collection, *Oppression and Liberty,* trans. Arthur Wills and John Petrie (Amherst: University of Massachusetts Press, 1973).

11. Given the personal and political investment made by many factions on the Left, this kind of critique was enormously dangerous. At the Trade Union Congress in Rheims in 1933, "Simone Weil asked to be allowed to speak in order to describe the plight of the German communists. Her request was refused." She spoke nonetheless, but probably could not be heard through what was described as the "uproar and disorder." During the last session of the Congress she was asked to speak again and read an article that "confirmed the reports that the Soviet Union had closed its frontiers to communist refugees [from Hitler's Germany]. At 4.30 in the morning the president cut her short . . . he declared the debate closed." Her speeches took great courage because "she was dealing with the unmentionable, the collusion between Hitler and Stalin. On two occasions [during the Congress] she was threatened with physical assault, but her comrades, the miners, were watching. . . . They surrounded her and kept the assailants at bay" (Cabaud, pp. 90–91).

this girls' lycee where she could do general chores such as weeding and milking. Once again she dug potatoes for a time, before actually hiring herself out as a servant to a farm family. Ochre paint was a product of the city and when Simone Weil was not teaching or writing, she studied how it was made.

The next year found her sent further away from Paris, even further to the south of France, to the manufacturing city of Roanne. By now she had come to know something of the reality of working class life, especially from the contacts she had made during her first teaching assignment at Le Puy. Then she had also taught at the Labor Exchange in nearby St. Etienne and while riding the train back and forth through this mining district, had had the opportunity to see and hear a great deal. Her helpfulness had led to the invitation—rare for a woman—to ride the cage to the bottom of a mine where, like Orwell, in muck, bent-over space, and dim light, she was taken by union colleagues who were miners and was shown how to work an airhammer at the coal face. While at Roanne she continued to travel to St. Etienne to take part in public meetings at the Labor Exchange, but as the school year advanced Simone Weil felt she needed to do something more than observe at a distance or participate marginally, something that would require leave for 1934–35.

Dorothy Day has often spoken about the boredom and suffering that results from the involuntary poverty forced upon large numbers of people and the freedom that results from poverty freely chosen. For all that she had already experienced, Simone Weil remained uncertain as to what her voluntary choice—the year she planned to devote to manual labor in the factories—would bring, or when and how, it would end. There were, however, three indications of what she anticipated. On the opening pages of a journal[12] in which she intended to relate her day-to-day

12. No less than Albert Camus and Hannah Arendt have praised this work highly. But the impression has been given by them and by others that *La condition ouvrière* (1951) is a formal study, a book rather than a compilation of sixteen different groups of materials such as letters, statements, essay fragments and the like, on work, unions, union organization, and Taylorism. The bulk of these thoughts were put on paper during the 1930s; her factory-work experience, by way of orienta-

factory experiences, she inscribed as a motto a line from Homer: *poll' aekadzomenē, kraterē d'epikeiset' anagkē* ("Much against your own will, since necessity lies more mightily upon you"). She also wrote to a former student, and then discussed her plans with her friend from Henri IV and the Ecole Normale, Simone Petrement. The letter to her student said, at one point, "I have taken a year's leave in order to do a little work on my own and also to make contact with the famous 'real life.'" A sensitive student might have concluded that underneath the obvious bravado, her teacher was anxious about what lay ahead. And as if underscoring its seriousness generally and its importance to her personally, Simone Petrement was told that the forthcoming year was to be more than a matter of learning how to endure something "unpleasant" for a time. This test was to have a timeless quality because, Simone Petrement recalled, "if she could not stand up under the work, she was determined to kill herself."

From December 4, 1934, to August 22, 1935, Simone Weil worked in three factories: the Alsthom Company, J. J. Carnaud et Forges de Basse-Indre, and the Renault plant. Two involved "light" manufacturing, as in the case of Renault, sub-assemblies for the major assembly line. Alsthom manufactured large-scale electrical machinery.

She was hired on, through a friend, as a "bench hand" but, like the transmutation of so many words since the industrial revolution—as critics such as Raymond Williams have shown—the actual meaning of the title was almost entirely other because Simone Weil neither worked at a bench nor used tools that were her own at a rate set by her. Instead, she stood long hours at a noisy, dangerous power press, and later, at a still noisier and more dangerous metal-shearing machine.[13] It was piece-work, and the

---

tion, was 1934–35. And her "Factory Journal," which is known to American readers by its publication in *Politics* and later reprinted in *Cross Currents,* is the fifth item in the Gallimard edition, occupying pp. 45–145.

13. Such machines are dangerous for any number of reasons, including the fact that they are rarely bolted to the shop floor in anything like a solid fashion, so that repeated vibration usually shakes the machine loose and it begins to "walk" into the unwary operator who cannot hear

pieces came without end. In 1934 there was no public outcry against "speed-up" for the Depression was on and workers were considered fortunate to have a job, no matter what its demands. Simone Weil does not say, specifically, but like the Ford factories where my father worked when Henry Ford announced his celebrated five dollars a day, her workday was continuous; there were no "breaks" for toilet or lunch, much less a twelve-minute period for coffee or tea twice a shift. Then, no reliefer came by to spell you, and like Charlie Chaplin in *Hard Times,* it *was* like being tied to a bobsled for the duration of the run downhill. And I suspect in Simone Weil's, as in my day and in my uncles' and father's day, foremen screamed in workers' faces or struck them, kicked crates—or equivalent work easers—out from under them (a kind of small managerial joke since for five dollars a day, you were expected to stand in Mr. Ford's factory when you worked), "accidentally" scattered their work kits or newspapers or clean "homebound" clothing, all under the pretext of safety regulations.

Or, worse than the insults and the violence, they ignored the workers' complaints about faulty machinery or dangerous working conditions as one would ignore the whining of an annoying child. The ultimate fear, which Simone Weil registered quite clearly was, of course, dismissal. The freedom to sell your labor on the free market in times of economic slowdown, lacking any agreements regarding seniority, was a chilling fear that kept you in complete (even anticipatory) obedience to your foreman or his supervisor. Fired and dejected, Simone Weil returned to the foreman at quitting time to ask "Why?", only to be told by him, "I don't have to account to you for anything."

---

a thing in the din. In this particular case, the metal-shearing machine lacked a hand guard: a cover over the massive blade to prevent a hand or fingers from being put under. It is also likely that the machine lacked a "double-trip lever," that is, a double set of operating buttons or levels such that a piece would have to be inserted and the operating buttons hit with both hands (usually spread widely apart), completely preventing the possibility that a piece could be fed with one hand while the other tripped the shearing blade. The need to make production or to advance one's earning on a piece-rate basis often encouraged workers to attempt such an operation, unless prevented by this or similar safety devices.

Like George Orwell, Simone Weil was uncomfortable in her body, and the resulting awkwardness made it impossible for her to make her rate at the first and second factories. This mechanical ineptitude (which will be considered as mis-education or lack of education further on) brought her to the attention not only of foremen but her fellow workers, and was another source of anxiety.[14] As a result, and as is commonly the case with new workers, she was shifted from one section to another within the factory in an effort not to waste the time taken hiring her. In terms of her earnings and in terms of her test, this was serious: not to make one's rate was to "muff the goodies," i.e., when one's salary, calculated on the basis of the number of pieces completed, was lower than the minimum salary.

At both Alsthom and Carnaud she was, in effect, demoted to supposedly easier tasks, although at Alsthom this meant nothing less than tending the furnaces; placing large copper bobbins inside huge ceramic and metal ovens and heating them for varying periods. She thereby shared, with her fellow workers, the headaches, burns, and terrific drain upon her energy such work exacted, and what sleep she got was simply not restorative. If it was a struggle to summon the energy to walk out of the plant at the end of her shift on the first day of this work, it was even a greater struggle to summon the energy to get up and return the next morning. She could not manage to strike an appropriate pace, which was essential, and her fatigue deepened. There were dazed moments when she sensed just what sort of fellowship she had joined; Cabaud describes one such time when "she could not lower the furnace door. The work inside was on the point of ruin when a smithy [nearby] leapt to her rescue." Of this she would later write, "How grateful you feel at such moments."

---

14. New workers who were in the least inept created major difficulties on an assembly line for their fellow workers since they not only slowed production but created safety problems. As a result, seasoned workers would "carry" the novices for a time, a brief time; but more often they would find ways, physical or psychological, to encourage the awkward offender to move along. Simone Weil was no doubt entirely aware of the pressure she was putting on others, and the pressures they were putting on her.

Yet such moments of grace passed quickly enough and a week later, she witnessed the kind of accident she had dismissed, earlier, as typical workers' gossip.

A woman's hair became caught in a machine. In an instant, the hair was taken up and a great patch of the woman's scalp was left raw. The accident occurred before noon, Simone Weil noted, and by afternoon the woman was back on her job, at the same machine. No one questioned what had happened, no one said a word. But in noticing this, Simone Weil noticed that she too had, imperceptibly, become part of the factory's rhythm and was torn, as were her co-workers, between two poles of behavior: the necessity workers feel to dull themselves to operations of mechanical repetition and to withdraw, using the least amount of mental or physical effort, and the conflicting necessity workers feel to remain constantly alert, and engaged, mentally and physically able to respond to unforeseeable but always possible error or danger. Exhausted by it all, her rate fell far too low and as a result, lay-off.

After a month of hunting for another job, running from one plant and one rumor to another, standing in the rain to be looked over, or passed by after a brief, humiliating appraisal, Simone Weil was hired on at Carnaud. This time her work card read "packer"; her job, in fact, was running a massive stamping press. Initially pleased, she quickly understood the crude logic behind her acceptance. The place was, in her words, "filthy, a very filthy workshop . . . a jail (frantic speedup, a profusion of cut fingers, layoffs without the slightest twinge of conscience)," and in spite of massive unemployment, few workers except the unskilled and most desperate would apply. Her foreman ("a very handsome fellow," she observed, "with an affable manner and voice") walked over to her after she had been working three-quarters of the shift, and said politely, "If you don't make eight hundred, I can't keep you on the job. If you make eight hundred in the two hours that are left, I would *agree perhaps* [his emphasis] to keep you on the job." And then he added, "Some of these workers do twelve hundred pieces." Enraged and determined, Simone Weil did her best, which kept her from being fired for a month.

Productivity was essential and no factory carried an "inefficient"

COLLEGE OF THE SEQUOIAS
LIBRARY

worker, so she pounded the pavements again. In June of 1935 she overheard someone saying that the man doing the hiring at the Renault plant was "swayed by the appearance of women workers and preferably those who were pretty." She had been there before, but borrowing some makeup from Simone Petrement (who relates the story), Simone Weil dutifully put "rouge on her lips and rose-colored makeup on her cheeks; she was transformed . . . this time, the clerk hired her without any difficulty." No one had invited her to join a picnic in the Luxembourg Gardens, however, and she was put on the afternoon shift running a milling machine (capable of doing enormous personal injury) and to the burns at Alsthom and the bruises at Carnaud, were added numerous lacerations: the end of her thumb was cut (nearly off), and metal shavings were driven into her hand and rapidly infected to become, as she worked, a painful abscess. The Vietnam veterans at Lordstown, Ohio, in the early 1970s may have worn their hair down to their shoulders and smoked dope as they misassembled the Vegas literally flying by, but it is doubtful whether their casual indifference insulated them, doubtful whether their experience differed much in kind from the tension, the pain, the indignities large and small, the fatigue *unredeemed* Simon Weil now knew day after day. In spite of her exhaustion from the work and the draining throb of her infection—and her own celebrated "mechanical inarticulateness"—she not only learned how to change and then to reset the cutter blade on her milling machine, but she was kept on past the thirty day trial period. Simone Weil was given "tenure" at the Renault works, where she remained until the school year began in the fall of 1935.

Two years would pass and she would be in Spain with the Anarchists, four years would pass and she would be attending the Easter services at the Benedictine monastery at Solesmes, and in another, she would be in Marseilles, several steps ahead of the Nazis who were occupying Paris. Five years later, Simone Weil would be meditating upon her voluntary choice of a winter, spring, and summer in those factories. During this period, she had become close to a Dominican, Father Perrin, and after all the questions she was raising about another mystery—Catholicism—

she was moved to ask him yet another favor. She needed to find work as a field hand, did the priest know of someone who would have her? Father Perrin did; some 150 miles to the north lived a farmer and lay philosopher by the name of Gustave Thibon. This man was deeply conservative, however, and had strong reservations about Jews, to say nothing of what he might think about radical Jews with strange ideas about a Christian God. Her earnestness must have moved Thibon, as evidenced from the first letter she wrote, saying, "I ardently wish to be able to do all that may be asked of me, without benefiting by any consideration. . . . I am not worrying about the consequences of the work."[15] And so it was "Yes," and Simone Weil moved to Saint-Marcel, in the Ardeche, and began working long days in Thibon's fields while studying and writing late into the night.

A touching friendship grew between them, a blend of mutual respect and affection, but her stay with the Thibon family was intended by her as only a way-station, "a few weeks," as Thibon writes, "in order to learn about the different kinds of agricultural work while she was waiting to become a real farm-hand under a large landowner of the district." Feeling the modest Thibon house "too comfortable," she "refused the room I was offering her and wanted at all costs to sleep out of doors." After no little vexation on Thibon's part, "a compromise" was reached. She agreed to stay in "a little half-ruined house" nearby, apart from the small amenities the Thibons might offer. Thibon initiated her to fieldwork while she provided instruction in Greek; together they read Plato and continued the discussions she had begun with Father Perrin. At the end of September 1941, Simone Weil became "weary," as Gustave Thibon put it, "of the 'fairy-tale' life she led with us, [and] joined a team of harvesters at Saint Julien de Peyrolas." There, from sunup to sundown, she bent over grapes, cultivated, picked, and cleaned grapes, until she came to exclaim that "Hell is a vineyard!"—not unlike our own United and un-United Farmworkers. And all the while she was doing this, she was pursuing her Greek, carefully reciting the Our Father, and

15. J. M. Perrin and G. Thibon, *Simone Weil As We Knew Her* (London: Routledge & Kegan Paul, 1953), p. 114.

poring over the great sacred texts of India and the wisdom literature of the Near East and the rest of Asia.

III   George Orwell was originally sent to Lancashire and Yorkshire by the 38,000-strong Left Book Club in order to report upon
the effects of the Depression in an industrial area, and the first
section of *The Road to Wigan Pier,* slightly more than half the
book, fulfilled the terms of his commission, more or less. The effects were everywhere, one could not help but see and feel and
smell them: homes are filthy and crowded, food is without nourishment and badly prepared, children play unattended and adults
find what work they can amid "the monstrous scenery of slag-
heaps, chimneys, piled scrap-iron, foul canals, paths of cindery
mud criss-crossed by the prints of cogs." The frustrated human
potential and the blasted human hopes are captured by an often-
cited passage, even more direct in Orwell's diary version:

Passed up a horrible side-alley, saw a woman, youngish but very pale
and with the usual draggled exhausted look, kneeling by gutter outside a house and poking a stick up a leaden waste-pipe, which was
blocked. I thought how dreadful a destiny it was to be kneeling in
the gutter in a back-alley in Wigan, in the bitter cold, prodding a
stick up a blocked drain. At that moment she looked up and caught
my eye, and her expression was as desolate as I have ever seen: it
struck me that she was thinking just the same thing as I was.

By documenting the devastation of social and personal life,
Orwell made a case not only for full employment but for the kind
of system—socialism—that would rationally plan for full employment, and for a great many other things, such as adequate
public housing, comprehensive health care, truly public schools
and, of course, strict industrial regulation that would prevent the
horrendous working conditions that led to the many injuries and
brutal deaths *The Road to Wigan Pier* made vivid. This was
strong medicine and fine, as far as it went. Yet even in passages
like the one just quoted, he went too far ("preoccupied," some
would say, with the *most* depressing aspects of working class life
when it was pushed to the edge), and unnecessarily provided am-

munition not only for the enemy, but invited severe criticism from his leftist sponsors as well.

Naturally the well-off would view George Orwell's account as "slumming," cheap, sensationalist stuff, or as "revolutionary intellectual dilettantism," more of that "proletarian cant." But in getting to know "the lowest of the low," as he put it, as well as what he called "the normal working class," hadn't Orwell documented the wrong ills, and in fact distorted the picture? What kind of socialist was it, who showed the future agents of social change so embittered and dispirited that they were indifferent to the conditions of their own environment? What kind of advertisement for socialism were Orwell's continual references to passivity, servility, and rank ignorance on the part of these workers, to the way they "smelled," or his tactless remark that around them, "one takes defilement for granted"? Leftists at their most charitable explained his pessimism as "excess," saw it as a purely personal reaction against his own middle-class social and educational background. "In trying to touch bottom," wrote Richard Hoggart, "Orwell most obviously was reacting against imperialism and against his own guilt as a former agent of imperialism."[16] Told he had given too much weight to the world of the outcasts, the lumpenproletariat instead of the proletariat, Orwell turned to criticism of those who *were* working, emphasizing their mindless consumerism while raising thorny questions concerning the lack

16. Richard Hoggart, "Introduction to *The Road to Wigan Pier*," in *George Orwell: A Collection of Critical Essays,* ed. Raymond Williams (Englewood Cliffs, N.J.: Prentice-Hall, Inc., 1974), p. 36. In addition to Hoggart's piece, this is an extremely useful collection, not least for the editor's thoughtful introduction and for his willingness to include views of Orwell divergent from his own. Williams is an independent Marxist up from the Welsh working class, currently resident at Jesus College, Cambridge. He speaks with a welcome authority on the issues of class privilege and political action; issues which contributors such as Lionel Trilling, E. P. Thompson, John Wain, Isaac Deutscher and Conor Cruise O'Brien join. Williams's own brief study, *Orwell,* in the Modern Masters Series (Viking Press, 1970), puts the case of Orwell's misuse by the Cold Warriors in a way Orwell himself would have respected. For a reply, see George Woodcock's review, "Half-Truths on Orwell," *Nation* (October 11, 1971), which, in its haste to argue Woodcock's position on Orwell, entirely misses Williams's.

of solidarity workers felt toward each other, the lack of opposition they directed against the ruling class of Great Britain. And Orwell, moreover, refused to engage the objection that his meeting with miners and arrangements for descent into the shafts were possible, after all, only because a network amongst the working class *was* a reality.

With the book's second section, leftist critics felt he showed his true colors, and they opened fire. There, the confused "liberal" rhetoric of George Orwell was revealed to be a cover for a clearly "reactionary" politics because, rather than continue with his somewhat flawed report, the author began a wild, mish-mash disquisition: part personal confession, part political diatribe; part jingo patriot speaking, part "soft" or "emotional" socialist speaking. For professional Leftists, someone like Victor Gollancz—who not only published Orwell but who had been one of the three Left Book Club members to send him North—it is difficult to say which part must have been the more disquieting. Orwell's acid characterization of the British Left as an amalgam of vegetarians sporting sandals and Talmudic Marxist intellectuals totally out of touch with the working class they purported to serve (and totally in touch with their own special interests) was outrageous. Intellectually insulting was his savaging of the principal tenet of the socialist creed—the idea of Progress—by treating it as only a secularized version of the worst of nineteenth-century Christianity, a badly-flawed successor *belief*. His drumming upon the class nature of modern society and class privilege, the corrupting effect of that privilege upon worker, manager, capitalist and intellectual, was so "obsessive" as to be personally offensive.[17] And his unyielding

17. Considering the position Orwell had put him in, Gollancz's Foreword to *The Road to Wigan Pier* was a restrained performance. Restraint departed, however, while Gollancz was toning down Orwell's class concerns, and Gollancz proved Orwell's case in the very act of arguing against it: ". . . Mr. Orwell embroiders the theme that, in the opinion of the middle class in general, the working class smells! I believe myself that Mr. Orwell is exaggerating violently: I do not myself think that more than a very small proportion of them have this quaint idea (I admit that I may be a bad judge of the question, for I am a Jew, and passed the years of my early boyhood in a fairly close Jewish community; and, among Jews of this type, class distinctions do not

skepticism about the superiority of "Socialist industrialism" over "capitalist industrialism" (Gollancz's phrases) and the absolute value he placed upon manual labor, were simply romantic notions, irrational and, worst of all, highly unscientific.

At bottom, what likely was most objectionable was the personal style in which Orwell wrote and the calculated uncomfortableness that arose whenever he said "I," and then, "you" or "we." *Self* was regarded as a vulgarity in the thirties; it was what modernist poets, for example, were trying to escape with their "masks" and "personae." So to generate a social analysis from a personal analysis, to insist upon an unbroken connection between subjective and objective experience, was to place one's own self at risk, and to threaten a great many intellectuals. Indeed, how much more could an intellectual risk than exposing the following about himself and, what was worse, by publishing it:

I was very young, not much more than six, when I first became aware of class distinctions. Before that age my chief heroes had generally been working-class people, because they always seemed to do such interesting things, such as being fishermen and blacksmiths and bricklayers. I remember the farm hands on a farm in Cornwall who used to let me ride on the drill when they were sowing turnips and would sometimes catch the ewes and milk them to give me a drink . . . and the plumber up the road with whose children I used to go out bird-nesting. But it was not long before I was forbidden to play with the plumbers' children; they were "common" and I was told to keep away from them.

Elsewhere, Orwell would question whether remaining "impersonal" allowed intellectuals of the Right and the Left to remain uncritical about industrialism and their own privilege with respect to it. He accomplished this by detailing the personal, not the corporate costs of mining coal; he told of his own ordinary hours in the darkness, damp, foul air, noise, confusion and the rapid, dangerous labor in unbearably cramped spaces. Then he mused aloud, "What different universes different people inhabit. . . . Here I am, sitting writing in front of my comfortable coal

exist [!] . . ." *The Road to Wigan Pier* [New York: Berkeley Medallion Books, 1967], p. x).

fire. It is April but I still need a fire. . . . It is only rarely, when I make a definite mental effort, that I connect this coal with that far-off labor in the mines." And remarking that there was a time when women, even pregnant women, worked as beasts of burden in those mines, concluded, "I fancy we should let them do it rather than deprive ourselves of coal. But most of the time, of course, we should prefer to forget that they were doing it. It is so with all types of manual labor; it keeps us alive, and we are oblivious of its existence."

That shift from the "I" of Orwell to the more inclusive "we" again, confronting the reader with what it meant to pay up personally; the costs from below, not above. He was aware that the mechanism that allowed "the privileged ones" (in Robert Coles's phrase) to forget about the work done for them by others, to remain oblivious to the complex structure of their privilege and its implications in terms of everyday benefits, was the function of an ideology; an unconscious program of "entitlement" formed in their minds from the day they were born.[18] He saw that one aspect of that ideology frequently surfaced as an assertion regarded as fact: those who do not have privilege do not have it for sound reasons, the chief one being that they are "lazy." The manual work George Orwell had experienced enabled him to discredit amply this assertion and to expose the self-serving nature of this ideology; *The Road to Wigan Pier* showed a society in which workers had no time to be idle since so many of their waking hours were taxed to the limit by the inconveniences and delays privilege allowed the upper classes to avoid. Comparing the socialism of Trotsky to that of Orwell in this respect, Dwight Macdonald wrote: "[Orwell] notes that when a miner leaves an elevator that takes him down into the mine, he must go through

18. The five volumes to date of Robert Coles's *Children of Crisis* series are extraordinary, among other things, for their demonstration that successful alliances between working-class people and professionals can be made on a principled basis. I have argued that his fifth volume, *Privileged Ones: The Well-Off and the Rich in America* (Boston: Atlantic-Little, Brown, 1977), is the most important inquiry into class yet to appear. See "The Plain Doctoring of Robert Coles," *The Catholic Worker*, March–April 1978.

one to three miles of twisting corridors, nearly always stooping and sometimes crawling. He notes that the miner is not paid for this journey, which may take an hour each way, the fiction being that it is the same as the office worker's journey to work on the bus." And on Orwell's ability to follow out the subtleties of privilege, he says, "This concern for the trivia of working-class life, which aren't so trivial if you are a worker, distinguishes Orwell's reporting [from Trotsky's theorizing]. Thus, it does not escape him that old miners don't get their pension checks in the mail but must report once a week to the colliery office, waiting in line for hours and wasting an afternoon—not to mention the sixpence for bus fare, a trifling sum unless one measures one's income in sixpences." By contrast, and anticipating Simone Weil, Orwell turned the (ethical) microscope upon himself:

It is very different for a member of the bourgeoisie, even such a down-at-heel member as I am. Even when I am on the verge of starvation I have certain rights attaching to my bourgeois status. I do not earn much more than a miner earns, but I do at least get it paid into my bank in a gentlemanly manner . . . this business of petty inconvenience and indignity, of being kept waiting about, of having to do everything at other people's convenience, is inherent in working-class life. A thousand influences constantly press a working man down into a *passive role*. He does not act, he is acted upon. He feels himself the slave of mysterious authority and has a firm conviction that "they" will never allow him to do this, that, and the other.[19]

But the most objectionable effect of George Orwell's personalism was that it threw into terrific doubt, ironically, what his critics most valued and thought was theirs exclusively, namely, intelligence. How intelligent was it, Orwell implied, to expect fundamental change to be had without sacrifice, moreover, to expect that someone other than the critics would be the ones sacrificing? "The high standard of life we enjoy in England," he wrote, "depends on our keeping a tight hold on Empire . . . to abolish class distinctions means abolishing a part of yourself."

19. All quotations are from "Trotsky, Orwell and Socialism" in Dwight Macdonald's *Discriminations: Essays and Afterthoughts, 1938–1974* (New York: Grossman Publishers, 1974).

And, "many people, however, imagine that they can abolish class-distinctions without making any uncomfortable change in their own habits and ideology." The very group that had prided itself upon its ability to locate deception was exposed by the man it had been criticizing as having been guilty of *self-deception*.

Upon her death in 1980, the *New York Times* reported that Dorothy Day had "opposed class politics," did not believe in "class struggle," and "did not seek the overthrow of capitalism and its network of property relationships." These statements present a deceptive picture to those unfamiliar with her. In truth, she had always been explicit about the fact that she, like George Orwell, sought "the lowest of the low," as much from a guilty awareness of the benefits she derived from her class privilege, as from the injunction in Matthew 25 that whatever is done "for the least of these," is done for Christ. The Catholic Worker Movement was directed toward the worker who is "systematically robbed of the wealth he produces" as an inevitable process of the society in which he labors. Although "we used the word in its broadest sense," she wrote in her autobiography, *The Long Loneliness* (1952), "meaning those who worked with hand and brain, those who did physical, mental or spiritual work, we thought primarily of the poor, the dispossessed, the exploited," that is to say, the most extreme victims of that process.

Should the *Times* reporter have asked victims of *what* process? he could have turned to the Catholic Worker "Positions," published from time to time by Dorothy Day, the first sentence of which reads that "the general aims" are nothing less than "realizing in the individual and in society the expressed and implied teachings of Christ." Now, just as few have ever seen who mines their coal much less where it is mined, few Christians, nominal or otherwise, have studied the teachings of Christ from the perspective of what they might cost to enact personally. So it is easy to see how one might walk away from the storefront on 36 East First Street with the impression that the poor are fed and the naked clothed in that part of the world, and in small towns and large cities other than New York, because a well-meaning old lady (who was once a firebreathing radical) turned to meek Jesus and with a rag-tag band of young volunteers, practiced the works of mercy, not in reaction to an oppressive system but rather, to assist a benevolent (but perpetually short-handed) welfare state.

Even the "Positions" themselves could be misleading, if one read only the first sentence of the first paragraph just quoted. Reading on, however, say the second sentence, one learns that our present society is to be "analyzed" by the Catholic Worker "to determine whether we already have an order that meets with the requirements of justice and charity in Christ." Needless to say, it does not pass muster, and the second paragraph is crisp on the classification and function of that society, which is "generally called capitalist, because of the method of producing wealth, and bourgeois, because of the prevailing mentality." The judgment is that it is not in accord with Christ's requirements because, in economics "the guiding principle is production for profit and because production determines need"; in psychology "capitalist society fails to take in the whole nature of man but rather regards him as an economic factor in production"; in morals "capitalism is maintained by class war." So technically, Dorothy Day did not *believe* in class struggle in the sense of approval, nor did she seek the order's overthrow, in anything like an active sense; she recognized the class nature of capitalist society as an objective reality, but her Catholic faith taught her that real or not it was wrong, and her experiences with workers and the dispossessed (whose condition inevitably proceeded, she believed, from that kind of society) persuaded her of the possibility of alternative social arrangements, both for production and for ownership. Overthrowing capitalist society was beside the point. In the light of the alternatives the Catholic Worker Movement posed, it would fall soon enough, and of its own sorry weight.

To achieve "a world in which it is easier for people to be good," as she would say, Dorothy Day pursued a program that she and her much older colleague and co-founder of the Catholic Worker, Peter Maurin, had evolved, and that continues to evolve. Self-educated, Peter Maurin possessed a determination Simone

Weil would have appreciated and although lacking anything like her academic sophistication, he would have been a source for her as he was for Dorothy Day, of the wisdom of which the Catholic Church is custodian. Having come from a peasant family in Southern France that could trace its origins a millennium and a half, he was entirely without shame before manual labor and he looked to these origins for his awareness of the spirituality of manual labor, especially as practiced in the fields. Well-rooted and well-read, Peter Maurin nevertheless had been neither crafts-man nor scholar (although he respected each as necessary and useful kinds of labor), but had spent his youth in service to the poor in the streets of Paris as a lay brother of a Catholic order, and had later travelled throughout Canada and the United States in the twenties as an unskilled laborer who knew at first-hand the uprootedness suffered by working men of all kinds and who him-self, "knew how to use an ax, a pick and shovel, how to break rocks and mend roads," as Dorothy Day recalls.

These two unlikely—some would say—collaborators enacted a program that had at its center three operational notions: the clarification of thought; houses of hospitality; and a green revolu-tion. The first was a short-hand way of saying that the issues they wished to engage—both theoretical and practical—had to be tested in thorough discussions in which any and all could partici-pate. Decisions were to be made by the entire community sitting together, Quaker style, and the right to obey was closely bound to the right to withdraw. Houses, whether urban soup kitchens and shelters or rural retreats and farms, had to be created where works of mercy could be performed in the course of which indi-vidual (not corporate), personal (not collectivist) commitments could be made and from which communities devoted to service would emerge. And the emphasis upon a return to the land, agrarian reform, was an attempt to strike a balance between manual and mental labor, radically to curb inflated needs by low-technology farming more congruent with life in human scale.

Running through the program were controversial (some would say contradictory or absurd) elements, including personalism, voluntary poverty, pacifism, anarchism, communitarianism, and a life centered on prayer and liturgy. Dorothy Day would part company, she said, those Leftists who held, with Lenin, that "atheism is an integral part of Marxism"; she would "admit to being fascinated by the lives of both Marx and Lenin," however, and warn that "there is an atheistic capitalism too, and an atheistic materialism which is more subtle and more deadly." And for those Christians who took Christ as a justification for the exploitation of others, she would say of their oppression, "we do not believe in violent revolution. Yet we do believe that it is better to revolt [citing the Cuban Revolution] than to do nothing." Adding, "we believe there must be new concepts of property," and that as far as possessions go, Peter Maurin had said, "there is a Christian communism and a Christian capitalism."

Dorothy Day's work experiences, her serving the sick and terminally ill as a nurse, and her religious convictions turned her to Christian Communism as embodied in the Catholic Worker Movement. As Hubert Jessup has noted, those convictions and that movement "did not signal an escape from the world so much as provide her with a *means* of encountering the world of injustice, suffering and meaninglessness." Haunted by the possibility of separation from God, she found her way by a path not dissimilar from Orwell's: by searching self-criticism and a life of service to others. Her deeply felt religious impulses found a home (though not without vexation and misgivings) in traditional Roman Catholicism, the same religious tradition that assisted Simone Weil in making sense of her working experiences but to which Simone Weil could not, as Dorothy Day did, submit herself. "Dorothy Day was able to create a Christian ethic," that was, according to Jessup,

based on the Church's sacraments and moral authority which would engage the evils of our capitalist-industrial-urban-mass society as well as providing an alternative that might convert that society, or at least individuals in it, to a way of life established by Christ Himself. To capitalism, The Catholic Worker offered a way of producing without exploiting; to socialism, The Catholic Worker offered an ethic that lifted man above his (often fratricidal) selfishness, based upon the sanctity of the individual; and to the Catholic Church itself The

Catholic Worker offered a challenge to live up to the ideals it preached, to stop sleeping with the powers and principalities of America, to become the enraged voice of the poor.[20]

Dorothy Day's critique of industrial society was neither poetic romanticism nor mindlessly antimachine so much as it was deep awareness of the hidden costs of a high technology society. Many an issue of *The Catholic Worker* noted how little has been heard of the massive land clearances in the old world and how very few have addressed the question as to whether, on balance, people feel more rather than less in control of their lives.

Workers have been horribly exploited in both locations, but on the land did they have to contend with greater crowding and personal alienation than in cities? Industrial society is also inherently harmful, she argued, because it requires unemployment as a condition of mass production and industrial profit requires that the earth's resources be aggressively exploited—what the Catholic Worker condemns as unfaithful stewardship. Shifting from social to personal costs, industrialism makes *more possible* the alienation of the worker from the product of his labor. With standardization and the cult of efficiency, labor loses its dignity and the separation of intellectual (and managerial and planning) labor from manual labor follows. The further division of labor encourages greater privileges for some workers than for others, discouraging community, and allowing the creation of artificial or false needs as compensations for this separation. Work, Peter Maurin believed, should be the expression of human value and result in the fulfillment of basic human needs but because of this process of industrialism, human value is stripped from the work as profit, and work and worker suffer unacknowledged but irreparable loss. Capitalism argues, by contrast, that Christ Himself said we would always have the poor with us (carefully distinguishing between the "deserving" and the "undeserving" or "lazy" poor), and that whatever minor outrages industrialism has

20. Hubert D. Jessup, "Dorothy Day and Simone Weil: The Fruits of Religious Conviction," in *Simone Weil: Live Like Her?*, ed. George Abbott White (Cambridge, Mass.: The Technology and Culture Seminar at the Massachusetts Institute of Technology, 1976).

wrought must be accepted as the price of Progress and human nature being what it is, Progress can not be attained without rewards in the form of substantial profits for those willing to take risks.

The work experiences that formed the ground of Dorothy Day's life along with the wisdom of the Church that informed those experiences, allowed her to reject both capitalist and Marxist positions as false; they were apologies for elite manipulation and centralized control of people's lives, all people's lives. She rejected their conception of human nature and human purpose (or human activity) as fundamentally naive because they were unbiblical (repudiating man as good-and-evil; capitalism choosing evil, Marxism good) and fundamentally ineffective because they were un-Christian (repudiating human forgiveness; capitalism choosing punishment, Marxism rehabilitation). According to Jessup, "While Marx wished to place the means of production in the hands of the workers [and while capitalism wished to place them in the hands of even fewer capitalists], the Catholic Worker would eliminate industrial production per se. It argues that *no* work within a divided and industrial context can be nonalienating. . . . The agrarian reform aspect assures the dignity of human labor by offering a concrete alternative to both Marxism and capitalism, and it places responsibility for work—for production, distribution and, by implication, for consumption—directly in the hands of those who work.

To the critics who insisted that the works of mercy were "a band-aid for cancer" or that the Catholic Worker program was fine for the Lower East Side or one or two small farms but not widely applicable, the response was immediate and to the point. "By establishing Houses of Hospitality," the Catholic Worker answered, "we can take care of as many of those in need as we can rather than turn them over to the impersonal 'charity' of the State. We do not do this in order to patch up the wrecks of the capitalist system but rather because there is always a shared responsibility in these things and the call to minister to our brother transcends any consideration of economics." As for the so-called larger picture,

We believe in a withdrawal from the capitalist system so far as each one is able to do so. Toward this end we favor the establishment of a Distributist economy wherein those who have a vocation to the land will work on the farms surrounding the village and those who have other vocations will work in the village itself. In this way we will have a decentralized economy which will dispense with the State as we know it and will be federationist in character as was society during certain periods that preceded the rise of national states.

Further, "We believe in worker-ownership of the means of production and distribution, as distinguished from nationalization. This is to be accomplished by decentralized co-operatives and the elimination of a distinct employer class. It is revolution from below and not (as political revolutions are) from above."

IV   "What did I gain from this experience [in the factories]?" Simone Weil wrote afterwards. And then continued, "The feeling that I do not possess any right, whatever it might be, to anything whatever. . . . The ability to be morally self-sufficient, to live without feeling inwardly humiliated in my own eyes. . . ."

Recalling what it had been like, she added, "I could have been shattered. I nearly was. . . . I arose each morning with anguish, I went to the factory with dread; I worked like a slave; the noonday interruption was like a laceration. . . . The fear—the dread—of what was to come never ceased oppressing me until Saturday afternoon and Sunday morning. And the object of this fear was the *orders.*" She had come to understand two things: the enterprise of manual labor, and the human enterprise, or the human condition. Like George Orwell and Dorothy Day, she learned that these enterprises were necessary and reciprocal but before we can appreciate her hard-won understanding, we must consider the *affliction* that, for Simone Weil, linked them, and her learning must be set within the context of what was already known by the people with whom she worked.

In her autobiographical letter to Father Perrin several years before the end of her life, she wrote:

After my year in the factory . . . I was, as it were, in pieces, body and soul. The contact with affliction had killed my youth. Until then

I had not had any experience of affliction, unless we count my own, which, as it was my own, seemed to me to have little importance, and which moreover was only a partial affliction, being biological and not social. I knew quite well that there was a great deal of affliction in the world, I was obsessed with the idea, but I had not had prolonged and first-hand experience of it. As I worked in the factory . . . the affliction of others entered into my flesh and soul. Nothing separated me from it, for I had really forgotten my past and I looked forward to no future, finding it difficult to imagine the possibility of surviving all the fatigue. What I went through there marked me in so lasting a manner that still today when any human being, whoever he may be and in whatever circumstances, speaks to me without brutality, I cannot help having the impression that there must be a mistake and that unfortunately the mistake will in all probability disappear. There I received the mark of slavery. . . . Since then I have always regarded myself as a slave.

A cruel but honest response would have to be that Simone Weil learned very little, in the sense that working people have known what she learned since the beginning of time. In his poem, "A Worker Reads History," Bertolt Brecht captures this by saying,

> Who built the seven gates of Thebes?
> The books are filled with the names of kings.
> Was it kings who hauled the craggy blocks of stone?

Working people have known to whom History awards credit from the time they were slaves doing another's labor so that a ruling class could rule without distraction, pursue philosophy, conspicuously consume, engage in games and sports, and amuse itself. Brecht again,

> Young Alexander conquered India.
> He alone?
> Caesar beat the Gauls.
> Was there not even a cook in his army?
> Philip of Spain wept as his fleet
> Was sunk and destroyed. Were there no other tears?

Working people know what this young intellectual came agonizingly to learn, in their tired muscles and aching bones, their

brown lungs and calcium-deficient teeth, their malformed or de-
formed or work-broken bodies. Brecht finally,

> Each page a victory.
> At whose expense the victory ball?
> Every ten years a great man,
> Who paid the piper?
>
> So many particulars.
> So many questions.

Yet in another sense Simone Weil learned a great deal because,
like George Orwell and Dorothy Day, she learned the particulars
by learning how properly to question her own experience. Now
she could become consciously obedient to the *necessity* intrinsic
to the human condition because she had become conscious of the
class distinctions that separated her from the common lot. And
she had become aware of the inadequacy of mind before the true
nature of a reality that encompassed spirit, by becoming aware of
the true, spiritual, nature of work itself. Her Platonism gained a
completeness its own conditions of origin had, paradoxically,
denied it.

There were many, many particulars. She learned of the chasm
that separated skilled from unskilled labor and she learned that
it mattered that workers were organized by distinct gradations
along a continuum from skilled to unskilled, paid separately according to gradation, and that labor practiced agriculturally differed in essential possibility from labor practiced industrially because the organic world's demands differed from those of the
machine's. Like Orwell, she came to see that the arrogance of
certain of her colleagues from the Left seriously undermined their
ability to organize workers, and that the theorizing of the elite,
even the most brilliant, lacked value because it lacked first-hand
experience, which kind those brilliant ones would think beneath
them or irrelevant to acquire. In one furious moment, she thun-
dered, "Only when I think that the great Bolshevik leaders proposed to *create* a free working class and that doubtless none of
them—certainly not Trotsky, and I don't think Lenin either—had
ever set foot inside a factory, so that they hadn't the faintest idea
of the real conditions that make for servitude or freedom for the

workers—well, politics appears to me a sinister farce." Was she furious with herself as well? Was she ashamed of the separations she had made between manual and mental labor? No matter, Simone Petrement recalled a conversation with Simone Weil on the changes that needed to be made, as a result of this new understanding: "One must find machines of a different kind [she recalled Simone Weil saying] than those that now exist, or in any case make a new study and appraisal of those that now exist, considering them not only in terms of their efficiency but also in terms of how much thought they permit or demand of the worker."

This was only a step from asking why factory workers did not appear to think, or certainly did not speak, about their condition. Robert Coles's work has shown us that what George Orwell learned about working people has remained depressingly consistent: working people in fact think a great deal but the conditions of class inhibit their speech, in the sense that working people have become self-censoring for lack of an audience beyond themselves. Their work had, as Simone Weil suggested, quite literally struck them *dumb;* like the frightened slave she had become, workers were taught they did not know how to speak of their slavery should society have granted them permission to speak in the first place.

Her account "Factory Work" appeared in *Politics* in December 1946. It opened with the hope that "conceivably a plant or a factory could fill the soul through with a powerful awareness of the collective," but went on, in piteous detail, to demonstrate why it did not, most fundamentally because the rhythm of the factory is set against human rhythm; machines are set against people. Machine rhythm does not admit irregularity or other than predetermined, hierarchical control. Once inside the plant, workers necessarily surrender outside ties and become discrete things commanded to perform specific tasks for specific periods of time. There is little sharing within this kind of organization, and the factory, to be efficient, must necessarily deny freedom of movement; in a hundred ways, large and small, *homo faber* is turned from the thinking *work* of a tool wielder to the unthinking *labor* of a machine tender following orders. Indeed, the orders that so distressed Simone Weil may well have done so because they actually excluded thought by design—the rationale being that it has already been done, by someone other than the worker.

After his period in the coal mines, George Orwell became dissatisfied with D. H. Lawrence's account of the same experiences. Lawrence had glorified the comradeship of suffering and the accomplishment below, making it more than it was; Orwell felt that experience as an end in itself—that or any other experience—was unacceptable, but until the end of his life he would continue to search for just what was acceptable. Living within the community of the Catholic Worker, Dorothy Day could know an acceptable end such that "we would accept dull work, and monotonous work, which was nevertheless useful work, as part of our human condition, necessary for the common good." Simone Weil would make the most penetrating formulation of just what it was that made the end acceptable by introducing into the equation "machine rhythm / man's rhythm" a third element, "God's rhythm."

Throughout her writings, Simone Weil stressed the individual and warns against collectivity. She goes so far at one point as to regard collectivity, after Plato and John of Patmos, as the Great Beast; perhaps her most devastating insight occurred in an essay that developed the parallels between the collectivity of Rome and that of Hitler's Germany. One can reconcile this extremely negative attitude with the attitude expressed at the beginning of her essay, "Factory Work," by wondering whether she rejected collectivity, in her time, because she understood, as George Orwell sensed and as Dorothy Day as a Catholic knew, that in a secular world such collectivities led to tyranny and individual oppression whereas in another, in a world where the example of Christ was operative, collectivities became communities that enabled not the reduction of individuals but their fulfillment.

Like Dorothy Day, Simone Weil admired certain aspects of medieval society, most especially the great cathedrals. This was less a regression to earlier, romanticized states of capitalism (the guild), than an admiration of collective efforts by individuals for ends beyond themselves. Put another way, the community that erected those glorious structures could be reconciled with the needs of individual craftsmen precisely because theirs was work that was not narrowly egocentric, but work that was lifted up to the glory of God. This, in turn, allowed the workers to transcend themselves and, ennobled, to be "gathered up," in Yeats's phrase, "into the artifice of eternity." Sending the intellectuals and the artists and the students into the Cuban cane fields and to the Chinese factories were attempts, perhaps, in this direction, but in Simone Weil's time and in ours, factories summon up no such transcendent ends, neither a common nor a spiritual good. They are dedicated, by contrast, to an immediate materialism that does not even focus upon the object being made, but on an impersonal third-party payment—cash or wages—that almost guarantees irresponsibility and shoddiness.

Hannah Arendt admired Simone Weil's *La condition ouvrière,* saying, "[it] is the only book in the huge literature on the labor question which deals with the problem without prejudice and sentimentality." In her own study, *The Human Condition* (1958), Arendt makes many useful arguments about the nature and purpose of human activity, not the least of which is the distinction between work and labor. It is a distinction, we learn, made by most languages, ancient and modern, and Hannah Arendt goes on to trace the historical development of this distinction from Greek and Roman times to our present. Her argument cannot be reproduced without injustice, but even the casual reader cannot avoid its affinity to what Simone Weil learned by doing—more properly titled, *factory labor.*

That is, factory workers are not workers in the sense that the word "work" has been understood in every age but our own. Factory workers are, as Hannah Arendt would have it, factory laborers because they do not make any *thing,* no memorable object, and because what they do make is a function of routine, rather than a function of human intent. Factory laborers perform actions that result in objects, to be certain, but objects that they do not see or if they do, see only the smallest fractions of; and even in this, they cannot easily discern the result of their action on the object before them. Some labor is of course unavoidable, it is necessary; many human services fall under this category of necessity and within the personal sphere, cleaning and caretaking are only the most common and clearly not the least important examples. But factory labor is more than necessity demands, so much more, Simone Weil labeled it *oppression* and rather than part of the human condition, held it to be understood economically as part of the inhuman condition of slavery and the function of a particular political system.

Because their lives paralleled their labor, divided to the smallest degree and subject to a false necessity, the existence of workers was thereby trivialized and their shame and withdrawal from efforts at change constituted an unconscious awareness, she believed, of that unredeemed state. She saw through the illusion, created from the top and the outside, of course, that workers were unfeeling and elastic, insensitive to great physical weariness. She pierced through it because she, like Orwell, experienced the bitter double-bind at first hand: again and again workers were "wounded" by industrial accidents, yet remained obedient to their understanding of necessity; a tacit agreement that workers were not to express their pain nor to share that pain with others. The structure of the factory world reinforced this agreement so that not only management or foremen would ignore them, but their fellow workers would taunt or humiliate them. (What's the matter, don't you like your work?) They, in turn, were expected to humiliate themselves by self-criticism for their lapse, for "weakening." ("Don't be a crybaby," they would tell themselves. "What did I expect from this job anyway? Who am I to expect anything?")

More than physical or psychological, this state had a dimension of spiritual weariness: in such situations, Simone Weil understood, workers hated more than their injuries or their work, they hated themselves. Self-hatred, misunderstood and suppressed, generated a terrible passivity.

A terrible rage accompanied it, just below the surface and occasionally breaking through in acts of industrial sabotage (in auto plants, for example, urinating in the paint, placing nuts and bolts where they would rattle, leaving parts out of engines) or in lashing out at fellow workers. Perhaps most terrible, however, was that the rage would generally be directed inward, against spouses and children, rather than outward, against foremen, managers, sellout unions and owners. While Simone Weil knew this to be true, it was George Orwell and Dorothy Day who detailed the domestic side of it and who concluded that these acts of violence issued from a core of meaninglessness.

Because the slaves rarely revolted, Simone Weil did not assume they had consented to their oppression. Closing her "Factory Work" essay, she had some thoughts, nothing so pretentious as solutions. They were not elaborate nor did they address working conditions only within industrial plants or shops; years later she would have more to say about work on the land. They were not couched in the fundamentalist Marxism-Leninism of the time (nothing about "point of production" or "surplus value," for example), nor in the buzzwords of the technocratic management engineers who were just emerging (nothing about "scientific management" or "worker input"), nor in the impenetrable abstractions of the industrial psychologist (nothing about "quantification of affect" or "authoritarianism"). She was unable to cast her suggestions into a language that was other than reciprocal, holistic and, ultimately, spiritual. "We must change the system concerning concentration of attention during working hours," she began,

the types of stimulants which make for the overcoming of laziness or exhaustion—and which at present are merely fear and extra pay—the type of obedience necessary, the far too small amount of initiative, skill and thought demanded of the workman, their present exclusion from any imaginative share in the work of the enterprise as a whole, their sometimes total ignorance of the value, social utility, and destination of the things they manufacture, and the complete divorce between working life and family life.

Here one sees seeds for the best of the "worker control" movement in Europe and America, the attempts at teamwork assembly and worker-management production groups. Intimated are what we have come to see as the rotation of workers from job to job within plants as a matter of free choice or the arbitration of disputes of all kinds, at all levels of production, including on the assembly line itself. "The list," as she prophetically stated, "could well be extended," but at the time she met with hostility and indifference, if not silence. Her socialist colleagues pulled

back, the technocrats judged her "soft" and "unrealistic," and her
sophisticated, cultured, liberal friends—safe in their research institutes, government agencies, the academy, or writing careers
(where, after all, one could be a little speculative by definition)—
smiled but worried privately, where this interest of hers in God
would lead.[21] Dwight Macdonald, editor of the World War II
American magazine that featured half a dozen of her essays, ap-
pended a note to her essay on work, in effect apologizing for her;
anyone who addressed solutions about alienated labor to the
bosses as well as the workers had to be living in another world.

Perhaps she was, and speaking to this one, but she was certain
that nothing would change more than cosmetically until labor
was once again in contact with deeply-felt emotions about labor
(an unrealistic notion held by Freud), until labor was once again
in contact with the most serious kind of thought (an unrealistic
notion held by Marx), until labor was seen as something more
than an end in itself. Those who purported to understand Freud
would restrict their clinical services to the articulate, privileged
ones who were motivated and who could, after all, pay. Or they
would sell their services to those in business or industry to enable
the managers to manage more efficiently. Those who purported
to understand Marx or who saw themselves as practitioners of
Marxism-Leninism were, by definition, largely unaware of their
own privilege and would change very little; Simone Weil had
seen them use Marx as a club with their critics, as a carrot-and-
stick with managers, and as a honey pot with the workers they
patronized. A new bureaucracy had been substituted for the old
one while the theorists pulled the strings or justified the operation. Their promise that one day, perhaps soon, workers would

21. Simone Weil's desire for the Absolute seems to have had its roots
in her childhood, as both Jacques Cabaud and Simone Petrement have,
in different ways, demonstrated. While organizing with the trade unionists in the late 1920s and early 1930s, Simone Weil was critical of
"God-language" and only with her essay, "Factory Work," does an
intimation that this language might be conceptually valid, appear. She
traces her own religious course vividly in her autobiographical letters
to Father Perrin, published as *Attente de Dieu* (1950), and *Waiting on
God* (1951). See especially, Letters 3–6.

run this new bureaucracy, left Simone Weil unimpressed. Profit might be gone, the word "capital" might have vanished, but she suspected that power remained. As an intellectual, she was not persuaded by the idea that more machines would equal more freedom, as though machines would manufacture the good, allowing human beings to escape necessity. Indeed, she saw this promised escape from necessity as the most dangerous Marxist illusion. She felt that the degree to which whole societies attempted to enact it would be the degree to which they would approach a very busy unfreedom.

V Simone Weil had been taught to separate manual work from mental work. In her time and class, it could hardly have been otherwise but in a profound sense, which she came to understand after much struggle, she was deprived by what she had been taught. A gap not only separated her from the great mass of working people, it separated her from a great portion of herself. Of this (potential) self she discovered, she wrote a student toward the end of her factory experiences,

Although I suffer from it all, I am more glad than I can say to be where I am. . . . After all, I feel I have escaped from the world of abstractions, to find myself among real men—some good and some bad, but with a real goodness or a real badness. Goodness, especially when it exists in a factory, is something real: because the least act of kindness, from a mere smile to some little service, calls for a victory over fatigue and the obsession with pay and all the overwhelming influence which drive a man in upon himself. And thought, too, calls for an almost miraculous effort of rising above the conditions of one's life.

Her splendid intellectual training and her protected personal background had provided her with the expectation of attention and the kinds of defenses that, in the vast world of working people, were self-limiting. Necessity pierced this privileged state,

What working in a factory meant for me [she wrote] was that all the external reasons (which I had previously thought internal) upon which my sense of personal dignity, my self-respect, was based, were radically destroyed within two or three weeks by the daily experience of brutal constraint. And don't imagine that this provoked in me any rebellious reaction. No, on the contrary; it produced the last thing I expected from myself—docility. The resigned docility of a beast of burden.

Gustave Thibon has written, "She wanted first to become empty of self by giving herself entirely to work—to find out from experience what soul and thought become in a being whose time and strength are ceaselessly used up by hard obligatory labor." "I want my time and the current of my thoughts," she wrote to Thibon,

in so far as they depend upon my body, to be subjected to the same necessities as those which weigh upon no matter what farm-hand— that is to say: weariness and the compulsory task. . . . I think that intellectual culture, far from giving a right to privileges, constitutes in itself a privilege which is almost frightening and which involves terrible responsibilities per contra. . . . I want to prove to myself that I think this way by shouldering, for a time at any rate, a burden such as those who have no share in this privilege have to bear all their lives.

Simone Weil became a beast and suffered the humiliation that, as Dorothy Day has written many times, working people know and suffer every day of their lives. They suffer it, moreover, knowing full well that for them there is no escape, no "for a time at any rate." Working people are denied the address to write for money to (which George Orwell had when he was entering the world of the London tramp), they lack the sympathy and support of concerned and able parents (which Simone Weil had until 1942, when she left New York for wartime London, alone). They lack professional careers to fall back upon, trust funds or stock incomes to tide them over economic dislocations, and no "connections" or old boy networks exist in their worlds.

Yet what moved Simone Weil most by her work experiences was not discovering necessity for herself, but seeing that the conditions of modern industrial society had increasingly turned everyone, in a subtle but relentlessly machinelike way, into slaves. Everyone was destined to become a machine tender, as George

Orwell well knew; everyone was obedient at that moment to a false necessity even as they, intellectuals like Dwight Macdonald included, believed only themselves to be free. This was indisputably the case because the structures of slavery had unconsciously become part of modern society. The old hierarchy of slave holders and slaves had become transformed into the new hierarchy of owners, experts and workers. And if the factories ruthlessly subdivided labor into micro-actions, what was one to make of the universities and research institutes where professors reduced smaller and smaller realms into thicker and less comprehensible books with denser and denser non-public lexicons?[22] If advancing mechanization—always in the name of greater freedom—had alienated factory workers and field workers from natural processes while substituting a false necessity, this had its parallel in the intellectual realm. Marxian or capitalist or whatever, that regarded human beings as bundles of impulses— quantifiable, predictable, infinitely manipulable—with no inalienable rights other than those determined by the expert or leader of the moment, and with no intrinsic purpose other than that determined by the State. Given such a situation, Simone Weil felt it made no sense whatsoever to call one system socialist or capitalist, when both were megamachine states going about the business of being more efficient, that is to say, more fully rationalized, megamachine states. Or for that matter, no sense to call one laborer an assembly line worker, and another laborer a nuclear physicist or doctor. Each system, she wrote, whether macro or micro, had as its end not human beings and some transcendent,

22. It is worth noting that Dorothy Day and George Orwell elected to use a plain style and an unspecialized vocabulary both in describing their experiences and in making sense of them. Each noted parallels between the clichés, willful confusions, and Newspeak of officialdom, and the often sinister operations that soon followed on the heels of such state communications—Orwell, particularly in novels such as *Animal Farm* and *1984,* and his celebrated essay, "Politics and the English Language," and Dorothy Day in the columns of *The Catholic Worker.* Simone Weil also aimed at simple language and direct expression, as her brother has remarked, the only difference being the fact that she engaged her experience at a more explicitly philosophical level of interrogation and in a more consistently philosophical level of analysis.

ultimate end, but a series of figures and a finitude that pretended the infinite and called it Progress; justifying this Progress, because it was rational.

Simone Weil may have been at her most penetrating as to what all this meant, when she wrote about her beloved *Iliad*—a text that engaged her entire being. She saw as the central flaw in Homer's poem that men appeared governed by what to them was necessity. Their behavior was directed by gods and by certain values that went unquestioned because they had been part of a long tradition, values such as bravery, honor, courage, and loyalty. Her reading of the poem convinced her that whatever glory the warriors may be said to have achieved was riddled by illusion, since no one in the poem had questioned the end of his actions and everyone in the poem had submitted, was bound and enslaved in her judgment, by a false necessity which she called *force*. The brutal actions that Ajax and Hector performed were not wrong, for example, because Ajax and Hector were immoral men. They were wrong because what each submitted to was not true necessity. In their unquestioning obedience, they offered up their lives and the lives of their posterity . . . to false gods and false values. She judged those Homeric heroes harshly in seeing them as slaves as, it seems, she would see us today. Who can deny the many false gods we serve?

Her solution, which was at once personal and public, Dorothy Day quoted in a letter she sent *Catholic Worker* subscribers, begging for funds. "Simone Weil does not talk of penance," wrote Dorothy Day, "she does not cry out against self indulgence. She says 'Renounce!' " For George Orwell, this imperative took the form of manual labor he engaged in and manual labor he observed, which allowed him to describe class privilege and which allowed him, through his writing, to share his descriptions with others. By choosing voluntary poverty and becoming a caretaker of the least privileged, Dorothy Day attempted to renounce, in Simone Weil's phrase, "all compensations." Where both described suffering and devoted themselves to what relief could be provided, Simone Weil chose to identify, physically and mentally, with those who suffered as well as to analyze the conditions that caused such suffering, whether temporal or eternal. Where George

Orwell and Dorothy Day countered the system of oppression, Simone Weil entered its jaws and spoke of necessity from the belly of the beast. Such radical, exemplary actions are beyond all but a few. Perhaps the greatest fear, the last thing that holds us back, is the fear that having taken Simone Weil to heart and having renounced everything, we ourselves will be left with nothing. Gustave Thibon plumbed this uncertainty by placing it within the framework of Christian paradox, the losing of one's life in order to save it. He said of Simone Weil, "She hoped—since emptiness attracts plenitude—that earth and nature, to which she wanted to give herself completely, would perhaps give themselves to her in return and, when she was at the extreme point of physical weariness which suspends the activities of the self, would allow her to taste their deep and ineffable reality." In confirmation of this, he quoted from a letter she wrote to him in which she said,

Perhaps it may be given to me, at least for a few moments, to receive the reward attached to work on the land and to none other, the feeling that the earth, the sun, the landscape really exist and are something more than mere scenery. This sense of reality, though it only lasts for a second, amply repays days and days of the bitterest fatigue and, to judge from my own experience, it is only granted when one has been working. But I do not allow myself to desire this, and scarcely even to think of it; for the earth only surrenders to those who have a claim . . . to those who have given their lives. . . .

Simone Weil's Bibliography:
Some Reflections
on Publishing and Criticism

✷

GEORGE ABBOTT WHITE

Any description of Simone Weil's writings as a whole must first engage one stubborn fact: no book by Simone Weil was published in her lifetime.

But had she lived longer than her thirty-four years, it is doubtful a book of hers would have been published, at least nothing resembling a lengthy elaborated study.[1] Simone Weil's mind was neither fragmentary nor disassociative; it was unintimidated by scholarship and wholly aware of specialized sources, and as an act of sheer will she likely could have written such a book. The thrust of her mind, however, may be said to have been other— more toward raising questions than providing answers.

Questions are necessarily briefer than the answers they attempt to provoke, and, on the whole, they play against already existing problems, situations, personalities, or texts. This interrogatory stance is not unique to Simone Weil. It is also characteristic of the modern sensibility, though a fundamental difference may be seen on the level of structure. If we compare the two we will see that while moderns gave way to questions and accepted fragments of truth because their world had given way to the imperative of popularized notions of "relativity," Simone Weil subjected the world to questions as a way of re-establishing a route back to classical first principles, the unitary truth of which she never

1. It might be argued that *The Need for Roots* was not only published as a book but conceived as one. Simone Weil felt otherwise, and not from any false modesty; she spoke of it as only "a draft" and in any event, as its spare and often eliptical nature suggests, her aim was to produce an outline intended to engender a programmatic discussion.

doubted, much as she felt them obscured by most of modern life.

This accounts for the uneasy situation where the books we know Simone Weil by are not books as such but collections of shorter forms—essays or letters—or compilations of materials that, at a glance, appear somewhat confusing when assembled together: journal entries, essay fragments, statements, book reviews, articles. Their meaning becomes more of a piece when they are viewed as part of a questioning process rather than as the ends of such a process. That these collections and compilations were themselves gathered from disparate sources—trade union pamphlets to literary magazines to left journals—may argue in support of Simone Weil's judgment of books, in her time, as premature or misleading forms. Equally plausible, such variety may be said to have demonstrated how far she would range in her search for truth as surely as it demonstrated her utter disregard for where truth might be found. Like Whitman, she recognized the profound in the mundane, in the rankest soil of whatever vineyard she happened to be working at that moment.

In the last letter she wrote to Father Perrin, Simone Weil asked the Dominican to turn from any consideration of her as a person, to what she had written. And in a letter to her parents, just before her death, she expressed a certain annoyance with those who praised ("eulogized," she wrote) her for her "intelligence" instead of asking whether what she had thought was true.

In the world of intellectual discourse, as in the world of social relations, truth is shaped by the way in which it is presented. Susan Sontag did not discover this, but she has been the critic who has most perceptively observed what "packaging" has meant for the truth in Simone Weil, since collections and compilations require not only editors to select and then to organize, but editors to title and to introduce, or to invite introductions.[2] Speaking at

2. Translations and translators are another matter. As the correspondence between Andre Weil and Sir Richard Rees—Simone Weil's brother and her most able and most attentive editor—illustrates, questions of selection, translation, entitlement, and grouping have quite naturally attended the posthumous publication of Simone Weil's works from the beginning. And until the Andre Weil-Rees collaboration, her work has not always been

a Princeton University symposium in 1978, Sontag reminded her audience that Simone Weil's earliest publication in English had been less than three years after her death and before the end of World War II, in Dwight Macdonald's *Politics* magazine with the essay entitled "Reflections on War" (February 1945), followed by four more powerful essays in as many years: "The *Iliad,* or The Poem of Force" (November 1945); "Words and War" (March 1946); "Factory Work" (December 1946); "What is a Jew? A Letter to a Minister of Education" (Winter 1949). Celebrated for its imagination and for its moral force, the imprint of *Politics* was nevertheless not decisive. "For in 1952," continued Sontag, *"The Need for Roots* appeared with a preface by none other than T. S. Eliot. In that dim and distant era, *anything* that had a preface by T. S. Eliot commanded attention; he was the 'king' of letters, the most famous literary figure, whose influence was enormous. . . . First Simone Weil was launched by Macdonald's left, anarchist-leaning *Politics,* then, only a few years later, under the auspices of the royalist, Anglican-conservative Eliot." Clearly, introductions mattered because, as a result, "people thought of her as a very original kind of Catholic mystic" and therefore, "the tendency was to interpret everything [of Simone Weil's] from a religious perspective."

How much of Simone Weil's reputation, how much of the reading done of her work was in the light of T. S. Eliot's introduction, and how much was due to what it was of hers that was assembled and actually published, are important issues for future critics to assess. (I will avoid for now, of course, the similarly difficult issues of what the publishers wanted, what the publishers assumed the public wanted, and what the public might have wanted had it known what might have been available.) What can be agreed to from a reading of the early list of publication in French is that while it was her "religious" side that was initially put forward, especially with *La pesanteur et la grace* (1947) and *Attente de Dieu* (1950), the more overtly "political" collections quickly followed, as was the case with *La condition ouvrière* (1951) and *Oppression et liberté* (1953):

---

served as well as it might—certainly not from the standpoint of appropriate grouping and felicitous translation.

La pesanteur et la grace. Preface by G. Thibon. Plon, 1947.
L'Enracinement. Gallimard, 1949.
Attente de Dieu. LaColombe, 1950.
La connaissance surnaturelle. Gallimard, 1950.
Cahiers I. Plon, 1951.
Intuitions prechretiennes. LaColombe, 1951.
La condition ouvrière. Gallimard, 1951.
Lettre à un Religieux. Gallimard, 1951.
Cahiers II. Plon, 1953.
La source grecque. Gallimard, 1953.
Oppression et liberté. Gallimard, 1953.
Venise sauvée. Gallimard, 1955.
Cahiers III. Plon, 1956.
Ecrits de Londres et dernières lettres. Gallimard, 1957.
Leçons de philosophie de Simone Weil. With a memoir on SW as
    teacher by Mme. Reynauld-Guerithault. Plon, 1959.
Ecrits historiques et politiques. Gallimard, 1960.
Pensées sans ordre concernant l'amour de Dieu. Gallimard, 1962.
Poèms. Gallimard, 1968.

Nothing like balance, much less the French completeness, has
attended English-language publication. Indeed, Simone Weil's
work has been published not only in a far more piecemeal fashion
in English, but in a chronologically awkward fashion, as Lawrence Cunningham suggested in a helpful *Cross Currents* article saying:*"Waiting for God,* published in 1951 (New York:
Putnam), was the first introduction to the thought of Simone
Weil for the English-speaking world [Cunningham refers to
published books]. This may have been somewhat misleading,
since it focused the attention of critics on writings most of which
were composed in her last years, often with no view to publication." Moreover, he wrote, "This may explain a certain diffidence
that one detects in the response of Catholic critics. *Gravity and
Grace* (New York: Putnam, 1952) appeared next and also rep-
resents the later part of her career." Mr. Cunningham's "Simone
Weil: A Selective Bibliography" (Spring 1973) mentioned
T. S. Eliot's introduction to *The Need for Roots* but without
sensing what Ms. Sontag did. He neglected the English-language
publications picture until the rich spate of Rees translations and

editions appeared, beginning in 1962 with the *Selected Essays,* though Sir Richard had translated some of Simone Weil's work for *Brave Men: A Study of D. H. Lawrence and Simone Weil* (1958), and he had translated and edited the *Selected Essays* in 1962.

It is also worth noting that although *Oppression and Liberty* was published in England in 1958, it was not until well after the New Left had read and widely quoted a far less enlightening critic on similar issues, Herbert Marcuse, that the book appeared in the United States, in 1973. A survey of the English-language publications of Simone Weil's work will demonstrate a number of other points, among them the understandable though important delays between English and American editions, and the not-so-understandable fact that *La condition ouvrière* has never been translated into English even though it was the sixth volume to be published in France, and does much toward focusing Simone Weil's work experiences. The many-million English and American trade unionists were thereby denied an important text, to say nothing of the English-speaking New Left with its resurgent Marxist-Leninist emphasis upon the working class.

Waiting on God. London: Routledge & Kegan Paul, 1951; *Waiting for God.* Preface by Leslie A. Fiedler. New York: Putnam's Sons, 1951. Paperback, England and United States, 1959. Emma Craufurd translated all editions.

Gravity and Grace. Preface by Gustave Thibon. Translated by Emma Craufurd. London: Routledge & Kegan Paul, 1952. Translated by Arthur F. Wills. New York: Putnam's Sons, 1952.

The Need for Roots. Preface by T. S. Eliot. Translated by Arthur F. Wills. London: Routledge & Kegan Paul, 1952; New York: Putnam's Sons, 1953. Paperback, Boston: Beacon Press, 1955; New York: Harper Colophon, 1971.

Letter to a Priest. Translated by Arthur F. Wills. London: Routledge & Kegan Paul; New York: Putnam's Sons, 1953.

The Notebooks of Simone Weil. Translated by Arthur F. Wills. London: Routledge & Kegan Paul; New York: Putnam's Sons, 1956.

Intimations of Christianity. Translated by Elizabeth Chase Geiss-buhler. London: Routledge & Kegan Paul, 1957.

Oppression and Liberty. Translated by Arthur F. Wills and John Petrie. London: Routledge & Kegan Paul, 1958; Amherst: University of Massachusetts Press, 1973. Paperback, Amherst: University of Massachusetts Press, 1977.

Selected Essays: 1934–1943. Edited, translated, and with a preface by Richard Rees. London: Oxford University Press, 1962.

Seventy Letters. Edited, translated, and with a preface by Richard Rees. London: Oxford University Press, 1965.

On Science, Necessity and the Love of God. Edited, translated, and with a preface by Richard Rees. London, New York, Toronto: Oxford University Press, 1968.

First and Last Notebooks. Translated, edited, and with a preface by Richard Rees. London, New York, Toronto: Oxford University Press, 1970.

The Simone Weil Reader. Edited, with an introduction, chronology, prefaces before sections, reference notes, and selected bibliography by George A. Panichas. New York: David McKay, 1977. Paperback, New York: David McKay, 1977.

Simone Weil: Lectures on Philosophy. Introductions by Peter Winch and Anne Reynauld-Guerithault. Translated by Hugh Price. London, New York: Cambridge University Press, 1978. Simultaneous paperback.

II. The Projected Complete Edition   Twenty years ago Sir Richard Rees was writing to Andre Weil, sympathizing with him about "the difficulties of getting your sister's writings organized." Sir Richard had been an executor of George Orwell's literary estate and also had lived through the dislocation and chaos of a world war. He was well aware of what flight from the Nazis to America had forced upon Simone Weil and upon her family, not only in personal terms, but in terms of locating and assembling her work. Even without the war, Sir Richard believed complications and difficulties inevitable when dealing with anything as complex as an author's estate, and he knew that the relationship between large amounts of unpublished material and pieces already in print, as was the case with Simone Weil's work, could not make matters any easier.

Additionally, Sir Richard was reacting to what he took to be obvious disagreements in the actual handling of Simone Weil's writings after her death, disagreements that made impossible a comprehensive plan of publication, based upon a "catalogue raisonne" of her manuscripts. Readers other than he had commented upon what amounted to rival publications from competing French publishing houses, where principles of organization and editorial involvement differed markedly.

But in translating and assembling her work for English-language publication, Sir Richard was to encounter difficulties of his own, not least with his publishers—Oxford University Press in London—and their "religious books editor," as Sir Richard put it. This person, he wrote to Andre Weil, "with typical religious unscrupulousness, wanted to present your sister as a sort of Student Christian Movement Group Leader." Nothing in Sir Richard's character made him unappreciative of the religious dimension in Simone Weil's work. His primary concern, however, was that this dimension, or any other dimension, be appropriately presented in terms of the particular materials an editor selected. Speaking of his work with her essays in 1963, "The ideal thing," he wrote to Andre Weil, "would be to make a coherent collection of the most important essays." "Coherence," then, was the operant value.

Having completed *Selected Essays: 1934–1943* (1962), Sir Richard turned to a collection of Simone Weil's letters. With an eye toward the future, he saw his present task of locating her letters in English-language publications as "a definite step towards the complete collection which will no doubt be made someday." It was in the course of putting together *Seventy Letters* that Sir Richard observed discrepancies in the French editions. ("I had noticed," he wrote to Andre Weil, "that there was some repetition in the letters [of Simone Weil] to you." He continued, "I think your mother does not always distinguish between drafts and letters that were actually sent.") This appears to have resulted in his actually increasing his concern with discrepancies, omissions, and possible misrepresentations of his own. Writing to Andre Weil a year later about his essay, *Simone Weil: A Sketch for a Portrait* (1966), Sir Richard said: "If you should happen to notice any place where I seem to have betrayed one of her ideas by presenting it inadequately or incompletely, I would be glad to know." He continued, "If there are too many such places, I shall not publish the book, as it would do more harm than good." His conclusion aptly underscored his aim: "On the other hand, if it *is* publishable it will be almost the only study of her that avoids a sickly religiosity."

Each of Sir Richard's four editions as well as his two critical studies of Simone Weil were well received, and these examples of high standards alongside the increasing critical attention directed toward her and her work could only encourage the formation of a larger, more sophisticated audience appreciative of the value of a complete edition done with similar attentiveness and evenhandedness.

Writing to me in late November 1980, Andre Weil said, "Any statement about the projected complete edition of my sister's writings would be premature." However, "What can be said is the following:

A team, jointly sponsored by the Bibliotheque Nationale in Paris and by the Centre National de la Recherche Scientifique, is at present at work on Simone Weil's manuscripts, published and unpublished, and on her correspondence. It is hoped that this may eventually lead to a full publication of her complete writings. In the meanwhile, her manuscripts are on deposit at the Bibliotheque Nationale, and a complete microfilm is on deposit at the Institute for Advanced Study, Princeton, New Jersey.

Professor Weil held out the hope that, "perhaps, within a year or two, one will be able to say more."

III. Simone Weil in Print The apogee for the availability of Simone Weil's writings likely occurred between 1976 and 1977. At this point, the publication of Simone Petrement's biography of Simone Weil in an attractive one-volume English edition focused interest that had been growing for many years, while at the same time much, if not most, of Sir Richard Rees's later collections remained in print from the Oxford University Press, and even *Selected Essays: 1934–1943* (1962) or the earlier Arthur

Wills's translation of *The Notebooks of Simone Weil* (1956), in two volumes, might be located in a good used bookshop. Within a year or so, however, an ironic situation had developed. Interest in Simone Weil encouraged the reprinting of paperbacks such as *Waiting for God* and *The Need for Roots,* the publishing of a new collection, *The Simone Weil Reader* (1977) in hardcover and paperback editions, and the translation into English of the *Lectures on Philosophy,* which became available in hardcover and paperback in 1978. But interest was not strong enough to keep by-now exhausted Rees collections from going out of print, or to support making those collections, or *Gravity and Grace,* available in paperback. *Oppression and Liberty* was put into paperback in 1977 as was Petrement's biography, but by the end of 1980, less of Simone Weil's writings were in print than at any time during the previous decade.

As of December 1980, *Gravity and Grace* and *The Need for Roots* were available in hardcover reprint (Octagon Press), and the following were available in paperback: *Gateway to God, Lectures on Philosophy, Oppression and Liberty, The Simone Weil Reader, Waiting for God.*

IV. Biographical Material on Simone Weil   Two major biographies of Simone Weil exist, as do a number of specialized studies. Jacques Cabaud, *Simone Weil: A Fellowship in Love* (London: Harvill, 1964; New York: Channel Press, 1965) appeared first, and it is regrettable that Cabaud's later research, which resulted in a second book on Simone Weil's last years, *Simone Weil à New York et à Londres* (Paris: Plon, 1967), was never translated into English. Simone Petrement's *Simone Weil: A Life* (Paris, Plon, 1973; New York: Pantheon, 1976), which appeared some time later, not only had the advantage of greater perspective, but of important personal material that surfaced with the passage of time.

Yet each study has its advantage. Cabaud's has the immediacy of the discoverer and the certain distance of the outsider; his photographs of Simone Weil and the places she lived or worked are superb, and more New York and London interviews make their way into his life of Simone Weil than into Simone Petrement's. On the other hand, though each tends to description and—at times—dreary catalog or summary of writing, Simone Petrement shows the greater political awareness, and her portrait of Simone Weil's relations with family, friends, colleagues, and opponents shows more complexity and—at times—more humor. Indeed, it is this latter element, in all its deft and ironic quality, that the reader will easily miss without a biographer's sensitive re-creation.

These two biographies may be supplemented by a half dozen other studies of varying length. One can deepen Cabaud's perspective, for example, with the very interesting memoir by her two closest friends from what Lawrence Cunningham calls her "Catholic" days, Joseph Marie Perrin, the Dominican priest of Marseilles with whom she had some of her most intense religious discussions, and Gustave Thibon, the farmer and lay theologian to whom she was sent by Father Perrin in answer to her request for an opportunity to labor in the Ardeche vineyards: J. M. Perrin and Gustave Thibon, *Simone Weil As We Knew Her* (London and New York: Routledge & Kegan Paul, 1953). Gustave Thibon speaks with a sharpness and a directness about his time with Simone Weil that, by comparison with the halo others have put about her, is refreshing.

Similar common sense may be found on nearly every page of E. W. F. Tomlin's sixty-two page essay, *Simone Weil* (New Haven: Yale University Press, 1954). Tomlin deals with thorny political and religious issues from a consistent psychological perspective; he separates truth from hearsay and misconception, and his intellectual sorting is crisp but just. ("Mysticism," he writes, "the 'glamour' of the spirit, always enjoys a good press" and "Much of *The Need for Roots* consists of demolition work. All the old nostrums are challenged. . . .")

Sir Richard Rees, whose superb translations have been discussed above, also made two studies—one an essentially literary comparison, the other more critical-biographical. *Brave Men: A Study of D. H. Lawrence and Simone Weil* (Carbondale: Southern Illinois University Press, 1958) is thoughtful, but Simone

Weil, who found D. H. Lawrence "completely uninteresting," would not have been pleased by the comparison. Another story altogether is his *Simone Weil: A Sketch for a Portrait* (Carbondale: Southern Illinois University Press, 1966). Written with his friend George Orwell's eye for apt detail (e.g., Sir Richard notes that Mrs. Francis, Simone Weil's landlady of three months at Holland Park, "travelled from London to Ashford [Kent] to attend the funeral"—no small distance, or inconvenience, during wartime), it also has an unsparing but ultimately committed response to the political dimension in Simone Weil's life. Thus Sir Richard's reading of the religious in light of the political is the most penetrating of any of her critics'.

The Rev. David Anderson's overview, *Simone Weil* (London: SCM Press, Ltd, 1971) is spare in style, about twice as long as E. W. F. Tomlin's, but on the whole the very best brief introduction to her life and work. To it might be added the account of Simone Weil's teaching in a provincial lycée, by a former student, which serves as one of the introductions to *Simone Weil: Lectures on Philosophy* (1978). Other studies, especially those on Simone Weil's "mysticism," strike this writer as mystifying and tedious, and to be avoided by those who wish to retain either their respect for religious experience or their sense of appropriate "awe" before the absolute.

V. Critical Commentary on Simone Weil A surprising amount of tedious and highly inaccurate things have been written about Simone Weil. The following is an alphabetical attempt to sort the wheat from the chaff, mainly based upon Professor J. P. Little's excellent bibliography, *Simone Weil*. London: Grant and Cutler, 1973; Supplement, 1980.

Allen, Louis. "French Intellectuals and T. E. Lawrence." *Durham University Journal,* December 1976, pp. 52–66.
Bliven, Naomi. "The Shadow and the Substance." *New Yorker,* August 1, 1966, pp. 104–10.
Bree, Germaine. "A Stranger in this World." *Saturday Review,* February 1965, pp. 26–27.

Camus, Albert. "La Condition ouvrière de Simone Weil." *L'Express,* December 13, 1955.
———. Extract from letter to Mme Selma Weil. *L'Express,* February 11, 1960.
———. Preface to *L'Enracinement* [unsigned]. *Bulletin de la Nouvelle Revue Francaise* (June 1949); Reprinted in Camus, *Œuvres completes* (Essais), Bibliotheque de la Pleiade, 2:1700–1702.
Coles, Robert. "Simone Weil: Prophet of Grace." *American Scholar,* Autumn 1973, pp. 692–96.
Cranston, Maurice. "Reactionary Mystic." *The Guardian,* October 19, 1962.
Cunningham, Lawrence. "Simone Weil: A Selective Bibliography." *Cross Currents,* Spring 1973, pp. 120–24.
Eliot, T. S. "Books of the Year." *Sunday Times* (London), December 24, 1950.
Fiedler, Leslie. "Simone Weil: Prophet Out of Israel, Saint of the Absurd." *Commentary,* January 1951, pp. 36–46.
Fremantle, Anne. "Soul in Search of Salvation." *New York Times Book Review,* December 16, 1956, p. 6.
Garvin, Michele. "Simone Petrement's *Simone Weil.*" *Telos,* Summer 1978, pp. 225–35.
Greene, Graham. "Waiting for God." In *Collected Essays,* pp. 372–75. London: Bodley Head, 1969.
Heppenstall, Rayner. "Worth Doing Badly." *Encounter,* April 1958, pp. 84–86.
Kazin, Alfred. "The Gift." In *The Innermost Leaf: A Selection of Essays,* pp. 208–13. New York: Harcourt, Brace, 1955.
Lichtheim, George. "Simone Weil." In *Collected Essays,* pp. 458–76. New York: Viking Press, 1973.
Macdonald, Dwight. "A Formula to Give a War-Torn Society Fresh Roots." *New York Times Book Review,* July 6, 1952, p. 6.
Marcel, Gabriel. "Simone Weil." *Month,* July 1949, pp. 9–18.
Merton, Thomas. "Pacifism and Resistance in Simone Weil." In *Faith and Violence,* pp. 76–84. West Bend, Ind.: University of Notre Dame Press, 1968.

Milosz, Czeslaw. Introduction to *Wybor Pism*. Paris: Instytut Literacki, Biblioteka 'Kultury,' no 33, 1958, pp. 9–23.

Muggeridge, Malcolm. "Agonies and Ecstasies." *Observer,* September 22, 1968, p. 31.

Murray, Michele. "The Passion of Simone Weil." *Cross Currents,* Summer 1973, pp. 213–18.

Nott, Kathleen. "Religious Humanist." *Observer,* June 19, 1966, p. 27.

Ottenmeyer, OSB, Hilary. "Simone Weil, 'Mystic' and lover of the poor." *American Benedictine Review* 15 (1964), pp. 504–14.

Peyre, Henri. "Simone Weil." *Massachusetts Review* 6 (1965), pp. 625–30.

Pierce, Roy. "Biography of a Generation," and "Simone Weil: Sociology, Utopia, and Faith." In *Contemporary French Political Thought,* pp. 24–48, pp. 89–121. London: Oxford University Press, 1966.

Raine, Kathleen. "The Frontiers of Religion." *Observer,* October 7, 1951, p. 7.

Read, Herbert. "Among the Saints." *Yorkshire Post,* May 19, 1966, p. 5.

Rees, Richard. "History." In *A Theory of My Time: An Essay in Didactic Reminiscence,* pp. 193–208. London: Seeker & Warburg, 1963.

Rexroth, Kenneth. "The Dialectic of Agony." *Nation,* January 12, 1957, pp. 42–43.

Rosenthal, Raymond. "Simone Weil's Politics" (Letter to the editors). *New York Review of Books,* November 10, 1977, pp. 45–46.

Sontag, Susan. "Simone Weil." In *Against Interpretation, and Other Essays,* pp. 49–51. New York: Farrar, Straus & Giroux, Inc., 1967.

Stoneburner, Tony. "Solidarity in Suffering." *Christian Century,* March 27, 1963.

Taubes, Susan A. "The Absent God." *Journal of Religion* 35 (1955), pp. 6–16.

Taylor, Mark. "History, Humanism & Simone Weil." *Commonweal*, August 24, 1973, pp. 448–52.

Thibon, Gustave. "Having and Being." *Time Literary Supplement*, January 15, 1949, pp. 33–34.

Times Literary Supplement. [Reviews] "Confrontation with Existence." October 17, 1968, p. 1174.

————. "Deprivation of the Ego." August 14, 1970, p. 904.

————. "The Ethos of Western Man." March 17, 1950, p. 168.

————. "In the Face of Suffering." December 26, 1962.

————. "The Love of God." February 22, 1963.

————. "No Escape Without Religion." August 4, 1966, p. 710.

————. "The Paradox of Simone Weil." May 5, 1955, p. 2775.

————. "The Road to Belief." October 26, 1951, p. 681.

————. "Seekers After Truth." May 19, 1966, p. 18.

————. "Two of a Kind." February 28, 1958.

Toynbee, Philip. "The Agony and the Ecstasy." *Observer*, July 5, 1970, p. 29.

Weil, Andre. "Letter to the Editor," *Commonweal*, May 25, 1973, p. 323.

————. "Letter to the Editor." *New York Times Book Review*, January 23, 1977, p. 33.

[Weil, Andre]. "Andre Weil, A Scientist, Discusses His Sister with Malcolm Muggeridge." *The Listener*, January 23, 1973, pp. 673–74, 678–79.

[Weil, Andre, and Coles, Robert, M.D.]. "MIT Examines the Life of a Saintlike Woman." Israel Shenker, *New York Times*, October 11, 1975.

————. "MIT Switches on to Weil." *Times Higher Education Supplement*, October 31, 1975, p. 14.

West, Paul. "Simone Weil." In *The Wine of Absurdity: Essays on Literature and Consolation*, pp. 143–57. University Park: Pennsylvania State University Press, 1966.

White, George Abbott. "A Life Paid Up." *Commonweal*, July 22, 1977, pp. 468–70.

————, ed. *Simone Weil: Live Like Her?* Cambridge, Mass.: Technology and Culture Seminar at MIT, 1976.

Wren-Lewis, John. "Breakthrough Wanted." *Guardian*, November 1, 1968, p. 6.

Notes on Contributors

JAMES MUNRO CAMERON, formerly Professor of Philosophy at the University of Leeds, Master of Rutherford College, University of Kent at Canterbury, and first University Professor at St. Michael's College, University of Toronto, is now retired and lives in London, Ontario. Among his publications are *Images of Authority* (the Terry Lectures at Yale for 1964) and *On the Idea of a University* (1978). He was for some years the English correspondent of *Commonweal,* and now frequently contributes to the *New York Review of Books.*

ROBERT COLES, M.D., is a child psychiatrist at the Harvard Medical School and the Harvard University Health Services who has worked in various parts of the United States and abroad. He is the author of *Children of Crisis,* in five volumes, and books on the work of Erik H. Erikson, William Carlos Williams, Walker Percy, and Flannery O'Connor.

MICHAEL K. FERBER helped organize draft resistance during the war in Vietnam, and stood trial with Dr. Spock and others in 1968 in Boston. With Staughton Lynd he wrote *The Resistance* (1971), and his articles on politics and literature have appeared in professional and general interest publications. He has a B.A. in Greek from Swarthmore and a Ph.D. in English from Harvard University. Now teaching at Yale University, he is at work on a book about William Blake.

STAUGHTON LYND participated throughout the 1960s in civil rights and antiwar activities. He is now a lawyer in Youngstown, Ohio, where he has been active in that community's resistance to steel mill closings. His recent writing includes *Rank and File:*

Personal Histories by Working-Class Organizers (edited with his wife Alice Lynd, 1981), *Labor Law for the Rank and Filer* (2d rev. ed., Singlejack Books: San Pedro, California, 1981), and a forthcoming book on the Youngstown experience.

MICHELE MURRAY was Book Review Editor of the *National Observer* from 1971 until her death in 1974 at age forty. Her published works include two novels for teenagers (one of which was selected by the Junior Literary Guild) and *The Great Mother* (1974), a collection of poems published posthumously. She also edited the anthology, *A House of Good Proportion: Images of Women in Literature* (1973), and her articles and reviews appeared in a wide variety of journals and newspapers. The essays included here are from a book she planned to write on Simone Weil, and which she was actively researching at the time of her death.

CONOR CRUISE O'BRIEN has ranged across the realms of politics and literature. Currently the Editor-in-Chief of the *Observer* (London), he has been in the Department of External Affairs for Ireland, Vice-Chancellor of the University of Ghana, Head of the United Nations Section for Ireland, and Schweitzer Professor of Humanities at New York University. His books include *Parnell and His Party* (1957), *Writers and Politics* (1965), *Camus* (1970), *States of Ireland* (1972), and *Herod: Reflections on Political Violence* (1978).

JOSEPH H. SUMMERS was a conscientious objector during World War II and spent two years in Civilian Public Service camps. He has taught at Bard College, the University of Connecticut, Washington University (St. Louis), Amherst College, Michigan State University, the University of Kent at Canterbury, and is now Professor of English at the University of Rochester. His *George Herbert: His Religion and Art* and *The Muses' Method: An Introduction to "Paradise Lost"* will be reprinted during 1981. This past year he has been working at the Huntington Library on a book about Shakespeare's plays.

GEORGE ABBOTT WHITE is a teacher and a clinical child psychologist practicing in the Boston area. He began reading Simone

Weil in the early 1960s working at the Ford Motor Company (River Rouge), and while he was involved in civil rights and antiwar activities. He edited the *Generation New Poet Series,* in four volumes (1964, 1965, 1966), *Literature in Revolution* (1972), and *Simone Weil: Live Like Her?* (1976). With John D. Stoeckle, M.D. he is preparing photographs of doctors and patients in the 1930s, *Plain Pictures of Plain Doctoring,* and is writing a biography of F. O. Matthiessen.

Index

Achilles, 64, 65, 70–72, 73
Adams, Henry, 52
Aeneid, 79
Aeschylus, 78
Agee, James, 29, 63
Alain. *See* Chartier
American Renaissance, 53
Anderson, Reverend David, 191
Andromache, 63
Animal Farm, 177 n
anorexia nervosa, 26, 33, 50
anti-draft, 132
Antigone, 39
Apollinaire, Guillaume, 14
Archimedes, 8
Arendt, Hannah, 12, 84–85, 146,
   147; on *La condition ouvrière,*
   171
Aristotle, 98
Aron, Suzanne Gauchon, 98 n
Ashford, Kent, 1, 27, 35. *See also*
   Grosvenor Sanatorium
Assisi, 5, 20
atomic bomb, 88, 131
attention, 64–65. *See also* "Reflec-
   tions on the Right Use of School
   Studies . . ."
Augustine, Saint, 55
Auschwitz, 58

Baudelaire, Charles, 28
Berlin, Sir Isaiah, 1
Bernanos, Georges, 22, 29, 32, 89.
   See also *The Diary of a
   Country Priest*

Bhagavad-Gita, 43–44, 60
Bible, the, 42, 43, 45, 65, 77
Bloom, Harold, 70
Bonhoeffer, Dietrich, 13, 21
Bourges (lycée), 19
Brecht, Bertolt, 167
British Left, 156
Brothers Karamazov, The, 39, 58
Buber, Martin, 23
bureaucracy, 115, 174–75; "bu-
   reauctratic collectivism," 128;
   modern, 117; Russian, 145
Burke, Edmund, 99, 102
Burnham, James, 116

Camus, Albert, 109, 115, 147
capitalist system, 17, 31, 128, 161
Cathars, 26, 42, 44–45, 57, 59–60,
   109
Catherine of Genoa, Saint, 45
Catherine of Sienna, Saint, 45
Catholic Church, Catholicism, 4,
   6, 11, 24, 30, 41; bishops of, in
   Germany, 104; and French nationalism, 104; midwestern
   (USA), 23; SW drawn to, 45–
   46; SW refuses baptism into,
   103; and social justice, 161–63
Catholic Worker, 2, 137 n, 170;
   criticizes high technology, 164;
   locations in New York City,
   141 n; newspaper operation,
   177 n; "Positions," 166; questions concept of Progress, 165;

Catholic Worker (*Cont.*)
quoted, 160–61. *See also*
Dorothy Day
Cervantes, Miguel de, 78
Chaplin, Charles, 149
Chartier, Emile-Auguste (Alain),
36, 37, 43
Chomsky, Noam, 131
Christ, Jesus, 68, 78, 83, 107; and
Catholic Worker, 160–61; and
Krishna, 43; SW's awareness
of, 15; SW believes in divinity
of, 42; SW encounters, 21, 38–
39; SW loves, 32; SW quotes,
105–6; SW recites Lord's
Prayer, 52; SW separates from
Judaism, 25, 33; SW and true
corporeality, 59. *See also*
Catholic Church
Christianity, 25, 29, 33, 41, 42,
53; Augustinian tradition, 27;
Dorothy Day, 141; dualistic
terminology, 75; and *Iliad,* 78;
Jansenism and Calvinist
"strands," 69; and Silone, 112;
SW and baptism into, 103; SW
sees as religion of slaves, 19;
will of God, 22. *See also*
Catholic Church
Claudel, Paul, 22
Coles, Robert, 5, 139, 169; on Orwell, 158; on privilege, 175–76
colonialism, 3, 7, 107
Communism, Communist Party, 2,
11, 16, 103, 109; anticommu-
nism 109; Christian communism, 163; *Communist Manifesto,* 120; and European Resistance movements, 129; German communists, 145; and
Silone, 112; SW's reputation as,
144; working-class influence,
130. *See also* Lenin; Marx;
Marxism-Leninism; Stalinism;
Soviet Union

Cuban cane fields, 171
Cunningham, Lawrence, 184–85

Dante, 65, 79
Darwin, Charles, 127
Day, Dorothy, 3, 32, 139, 140,
166, 168, 170, 173, 178, 179;
caretaker of dispossessed and
sick, 140 n; cites Cuban Revolution, 163; critique of industrial
society, 164; as journalist,
140 n; manual labor a central
value, 141; necessary work,
170; as nurse, 163; parts with
Marx and Lenin, 163; quotes
SW on privilege, 178; on volun-
tary and involuntary poverty,
147; works of mercy, 141, 165;
writing style compared with
Orwell and SW, 177 n. *See also*
Catholic Worker
"Death of Ivan Ilych, The," 39
de Beauvoir, Simone, 14
de Gaulle, Charles, 1, 96, 97, 108;
judges SW "mad," 97
Deiphobus, 73
Dellinger, David, 113, 132
Descartes, Rene, 37, 39, 43, 44,
144
Deutscher, Isaac, 155 n
Diary of a Country Priest, The,
32, 89. *See also* Georges
Bernanos
Divine Comedy, The, 79
Dodds, E. R., 74
*Down and Out in Paris and
London,* 139
Dreyfus Case, 14
Durruti, Buenaventura, 41. *See
also* Spanish Civil War
Ecole Normale Superieure, 15, 16,
36, 43, 137, 143, 148; SW re-
ceives diploma, 145
Eliot, T. S., 22, 24, 183; intro-

duces *The Need for Roots*,
95–96

Engels, Friedrich, 40; *See also*
Marx

"Essay on Criticism," 65

"Factory Work," 1, 122–23, 169–
71, 173

factory work, 2, 4, 11, 18, 29, 38,
116, 137; under capitalism, 127;
in China, 171; and individual
oppression, 121; New Left's experience of, 137–38; SW's experience of, 121–24; SW recalls
and analyzes, 166–78

fascism, fascists, 29, 115; and
Franco's troops, 20, 41; and
French nationalism, 107; Ger-
man army, 87; occupation of
Ethiopia, 112; SW compares to
Rome, 106, 170. *See also* Hitler;
National Socialist Party

Fest, Joachim, 145

Fiedler, Leslie, 24, 69, 77

force, 84, 178; SW quoted, 88,
90; SW's theory of, 81–83. *See
also* nonviolence; pacifism

Ford, Henry, 149

forgiveness, 83–84

Francis of Assisi, Saint, 5, 20

Free French, 23, 25, 48, 51, 105;
recovering French Empire, 108;
SW has serious reservations
about, 88; SW writes for their
post-WWII reconstruction, 34,
96–98

Freud, Sigmund, 29, 30, 52, 56;
paralleled with Marx, 174

Gandhi, Mohandes, 84

general strikes, 121. *See also*
workers

Gitlin, Todd, 128

Gnosticism, 6, 28, 42, 44, 57–61

Goodman, Paul, 111, 130–31

Gorz, Andre, 122, 125–26

Gospels, 43. *See also* the Bible;
Christianity

Gravity and Grace, 24, 27, 31, 32,
35, 76

Great Beast, 58, 96, 109, 170, 179

Greek philosophy, 4, 18, 28, 59;
and Judaism, 43. *See also* Plato

Grosvenor Sanatorium, 1, 50, 54

Hardwick, Elizabeth, 2

Hector, 63, 73

Hemingway, Ernest, 54

Henri IV (lycée), 16, 36, 37, 137,
148

Herbert, George, 11, 21, 34, 38–39

Hinduism, 26, 59

Hiroshima, 89

Hitler, Adolph, 40, 87, 106, 145;
Prague entry key for SW, 104;
and Rome, 106. *See also* National Socialist Party

Hoggart, Richard, quoted on
Wigan Pier, 155

Holocaust, 80

Homer, 8, 48, 178

Human Condition, The, 171

Iliad, 44, 63–85, 87–93, 178

"*Iliad*, or, The Poem of Force,
The," 2, 8, 43; in Ferber, 63–
85; in *Politics*, 131; in Summers, 87–93

industrial health and safety, 168

Industrial Workers of the World
(I.W.W.), 129, 133

Inferno, 79

intellectuals, intellect, 1, 3, 5, 11,
13, 137; and experiential deprivation, 175–78; SW's anti-
intellectualism, 32, SW's contempt for, 6; SW as "Jewish
female intellectual," 51; SW
as "pure" intellectual, 99–101,

intellectuals, intellect (*Cont.*)
   SW's relationship to, 30–31.
   See also Weil, Andre

Jansenism, 69, 89. *See also*
   Cathars
Jeremiah, Saint, 19
Jessup, Hubert, on Dorothy Day,
   163–64; critique of Marxism, 165
John, Saint, 55
John the Baptist, Saint, 19
John of the Cross, Saint, 22
Judaism, Jews, 14, 31, 36, 41, 51,
   87; as chosen people, 105; and
   Christ, 33; Victor Gollancz
   quoted, 156 n; Hellenized, 43;
   role in Christian development,
   25, 58–59; and SW's back-
   ground, 102; Thibon's attitude
   toward, 153
Joan of Arc, 105
Jung, C. G., 56

Kant, Immanuel, 39, 43
Kierkegaard, Soren, 23, 33
King, Martin Luther, 84
Kolakowski, Leszek, 115
Krishna, 43

labor (manual). *See* factory
   work; workers
Languedoc, 26. *See also* Cathars
Lawrence, D. H., 170, 185; SW
   finds "completely uninterest-
   ing," 191
Lawrence, T. H., 3
Lecarpentier, Marcel, 145
Left Book Club, 154, 156
Lenin, Leninism, 40, 125, 168; SW
   contrasts unfavorably with
   Marx, 102; SW criticizes, 101,
   146. *See also* Marx; Marxism-
   Leninism
"Love" (George Herbert), 21,
   38–39

Le Puy (lycée), 17, 37
Lewis, C. S., 75
London, 1, 33, 47, 51; SW in love
   with, 48
Long Loneliness, The, 160
Luxemburg, Rosa, 125
Lynn, Conrad, 111

Malraux, Clara, 14
McCarthy, Abigail, 23
McCarthy, Mary, 63, 87; Ferber
   criticizes as translator of SW, 81
Macdonald, Dwight, 1, 87, 111,
   128, 133, 183; apologizes for
   SW, 1, 174; on Trotsky and
   Orwell, 158–59; writings, 131.
   See also *Politics* magazine
Mallarme, Stephane, 28
Managerial Revolution, The, 116
Mao Tse-tung, 83
Marcel, Gabriel, 22, 23
Marcuse, Herbert, 185
Maritain, Jacques, 22, 96
Mark, Saint, 43
Marseilles, 8, 57, 152
Marx, Marxism, 4, 5, 40, 85, 101,
   115, 174; and alienation, 119–
   20; as false science, 125; and
   illusions, 175; kinds of, 127; as
   religion, 118; and violent revo-
   lution, 124; and working class,
   134. *See also* workers
Marxism-Leninism, 3, 7, 173, 174;
   and cadre, 138; language prob-
   lems with, 126; vanguards
   criticized, 125
Matthew, Saint, 43
Matthiessen, F. O., 3, 53, 54
Maurin, Peter, 137, 161–62. *See
   also* Catholic Worker; Dorothy
   Day
Mauriac, Francois, 22
Maurras, Charles, 41
medieval society, 57, 170
Merton, Thomas, 22

Middlemarch, 39
Mills, C. Wright, 111, 115, 130
Milton, John, 79
Moliere, 78
"Morality and Literature," 79
Muste, A. J., 112; Brookwood
  Labor College, 113; Lawrence
  Textile Strike, 113; relationship
  to Marxist parties, 113; United
  Labor Party, 132
mysticism, 22, 35, 60, 109; SW
  and experience of, 21, 38–39;
  SW's vocation, 45

Nagasaki, 58
nationalism, 32, 107; French versions, 104–5; SW's critique of,
  110
National Socialist Party, Nazis,
  25, 33, 96, 115, 145; SW con-
  siders as supreme embodiment
  of nationalism, 105
necessity: 170–72. *See also* intellectuals; privilege
Need for Roots, The, 23, 24, 25,
  31, 35, 48, 50, 51, 52; not intended as a finished book,
  181 n; publication dates and
  titles, 95
New Deal, 115
New Left, 13, 28, 118, 126, 185;
  first, 111; and participatory
  democracy, 111, 119; SDS, 120;
  second, 134; working-class
  contact, 131; work experiences
  compared to SW, 137–39
New Testament, 43, 77
Nietzsche, Friedrich, 13
nonviolence, 84, 89, 162; nonviolent revolution, 126; SW
  quoted on, 91. *See also* pacifism
Notebooks, The, 24, 35

O'Brien, Conor Cruise, 9, 155 n;
  as Donat O'Donnell, 23

O'Connor, Flannery, 29
Odyssey, 73, 79
Old Testament, 77. *See also*
  Judaism
"On the Contradictions of
  Marxism," 102, 124
*On Science, Necessity, and the
  Love of God,* 24; Sir Richard
  Rees's editorial procedures,
  186–88
Orwell, George, 3, 29, 139, 166,
  170–78, 191; class privilege examined, 158–59, 178; fieldwork experiences, 140 n; "liberal" and "reactionary" labeling, 156; manual labor as central value, 141, 145; nature of
  class distinctions, 157; physical
  awkwardness compared to SW,
  150; restaurant work experiences, 139–40; sent to Lancashire and Wigan Pier, 154;
  SW's mine experience paralleled, 147; writing style compared to SW and Dorothy
  Day, 177 n

pacifism, 3, 16, 61, 128–29, 131,
  162; SW abandons, 20; SW's
  position on, 91–92
Paris, in period of SW's childhood 13–15; Red Belt, 139
Paris Commune, 121
Pascal, Blaise, 36, 39
patriotism, 9, 88: O'Brien examines, 95–110. *See also*
  nationalism
Patroclus, 64, 65
Paul, Saint, 43
Peguy, Charles, 22
Perrin, Father (Joseph Marie),
  41, 42, 45, 98 n, 152, 153,
  174 n, 190; quotes SW letter on
  work, 166–67

Petrement, Simone, 35, 43, 45, 143 n, 174 n, 189, 190; judged as SW's second biographer, 2–5; handling of SW material compared with Cabaud, 143 n; quotes SW on work experiences, 148, 149
Picasso, Pablo, 14
Plato, Platonism, 3, 7, 25, 39, 43, 60–61, 144; and Cathars, 58; enriched by manual work experiences, 168. See also Greek philosophy
"Politics and the English Language," 177. See also Orwell
Politics magazine, 63, 87, 111, 131–32; "Factory Work," 1, 169; first issue of, 128; humorous qualities, 130; important labor movements missed, 131–33; newness of political language, 127–30; persons associated with key to Left, 134; resistance movements observed, 129–30; SW, 131; SW's appearance listed, 183. See also Macdonald
Pope, Alexander, 65
Port Huron Statement: freshness of analysis and language, 120; on work and work experiences, 123
Posternak, Jean, 103
prayer, 24, 52, 64; SW's "terrible prayer," 45–46, 54–55
Priam, 70, 71–72
privilege, 3, 5, 123–24, 156; Dorothy Day's comment upon, 141; Orwell's analysis of, 158–60; SW's analysis of, 175–76; white skin and New Left organizing, 138

Racine, Jean, 43, 78

racism, 2, 23; SW's awareness of, 106–7, 137–39
Rees, Sir Richard, 35; as editor of SW material 185–91; and Andre Weil, 186–87
"Reflections on the Right Use of School Studies with a View to the Love of God," 40, 64
Retz, Cardinal de, 38
Resistance (French), 107, 129
resistance, in U.S. prisons, 128
"Responsibility of Peoples," 131
revolution and reform, quantitative and qualitative versions, 125–26
Rexroth, Kenneth, 27
Rilke, Rainer Maria, 14
Road to Wigan Pier, The, 154, 155 n, 156 n, 158
Rome, Roman thought, 3, 11, 41, 44, 58; and Hitler, 106, 170; and modern French state, 106; and plebeians, 126; SW hates, 53
"Root is Man, The," 131

sainthood: Dorothy Day explains, 32; "secular sainthood" and religionless Christianity, 21; and SW's youth, 36; Andre Weil discusses in relation to SW, 9–10
saints, 19, 20, 22, 43, 45, 55
Sartre, Jean-Paul, 14, 23, 28
Schweitzer, Albert, 98; effect upon nuclear testing and SW, 109
Selected Essays: 1934–1943, 57
Shakespeare, 78
Silone, Ignazio, 3; Bread and Wine as protest, 112–13; and Communist Party, 112
Solesmes (Benedictine monastery), 5, 21, 152
Sontag, Susan, 185; Princeton Symposium on SW, 182–83;

comments upon T. S. Eliot's
influence, 183
Sophocles, 78
Souvarine, Boris, 40
Soviet Union, 113, 114, 128, 145
Spanish Civil War, 4, 20, 38, 41,
121, 152
Stalinism, 115, 130
Stein, Gertrude, 14
Steiner, George, 1
Strategy for Labor, 125
Swift, Jonathan, 98

Tate, Allen, 22
Taylorism, 4, 119, 146; SW faults
Lenin for approval of, 146 n
Teresa of Avila, Saint, 45
Thibon, Gustave, 27, 42, 45, 57,
153, 176, 190; quotes SW on
work, 179
Thompson, E. P., 115, 155 n
Thucydides, 43, 44
Torah, 42
totalitarianism, 146
trade unions, 3, 9, 17, 40, 113;
acquiring influence in, 117;
Labor Exchange (St. Etienne),
147; Lawrence Textile Strike,
113; historical revolts in Europe, 124; SW addresses
Rheims Congress, 146 n; sit-
down strikes (France), 121;
wildcat strikes (USA), 132
Trilling, Lionel, 155 n
Trojan War, 74
Trotsky, Leon, 31, 92–93, 168;
compared with Orwell, 158;
Ohio organizers, 133; SW chal-
lenges, 115; strategic failures
as socialist, 129; encounter of,
with SW, 92

UAW (United Automobile
Workers), 132
United Farmworkers (USA), 153

United Labor Party (USA), 132,
133
Upanishads, 44

vanguards, criticized by SW, 133
Viete, Andre Weil comments
upon, 8
Vietnam war, 131
Virgil, 65, 66
voluntary poverty, 162

Wahl, Jean, 66
Wain, John, 155 n
Waiting for God, 21, 24, 35, 76
war, 1, 17, 20, 33, 41, 48, 88, 103,
108–9, 117, 131; Dorothy Day
on class war, 161; permanent
war economy, 117; SW's views
on, 103; total war considered,
87
Weil, Professor Andre (brother),
36, 137; at MIT, 6; Sir Richard
Rees correspondence, 182–83 n,
186–87; on SW and mathe-
matics, 7–8; on SW and sainthood, 9; on SW and Trotsky,
92; tentative comments upon
complete edition, 188
Weil, Dr. Bernard (father), 142
Weil, Selma Reinherz (mother),
144 n
Weil, Simone (SW): agricultural
laborer, 42, 57, 137, 144–45,
153, 179; with Anarchist troops
in Spain, 20, 41; on anti-
Semitism, 102–3; asceticism,
49; assertive upbringing, 144 n;
baptism, resistance to, 42, 43,
98 n, 103; childhood of, 13–15;
and Christ, 15, 21, 32, 42, 52,
105–6; Christianity, 19, 22;
Communism, 2, 11, 16, 103,
109, 144; cooperation possibilities, 119; death, 25, 34; early
home described, 142; factory

Weil, Simone (SW): (*Cont.*)
work experience, 2, 4, 18, 30,
37, 40, 121–27, 147–52, 166–
79; family support, 15, 50;
feminism, 36; femininity (lack
of), 16, 20, 26, 38, 47, 50, 53;
force, 63, 81–85, 88, 90, 178;
Free French, 4, 25, 34, 88; on
Freud, 30; Gospels, 43, 55;
Henri IV (lycée), 16, 36, 37,
137, 148; illness, 21, 26, 50, 61;
and mathematics, 7; Marx/
Marxism, 17, 31, 118, 125, 175;
and mysticism, 21, 38–39, 45;
and pacifism, 3, 20, 91–92; as
parachute nurse, 33; on patriotism, 9, 88, 95–110; and
Simone Petrement, 2–4, 35, 43,
45, 92, 92 n, 97 n, 99 n, 103,
103 n, 109 n, 142, 143 n, 144 n,
148–49; Platonism of, 3, 7, 25,
39, 43, 60–61, 144; as political
analyst, 3, 12, 85, 87–89, 96–97,
100–101, 102, 103, 106, 114–18,
119–27, 146 n, 177–79; as "pure
intellectual," 100; and problem
of evil, 79–80; and racism,
106–7, 137–39; readings in
Greek, 19; religious feelings of,
15, 174 n; on "rootlessness," 31;
Russian Revolution, 82; and
sainthood, 9–10, 21, 32; sexuality of, 19, 37, 53; and socialism, 40–41; and Spanish
Civil War, 4, 20, 38, 41, 121,
152; and Stalinism, 30, 115,
130; and suicide, 25, 27, 34, 52–
53; as teacher, 17, 39; "terrible
prayer" of, 45–46, 54–55; on
tragedy, 78; and Leon Trotsky,
31, 92–93, 115; and vanguards,
133; and vocation, 9, 46; on
war, 1, 17, 20, 33, 41, 71,
85, 88, 103, 108–9, 131; work
experiences, 1, 3–5, 11, 16, 18,

29, 30, 37, 92, 116, 119, 121–24,
134, 137, 144–54, 166–79 (locations: Alsthom plant, 148;
Auxerre, 146; J. J. Carnaud,
148; Renault plant, 148; Reville, 144–45; Saint-Marcel,
153; St. Malo de la Lande,
144); work-journal (*La condition ouvrière*), 147–48
Weil, Simone, writings of, 181–94;
"Are We Heading for the Proletarian Revolution?", 114–20;
"Factory Work," 1, 122–23,
126, 147–48, 169–71, 173; *First
and Last Notebooks, The*, 77 n;
Gravity and Grace, 24, 27, 31,
32, 35, 68 n, 76; "*Iliad*, or, The
Poem of Force, The," 2, 8, 12,
43, 63, 87–93, 131, 178; "Morality and Literature," 78 n, 79;
Need for Roots, The, 23, 24,
25, 31, 32, 35, 48, 50–51, 52,
76, 95 n, 96–98, 105, 106, 107–
8, 181 n; *Notebooks, The*, 24,
35, 70, 78; "On the Contradictions of Marxism," 78, 102,
124; *On Science, Necessity and
the Love of God*, 24, 186–88;
Oppression and Liberty, 82 n,
101 n, 111 n, 146 n; "Reflections
on the Right Use of School
Studies with a View to the Love
of God," 40, 64; "Reflections
on War," 131; "Romanesque
Renaissance, The," 57; *Selected
Essays: 1934–1943*, 57; *Seventy
Letters*, 77 n; *Waiting for God*,
21, 24, 35, 64 n, 67, 68, 69, 76,
77 n, 166–67, 174 n, 175;
Working Condition, The (*La
condition ouvrière*), 147–48, 171
Williams, Raymond, 148, 155 n
Wittgenstein, Ludwig, 13
Wobblies, *See* Industrial Workers
of the World (I.W.W.)

Woodcock, George, 155 n
work experiences, 1, 3–5, 11, 16,
18, 29, 30, 37, 92, 116, 119,
121–24, 134, 137, 144–54, 166–
79; Alsthom factory, 148; Auxerre printing press, 146; as
bench hand, 148–49; J. J. Carnaud factory, 148; criticizes
Lenin and Trotsky on work
involvement, 168–69; "Factory
Work," 1, 147–48, 169–71, 173;
letter to Father Perrin on factory work, 166; mechanical
skills acquired, 152; milling
machine work, mine experience,
147; necessity and work, 166–
67; reflections on factory work,
166; Renault factory, 148;
Reville (fishing experience),
144–45; Saint-Marcel (agricultural labor), 153; St. Malo de
la Lande (potato digging), 144;
stamping press work, 141–52;
Thibon farm (Ardeche), 153;
workers' injuries, 151; workers'
silence, 169
workers, 99 n, 117; and French
sit-down strikes, 121; and human services, 171; inarticulateness of, 169; milieu of, 147;
reading classics, 144; soviets,
116; and Third World, 125;
and worker control, 173
Working Condition, The (*La condition ouvrière*), 171; Camus
and Arendt on, 147 n
World War I, 15, 23
World War II, 23, 87–88
Worthy, William, 111

Yahweh, 42–43
Young-Bruehl, Elizabeth, 80